E. RICHARD LARSON has been litigating the rights of racial minorities, primarily in employment and education, since 1970. He has written numerous law review articles on civil rights issues, and is the author of a book on employment discrimination law entitled *Sue Your Boss*. For the past five years, Mr. Larson has been a National Staff Counsel with the American Civil Liberties Union. Before that, he was Senior Attorney at the National Employment Law Project.

LAUGHLIN McDONALD has been Director of the American Civil Liberties Union Southern Regional Office since 1972. Both as an ACLU lawyer and a private practitioner, he has tried many cases contesting racial discrimination in voting, jury selection and service, bar admissions and disciplinary proceedings, education, employment and the administration of justice. He has written a book entitled *Racial Equality* and contributed numerous articles and reviews involving minority rights to scholarly journals and publications for general audiences.

Also in this Series

THE RIGHTS OF ALIENS	44925	$1.95
THE RIGHTS OF CANDIDATES AND VOTERS	28159	$1.50
THE RIGHTS OF EX-OFFENDERS	44701	$1.95
THE RIGHTS OF GAY PEOPLE	24976	$1.75
THE RIGHTS OF GOVERNMENT EMPLOYEES	38505	$1.75
THE RIGHTS OF HOSPITAL PATIENTS	39198	$1.75
THE RIGHTS OF MENTAL PATIENTS	36574	$1.75
THE RIGHTS OF MENTALLY RETARDED PERSONS	31351	$1.50
THE RIGHTS OF MILITARY PERSONNEL	33365	$1.50
THE RIGHTS OF OLDER PERSONS	44362	$2.50
THE RIGHTS OF THE POOR	28002	$1.25
THE RIGHTS OF PRISONERS	35436	$1.50
THE RIGHTS OF PHYSICALLY HANDICAPPED PEOPLE	47274	$2.25
THE RIGHTS OF REPORTERS	38836	$1.75
THE RIGHTS OF STUDENTS	47019	$1.75
THE RIGHTS OF SUSPECTS	28043	$1.25
THE RIGHTS OF TEACHERS	25049	$1.50
THE RIGHTS OF VETERANS	36285	$1.75
THE RIGHTS OF UNION MEMBERS	46193	$2.25
THE RIGHTS OF WOMEN	27953	$1.75
THE RIGHTS OF YOUNG PEOPLE	42077	$1.75

Where better paperbacks are sold, or directly from the publisher. Include 25¢ per copy for mailing; allow three weeks for delivery.

Avon Books, Mail Order Dept., 250 West 55th Street, New York, N.Y. 10019

AN AMERICAN
CIVIL LIBERTIES
UNION HANDBOOK

THE RIGHTS OF RACIAL MINORITIES

E. Richard Larson
Laughlin McDonald

General Editor of this series
Norman Dorsen, *Chairperson ACLU*

A DISCUS BOOK/PUBLISHED BY AVON BOOKS

THE RIGHTS OF RACIAL MINORITIES is an original publication of Avon Books. This work has never before appeared in book form.

AVON BOOKS
A division of
The Hearst Corporation
959 Eighth Avenue
New York, New York 10019

Copyright © 1980
by The American Civil Liberties Union
Published by arrangement with
The American Civil Liberties Union
Library of Congress Catalog Card Number: 79-55397
ISBN: 0-380-75077-5

All rights reserved, which includes the right
to reproduce this book or portions thereof in
any form whatsoever. For information address
Avon Books.

First Discus Printing, January, 1980

DISCUS TRADEMARK REG. U.S. PAT. OFF. AND IN
OTHER COUNTRIES, MARCA REGISTRADA, HECHO EN
U.S.A.

Printed in the U.S.A.

Acknowledgments

We would like to express our appreciation to the many people who assisted us with the preparation of this book. Special thanks go to: Neil Bradley, for his critical review and comments; and to Deborah Spector, Donna Matern, and Marilyn Bright, for their careful editing, typing, and copying of the manuscript.

Contents

	Preface	11
I	Introduction and Overview	13
	The Reconstruction Constitutional Amendments	16
	The Surviving Reconstruction Civil Rights Acts	19
	The Modern Civil Rights Acts	21
II	Voting	34
	Protection of Voting Rights Generally	35
	The Voting Rights Act of 1965	44
	Election Procedures	55
III	Employment	63
	Prohibited Discriminatory Practices	65
	Remedies for Employment Discrimination	72
	Procedures under Title VII of the Civil Rights Act of 1964	75
	Affirmative Action	83
IV	Education	95
	Public School Segregation	96
	School Financing and Bilingual Education	104

CONTENTS

	Discrimination in Private Schools	107
	Affirmative Action in Admissions	109
V	Housing	116
	Prohibited Real Estate Practices	118
	Remedies and Procedures under Title VIII and the Civil Rights Act of 1866	122
	Exclusionary Zoning and Other Governmental Discrimination	129
VI	Public Accommodations	142
	The Thirteenth and Fourteen Amendments and the Civil Rights Act of 1866	143
	The Interstate Commerce Act	150
	Title II of the Civil Rights Act of 1964	153
	Title III of the Civil Rights Act of 1964	160
VII	Federally Assisted Discriminations	167
	The Fifth and Fourteenth Amendments	170
	Title VI of the Civil Rights Act of 1964	172
	The Revenue-Sharing Act of 1972	176
	The Crime-Control Act of 1968	179
VIII	Jury Selection and Trials	186
	Constitutional Protection against Discrimination in the Administration of Justice	187
	Statutory Protection against Discrimination in Jury Selection	197
	Additional Protections against Racially Biased Trials	202
IX	Federal Criminal Statutes Protecting the Rights of Minorities	215

CONTENTS

Reconstruction-Era Criminal Statutes 216
Criminal Statutes Prohibiting Slavery, Involuntary Servitude, and Peonage 220
Modern Criminal Statutes 222

Appendix A: Federal Agencies Responsible for Enforcing the Rights of Racial Minorities 227

Appendix B: Legal Resources for Racial Minorities Who Need Legal Assistance 237

Preface

This guide sets forth your rights under present law and offers suggestions on how you can protect your rights. It is one of a continuing series of handbooks published in cooperation with the American Civil Liberties Union.

The hope surrounding these publications is that Americans informed of their rights will be encouraged to exercise them. Through their exercise, rights are given life. If they are rarely used, they may be forgotten and violations may become routine.

This guide offers no assurances that your rights will be respected. The laws may change and, in some of the subjects covered in these pages, they change quite rapidly. An effort has been made to note those parts of the law where movement is taking place but it is not always possible to predict accurately when the law *will* change.

Even if the laws remain the same, interpretations of them by courts and administrative officials often vary. In a federal system such as ours, there is a built-in problem of the differences between state and federal law, not to speak of the confusion of the differences from state to state. In addition, there are wide variations in the ways in which particular courts and administrative officials will interpret the same law at any given moment.

If you encounter what you consider to be a specific abuse of your rights you should seek legal assistance. There are a number of agencies that may help you, among them ACLU affiliate offices, but bear in mind that the ACLU is a limited-purpose organization. In many communities, there are federally funded legal service of-

PREFACE

fices which provide assistance to poor persons who cannot afford the costs of legal representation. In general, the rights that the ACLU defends are freedom of inquiry and expression; due process of law; equal protection of the laws; and privacy. The authors in this series have discussed other rights in these books (even though they sometimes fall outside the ACLU's usual concern) in order to provide as much guidance as possible.

These books have been planned as guides for the people directly affected: therefore the question and answer format. In some of these areas there are more detailed works available for "experts." These guides seek to raise the largest issues and inform the non-specialist of the basic law on the subject. The authors of the books are themselves specialists who understand the need for information at "street level."

No attorney can be an expert in every part of the law. If you encounter a specific legal problem in an area discussed in one of these handbooks, show the book to your attorney. Of course, he will not be able to rely *exclusively* on the handbook to provide you with adequate representation. But if he hasn't had a great deal of experience in the specific area, the handbook can provide helpful suggestions on how to proceed.

Norman Dorsen, Chairperson
American Civil Liberties Union

The principle purpose of this handbook, and others in this series, is to inform individuals of their legal rights. The authors from time to time suggest what the law should be, but the author's personal views are not necessarily those of the ACLU. For the ACLU's position on the issues discussed in this handbook, the reader should write to Librarian, ACLU, 22 East 40th Street, New York, N.Y. 10016.

I
Introduction and Overview

American democracy was founded on a contradiction —that all people were equal but that human slavery was tolerable. The nation's belief in equality was written into the Declaration of Independence, which claimed that "all men are created equal." Its tolerance of slavery was contained in three original provisions of the Constitution of 1787, which counted a slave as only three-fifths of a person for purposes of apportionment of the House of Representatives, prohibited Congress from abolishing the slave trade prior to the year 1808, and provided for the return of fugitive slaves. The subsequent history of this nation has been in large measure the story —often violent, sometimes heroic, and always traumatic— of its attempts to reconcile its stated beliefs with its actual racial practices.

In 1857, the Supreme Court squarely confronted the issue of whether slavery was lawful in the infamous case of *Dred Scott* v. *Sanford*.[1] The court held that slaves were not citizens and thus had no access to the federal courts, that temporary residence in a free state or territory did not make a slave free, and that the Missouri Compromise of 1820 abolishing slavery in portions of the Louisiana Territory was unconstitutional, since it violated the property rights of slave owners. *Dred Scott* further divided a nation already torn on the issue of slavery and foreshadowed the Civil War, which erupted four years later. Out of that war came the Thirteenth Amendment and the eventual end of "the peculiar institution."[2] The Thirteenth Amendment did not, however, bring to fulfillment the national commitment to equality.

THE RIGHTS OF RACIAL MINORITIES

Many of the states responded to abolition by enacting laws known as "black codes" which imposed upon blacks a status different from slavery in name only. The black codes contained crippling restrictions on the rights of freedmen to own, purchase, inherit, or convey property, to have access to the courts, and to contract and pursue employment. Partly in response to the black codes, the Congress enacted in 1866 a sweeping civil rights act designed to confer full and equal citizenship upon blacks. Then, on July 9, 1868, the Fourteenth Amendment was ratified, which among other things guarantees to all persons without regard to race the equal protection of the laws. The last of the great post–Civil War constitutional amendments was the Fifteenth Amendment, ratified on March 3, 1870, guaranteeing the equal right to vote.

The Civil War amendments were implemented by a number of congressional acts which essentially sought to wipe out racial discrimination, whether supported by local legislation, the courts, or custom and practice. Had the amendments and implementing legislation been effectively enforced, much of the racial division and injustice that ensued over the next hundred years could have been avoided. But Reconstruction, as far as racial minorities are concerned, was a failure. Within only a few years after its passage, the Supreme Court declared that much of the legislation designed to enforce the Civil War amendments was unconstitutional, and it severely limited the application of the amendments themselves. Civil rights legislation was further weakened by the Congress, which eventually repealed major portions of the remaining Reconstruction laws.

Following the Compromise of 1877, and the withdrawal of federal troops from the confederate states, Reconstruction ended. The states were left free to adopt their own "local" solutions to race relations. Many states opted for separate-but-equal laws, known as "Jim Crow" legislation. A necessary condition for Jim Crow was political disfranchisement of minority voters. Accordingly, the years following Reconstruction saw the systematic elimination of blacks from the electorate by state legislatures through such discriminatory devices as literacy tests and the poll tax for registering and voting.

The inevitable result of Jim Crow and racial discrimination was injustice, bitterness, and violence. There were some 5000 reported lynchings in the United States after 1859 and full-blown race riots across the nation— in New York in 1900; in Springfield, Ohio, in 1904; in Statesboro and Atlanta in 1906; in Greensburg, Indiana, in 1906; and in Brownsville, Texas, and Springfield, Illinois, in 1908. But the forces for racial change in the United States were never entirely stilled.

In 1905, responding to black lynchings and other forms of racial discrimination, W.E.B. DuBois and others, many of whom were former abolitionists, met at Niagara Falls, New York, and founded the Niagara Movement. Later, in 1909 and 1910, the group formed the National Association for the Advancement of Colored People and adopted an agenda for racial reform that served as a blueprint during the next fifty years. The Supreme Court was also beginning slowly and sporadically to chip away at Jim Crow in a series of cases declaring a number of laws and practices unconstitutional: a city ordinance requiring racial segregation in neighborhood housing, the enforcement by state courts of racially discriminatory covenants in deeds to real estate, and racial segregation in interstate transportation.

The most dramatic modern breakthrough in racial reform came in 1954 when the Supreme Court handed down its decision in *Brown* v. *Board of Education*,[8] involving separate but equal public schools. The Court concluded that separate educational facilities were "inherently unequal" and ruled that Jim Crow schools deprived blacks of equal protection of the laws guaranteed by the Fourteenth Amendment. The *Brown* decision marked the beginning of the end of the formal aspects of Jim Crow. The decade following *Brown,* with its renewed promise of racial equality, has aptly been called the second Reconstruction. But if *Brown* held out hope, it also drew intense resistance from states that stood to be most affected by it. School desegregation was not in fact significantly implemented until the 1970s, more than fifteen years after the historic *Brown* opinion.

In response to the growing demand for equal rights

of blacks and the relentless pressure being mounted by the Civil Rights Movement, Congress enacted major pieces of modern civil rights legislation during the 1960s which have taken the country an enormous step closer to realizing the promises of the first Reconstruction. These modern statutes, discussed in detail in this book, protect racial minorities against most forms of public and private discrimination in employment, housing, accommodations, federally assisted programs, education, voting, and the administration of civil and criminal laws.

The existence of extensive federal protection, of course, does not mean that the law has been translated into nondiscriminatory behavior. Such was the lesson of the first Reconstruction. Actual enforcement of the right of racial minorities is crucial to realizing equality. Unfortunately, enforcement, even in the modern era, has been markedly slow and uneven. In 1968, a century after adoption of the Fourteenth Amendment, the Kerner Commission reported on our lack of progress: "Our nation is moving toward two societies, one black, one white—separate and unequal." [4]

Our constitutional and statutory scheme provides the means to ensure equality and eradicate the continuing effects of past discrimination accumulated over more than two centuries. The challenge to the nation is to make the Constitution and the federal statutes work in order to bring to reality, at long last, the declaration of principle that all persons are created equal.

THE RECONSTRUCTION CONSTITUTIONAL AMENDMENTS

The first basis for the rights of racial minorities was provided by three constitutional amendments adopted after the Civil War during Reconstruction: the Thirteenth Amendment, which outlaws slavery and involuntary servitude; the Fourteenth Amendment, which prohibits states from denying to any person "equal protection of the laws"; and the Fifteenth Amendment, which prohibits denial or abridgement of the right to vote.

What are the Thirteenth Amendment's prohibitions against discrimination and how are they enforced?

The Thirteenth Amendment, with its narrow prohibition only of "slavery" and "involuntary servitude," has not been widely used in civil rights enforcement. This has changed only slightly in recent years subsequent to the Supreme Court's 1968 decision in *Jones* v. *Alfred H. Mayer Co.*, where the Court indicated that the amendment was intended to prohibit not just slavery but also the "badges and incidents of slavery."[5] The amendment's prohibitions are directed not only against governments but also against private entities and private persons.[6] The amendment, however, probably prohibits only practices which are intentionally discriminatory rather than unintentional practices which have a discriminatory effect.[7]

The main way the Thirteenth Amendment is enforced is through private lawsuits based on the Civil Rights Act of 1866 (the act is discussed later). In these lawsuits, people discriminated against can obtain court orders ending the prohibited activity and awarding damages to those whose rights were violated.[8] There are no administrative procedures that must be complied with before filing a lawsuit to enforce the Thirteenth Amendment. However, the lawsuit must be filed within the time specified by the applicable state statute of limitations (usually within several years of the discriminatory activity).[9]

What are the Fourteenth Amendment's prohibitions and how are they enforced?

The Fourteenth Amendment broadly prohibits states from intentionally denying to any person the "equal protection of the laws." Although the amendment is directed primarily at the actions of state and local governments, it also prohibits intentional private discrimination if it is closely tied to actions of the government or of government officials. For example, racial segregation of a private lunch counter is prohibited where that segregation is enforced by the local police.[10] Similarly, racial discrimination in a private restaurant is prohibited where the property is leased by the restaurant from the state.[11]

A major limitation on Fourteenth Amendment coverage

is that it prohibits only intentional discrimination and not unintentional discrimination that has a discriminatory effect. For example, a government employment test that screens out a disproportionate number of minority applicants but which is not used with an intent to discriminate is not prohibited by the Fourteenth Amendment.[12] Similarly, suburban exclusionary zoning that has a discriminatory impact against potential minority residents but which was not adopted with an intent to discriminate is not prohibited by the Fourteenth Amendment.[13]

Where intentional discrimination is practiced, however, it almost always will be found to be unconstitutional. Such discrimination will be allowed only if it is justified by a "compelling state interest."[14] It is virtually impossible for any discriminator to meet this standard of *compelling* state interest. According to Chief Justice Warren Burger of the U.S. Supreme Court, no discriminator "has ever satisfied this seemingly insurmountable standard."[15]

The main method of enforcing the Fourteenth Amendment is through private lawsuits based on the Civil Rights Act of 1871 (discussed later). In these lawsuits, people discriminated against can obtain court orders ending the intentional discrimination and awarding damages to those whose rights were violated.[16]

As with the Thirteenth Amendment, there are no administrative procedures that must be complied with before filing a lawsuit to enforce the Fourteenth Amendment.[17] However, the lawsuit must be filed within the time specified by the applicable state statute of limitations (usually within several years of the discriminatory act).[18]

What does the Fifteenth Amendment prohibit? How is it enforced?

The Fifteenth Amendment prohibits denial or abridgment of the right to vote at all levels of the political process by federal, state, and local officials on the basis of race, color, or previous condition of servitude. The amendment was enacted as a limitation on public officials, but the acts of private individuals have been held unconstitutional under it where they perpetuate or act as a substitute for official discrimination.[19]

The Supreme Court has never held that a showing of

intentional racial discrimination is required for a violation of the Fifteenth Amendment, although racial motive has been abundantly apparent in the voting cases it has decided.[20]

The Fifteenth Amendment is enforced through lawsuits brought by private individuals or by the U.S. Department of Justice pursuant to implementing legislation such as the Voting Rights Act of 1965, through administrative proceedings before the Department of Justice, and through prosecutions under criminal statutes protecting the equal right to vote. As with the Thirteenth and Fourteenth Amendments, there are no administrative procedures which must be exhausted before filing a lawsuit to enforce the Fifteenth Amendment.[21] Remedies include court orders ending the discrimination and awarding damages.[22]

THE SURVIVING RECONSTRUCTION CIVIL RIGHTS ACTS

Each of the Reconstruction amendments, besides prohibiting various forms of discrimination, authorized Congress to enforce the amendments "by appropriate legislation." Congress did so immediately and on a number of occasions. The most important of the Reconstruction laws were the Civil Rights Act of 1866, the Civil Rights Act of 1871, and the Civil Rights Act of 1875.[23] Major portions of the first two have survived. The third, the nation's first prohibition against discrimination in public and private accommodations, was declared unconstitutional by the Supreme Court in 1883.[24]

What is the Civil Rights Act of 1866 and how is it enforced?

The Civil Rights Act of 1866, dormant for nearly a century, was long thought to apply only to state-enforced discrimination. In 1968, however, in *Jones* v. *Alfred H. Mayer Co.*,[25] the Supreme Court revived the 1866 act by declaring that it prohibits private discrimination as well as public discrimination.

The act is divided into two parts, Sections 1981 and

1982.[26] Each section prohibits specific acts of discrimination. It is not yet clear whether the sections prohibit all specified forms of discrimination or just specified forms of *intentional* discrimination.[27]

Section 1981 provides that all persons shall have the same right to "make and enforce contracts" as is enjoyed by white citizens.[28] This guarantee has been most widely used to prohibit discrimination in employment.[29] It also has been used to prohibit discrimination in the use of recreational facilities [30] and in admissions to private schools.[31]

Section 1982 provides that all citizens shall have the same right as is enjoyed by white citizens "to inherit, purchase, lease, sell, hold and convey real and personal property." [32] This guarantee has been used to prohibit most forms of housing discrimination against racial minorities.[33]

Sections 1981 and 1982, like the Thirteenth Amendment on which they are based, are enforceable through private lawsuits. The remedies in such lawsuits include court orders terminating the discrimination,[34] awarding damages, and awarding attorneys' fees to the prevailing party.[35]

There are no administrative procedures to complete before filing a lawsuit to enforce Sections 1981 and 1982.[36] The lawsuit, however, must be filed soon after the discriminatory action in order to be filed within the applicable state statute of limitations.[37]

What is the Civil Rights Act of 1871 and how is it enforced?

The central provision of the Civil Rights Act of 1871 is known as Section 1983.[38] It is a statutory parallel to the Fourteenth Amendment. Section 1983 makes liable any "person" acting under color of state law who causes another person to be deprived "of any rights . . . secured by the Consitution and laws" of the United States.[39] The word "person" includes not only government officials and persons and entities acting in concert with them [40] but also municipalities, states, and their agencies.[41]

Since Section 1983 parallels the Fourteenth Amendment, it shares the limitation of prohibiting only intentional discrimination rather than also prohibiting unintentional discrimination which has a discriminatory effect.[42] Similarly, it permits such intentional discrimination only in the very rare situation where it can be justified by a compelling state interest.[43]

Like the Fourteenth Amendment, Section 1983 is enforced only through private lawsuits. The remedies in such lawsuits include court orders ending the discrimination, awarding damages,[44] and awarding attorneys' fees to the prevailing party.[45] There are no administrative procedures which must be complied with before filing a lawsuit,[46] but the lawsuit must be filed within the time period specified by the state statute of limitations.[47]

Another part of the Civil Rights Act of 1871, Section 1985(3), prohibits conspiracies to deprive others of equal protection of the laws.[48] Enforcement of Section 1985(3) does not depend upon the involvement of state officials or agencies; the Supreme Court has held that Section 1985(3) prohibits purely private conspiracies that deprive others of their civil rights.[49] For example, private persons who conspire to deny employment to minorities are in violation of Section 1985(3).[50]

Although private persons need not necessarily engage in intentional discrimination in order to violate Section 1985(3), such persons must have intentionally conspired to violate the civil rights of others.[51]

Section 1985(3) is enforced in the same way that Section 1983 is enforced (by private lawsuits, etc.).[52]

THE MODERN CIVIL RIGHTS ACTS

The Civil Rights Movement of the 1960s reflected the glaring reality that neither the Reconstruction amendments nor the surviving Reconstruction civil rights acts were being enforced well enough to protect the rights of racial minorities. Responding in part to this reality, Congress enacted and thereafter amended a number of very significant Civil Rights Acts. Most civil rights enforcement in recent years has been under these modern laws.

Since the acts resulted from legislative compromise,

they contain many exceptions and frequently include complicated administrative procedures. They are significant, however, in two ways. First, they do not rely principally upon private lawsuits for enforcement; instead, they also authorize federal enforcement, both through administrative procedures and through lawsuits. Second, they have been interpreted by the federal courts as prohibiting not only intentionally discriminatory practices but also those practices which have a discriminatory effect.

Does Title II of the Civil Rights Act of 1964 prohibit discrimination in accommodations? How is it enforced?

In the Civil Rights Act of 1875, Congress prohibited discrimination in public and private accommodations.[53] Eight years later, the Supreme Court voided the act by declaring it unconstitutional.[54] In Title II of the Civil Rights Act of 1964, Congress again prohibited discrimination in public and private accommodations.[55] The same year, Congress upheld Title II as constitutional.[56] The difference to the Supreme Court was not in the Constitution, but in eighty years of experience.

Title II prohibits discrimination in the enjoyment of services, facilities, privileges, etc., in any place of public accommodaton.[57] Covered establishments which provide accommodations open to the public, and hence are prohibited from engaging in discrimination, include inns, hotels, and motels; restaurants and lunch counters; and theaters, sports arenas, and other places of entertainment.[58] Specifically exempted from Title II, and hence not prohibited from engaging in discrimination by Title II, are private clubs.[59]

Title II is enforced by three methods. First, administrative enforcement may be undertaken by the federal Community Relations Service (CRS).[60] Second, the Department of Justice is authorized to sue violators of Title II.[61] Third, private individuals are authorized to sue violators of Title II.[62]

There is only one administrative prerequisite to a private lawsuit under Title II. If the discrimination occurred in a place where there is a state or local agency that is authorized to seek relief from such discrimination—and there is such an agency in nearly every state—the individual must give written notice of the discrimination to the state or local agency thirty days before filing the lawsuit.[63] No other administrative procedures must be met.[64]

In a private lawsuit, the individual may obtain termination of the discrimination but no damages.[65] Attorneys' fees, authorized for the prevailing party, ordinarily must be awarded to a prevailing plaintiff.[66]

Does Title VII of the Civil Rights Act of 1964 prohibit employment discrimination? How is it enforced?

Title VII of the Civil Rights Act of 1964, as initially enacted, prohibited discrimination only in private employment. In 1972, Congress amended Title VII to prohibit discrimination also in local, state, and federal employment.[67]

Title VII contains a number of exemptions. For instance, it covers only employers with fifteen or more employees, and unions with fifteen or more members.[68] Covered employers, unions, etc., however, are prohibited from engaging in a wide variety of specific discriminatory practices, such as discrimination in hiring, promotion, transfers, discharge, or payment of compensation, as well as discrimination in any other terms, conditions, or privileges of employment.[69]

Most significantly, Title VII prohibits not only practices that are intentionally discriminatory but also practices that have a discriminatory effect and are not job-related. For example, the Supreme Court has found unlawful under Title VII an employer's good faith use of a standardized written test and of a high school diploma requirement where these criteria discriminated against minorities and were not manifestly related to job performance.[70] Similarly, the Supreme Court has found unlawful under Title VII the use of a height requirement which had a discriminatory effect and which was not related to job performance.[71]

Title VII is enforced by three methods. First, administrative enforcement through investigation and conciliation is pursued by a federal agency, the Equal Employment Opportunity Commission (EEOC).[72] Second, the EEOC and the Department of Justice are au-

THE RIGHTS OF RACIAL MINORITIES

thorized to sue violators of Title VII.[73] Third, and still most important, private individuals may sue violators of Title VII.[74]

Private individuals may sue, however, only after going through several administrative procedures. Most importantly, the individuals must file administrative charges of discrimination with the EEOC within 180 days of the discriminatory action; and, after the EEOC has had an opportunity to investigate the charges, the individuals must sue within 90 days after receiving a "right-to-sue" letter from the EEOC.[75]

Remedies under Title VII include ending the discrimination and awarding back pay from two years before the administrative charges were filed with the EEOC.[76] Damage awards are not authorized, but attorneys' fees may be recovered by the prevailing party.[77]

What are the major provisions of the Voting Rights Act of 1965 and how are they enforced?

The Voting Rights Act of 1965, amended in 1970 and 1975,[78] contains several major provisions. It suspended "tests or devices" for voting which had been used in the past to disfranchise racial minorities.[79] The term "test or device" includes literacy tests, educational requirements, good-character tests, and exclusively English language registration procedures or elections where a linguistic minority comprises more than 5 percent of the voting-age population of the jurisdiction. A second provision, known as Section 5, requires jurisdictions that have used a "test or device" and in which voter registration is disproportionately low to gain approval or pre-clearance from either the Department of Justice or the federal courts before making changes in voting laws or procedures.[80] The purpose of pre-clearance is to make certain that the changes do not have the purpose or effect of abridging the right to vote on account of race, color, or membership in a language minority. Other important sections of the act provide for federal voter registrars and observers, absentee balloting in presidential elections, and bilingual ballots for linguistic minorities.[81] The act has been held constitutional by the Supreme Court.[82]

The Voting Rights Act is enforced through administrative pre-clearance procedures before the Department of Justice,[83] by lawsuits brought by the Department of Justice or by private individuals,[84] and by criminal prosecutions instituted by the federal government.[85] There are no administrative requirements with which an individual must comply before bringing suit.[86] Remedies include orders requiring compliance with the Voting Rights Act and payment of attorneys' fees to the prevailing party.[87] Damages are not authorized.

Does Title VIII of the Civil Rights Act of 1968 prohibit discrimination in housing? How is it enforced?

Three months before the Supreme Court revived the Civil Rights Act of 1866 by declaring that it prohibits discrimination in private housing transactions, Congress enacted Title VIII of the Civil Rights Act of 1968 (also known as the Fair Housing Act).[88]

Title VIII contains a number of exemptions, such as not prohibiting discrimination in the sale of a single-family dwelling by an owner not using commercial real-estate services.[89] But most housing transactions are covered by Title VIII's prohibitions against discrimination. Specifically prohibited are refusals to sell, to rent, or even to negotiate for the sale or rental of a dwelling;[90] representations that a dwelling is not available when it in fact is available;[91] and notices and advertisements indicating a racial preference.[92]

Like the other modern civil rights acts, Title VIII has been interpreted by the courts to prohibit not merely intentionally discriminatory practices but also practices that have a discriminatory effect. For example, suburban exclusionary zoning practices which might not be intentionally discriminatory, and hence are constitutional under the Fourteenth Amendment and Section 1983,[93] nonetheless are unlawful under Title VIII if they have a discriminatory impact upon racial minorities.[94]

Title VIII is enforced by three methods. First, administrative enforcement through investigation and conciliation is pursued by the federal Department of Housing and Urban Development (HUD).[95] Second, the Department of Justice is authorized to sue violators of Title

VIII.[96] Third, and still most important, private individuals may sue violators of Title VIII.[97]

There are two methods of private enforcement under Title VIII. Under one method, private individuals must comply with many complicated procedural prerequisites; in lawsuits pursued under this method, individuals may obtain a court order only terminating the unlawful discrimination.[98]

Under the second and preferred method of private enforcement under Title VIII, individuals must comply with only one procedural requirement: they must file their lawsuits within 180 days of the discriminatory housing practice.[99] In such lawsuits, the individuals may obtain court orders not only terminating the discrimination but also awarding actual damages, awarding punitive damages up to $1000, and awarding attorneys' fees.[100]

Do monetary penalties help stop prohibited discrimination?

Yes. And there is an obvious reason for this. People and institutions are likely to stop their discrimination if they will lose money because of it.

It has been hard to enforce many federal civil rights laws effectively because the penalties for practicing illegal discrimination were not sufficiently severe. All too often, illegal discrimination is halted only after long and tedious lawsuits which result in no more than a court-ordered end to discrimination. Without severe monetary penalties, there too often is little incentive for violators to change their ways.

In recent years, monetary remedies have been viewed as an important incentive for violators not to discriminate. As the Supreme Court stated in a lawsuit against private-employment discrimination under Title VII:

> It is the reasonably certain prospect of a backpay award that "provides the spur or catalyst which causes employers and unions to self-examine and to self-evaluate their employment practices and to endeavor to eliminate, so far as possible, the last vestiges of an unfortunate and ignominious page in this country's history." [101]

The certainty of having to pay attorneys' fees to prevailing plaintiffs in private civil rights lawsuits is also strong incentive for civil rights compliance.[102]

Another remedy which recently has been recognized as an even more potent threat to discriminators is the threatened or real termination of federal financial assistance. In a recent lawsuit, involving the suspension of revenue-sharing funds to a discriminatory local government, a federal judge remarked that: "Certainly the withholding of millions of dollars from financially plagued [government agencies and private contractors] is a device designed to bring them quickly to their knees."[103] As the judge recognized: "Stopping the flow of lifeblood to a body is certainly more fatal than enjoining that body from certain activity."[104]

What federal laws authorize cutting off federal assistance to discriminatory recipients?

The three most important federal statutes authorizing the cutoff of federal assistance either through administrative enforcement or through litigation are:

1. Title VI of the Civil Rights Act of 1964, as amended,[105] authorizes the cutoff of federal funds generally to discriminatory recipients. Title VI is enforced by twenty-six separate federal agencies against their recipients.
2. Section 122 of the Fiscal Assistance to State and Local Governments Act of 1972, as amended in 1976,[106] authorizes the cutoff of federal revenue-sharing funding to discriminatory state and local governments. Section 122 is enforced by the federal Office of Revenue Sharing against all state and local governments.
3. Section 518(c) of the Crime Control Act of 1968, as amended in 1976,[107] authorizes the cutoff of federal grants from the Law Enforcement Assistance Administration (LEAA) to discriminatory state and local law enforcement agencies. Section 518(c) is enforced by LEAA.

These laws are becoming increasingly significant in enforcing the rights of racial minorities. First, they usually prohibit practices which have a discriminatory effect. Second, they can be enforced merely by filing administrative charges of discrimination with the appropriate federal agencies. Third, they can cause immediate civil rights compliance through the threatened or real cutoff of federal assistance. And fourth, other remedies, such as lawsuits, can be pursued at the same time to enforce the rights of racial minorities.

Can a victim of discrimination seek remedies under more than one of the foregoing laws?
Yes. Persons who have been discriminated against may pursue their rights under as many laws as are relevant. Sometimes choices have to be made, but in general a person should try to use as many options as are available.

Chapters II to VIII explain the federal civil laws and procedures protecting the rights of racial minorities in voting, employment, education, housing, public accommodations, federally assisted programs, and jury selection and trials. The last chapter surveys the relevant criminal statutes.

NOTES

1. 60 U.S. (19 How.) 393 (1857).
2. KENNETH M. STAMPP, THE PECULIAR INSTITUTION (New York: Alfred A. Knopf, 1969).
3. 347 U.S. 483 (1954).
4. REPORT OF THE NATIONAL ADVISORY COMMISSION ON CIVIL DISORDERS 1 (New York: Bantam, 1968).
5. 392 U.S. 409, 441 (1968).
6. *E.g.*, Johnson v. Railway Express Agency, 421 U.S. 454 (1975).
7. *See* note 27, *infra*.
8. *E.g.*, Sullivan v. Little Hunting Park, 396 U.S. 229 (1969).
9. *Cf.* Johnson v. Railway Express Agency, 421 U.S. 454 (1975), applying a state statute of limitations to a case

brought to enforce part of §1 of the Civil Rights Act of 1866, now codified as 42 U.S.C. §1981.
10. Adickes v. S. H. Kress & Co., 398 U.S. 144 (1970).
11. Burton v. Wilmington Parking Auth., 365 U.S. 715 (1961).
12. Washington v. Davis, 426 U.S. 229 (1976).
13. Arlington Heights v. Metropolitan Hous. Dev. Corp., 429 U.S. 252 (1977).
14. *See* notes 12 and 13, *supra*.
15. Dunn v. Blumstein, 405 U.S. 330, 363–64 (1972) (Burger, C.J., dissenting). Chief Justice Burger is not entirely correct in that the compelling state interest standard has been met on two occasions. During World War II, the Supreme Court upheld discrimination against Japanese-Americans in the context of "gravest, imminent danger to the public safety," Korematsu v. United States, 323 U.S. 214, 218 (1944), and in "conditions of great emergency," Hirabayashi v. United States, 320 U.S. 81, 111 (1943) (Murphy, J., concurring).
16. Monell v. Department of Social Services, 436 U.S. 658 (1978).
17. Part of Monroe v. Pape, 365 U.S. 167 (1961), holding that administrative remedies need not be exhausted, was not affected by the overruling of another part of Monroe in Monell v. Department of Social Services, 436 U.S. 658 (1978).
18. *Cf.* O'Sullivan v. Felix, 233 U.S. 318 (1914), applying a state statute of limitations to a case brought under part of the Civil Rights Act of 1871 now codified as 42 U.S.C. §1985. *See also* note 9, *supra*.
19. Terry v. Adams, 345 U.S. 461 (1953).
20. *See, e.g.,* Guinn v. United States, 238 U.S. 347 (1915); White v. Regester, 412 U.S. 755 (1973).
21. Reddix v. Lucky, 252 F.2d 930 (5th Cir. 1958).
22. Lane v. Wilson, 307 U.S. 268 (1939).
23. The Civil Rights Act of 1866 is the Act of April 9, 1866, ch. 31, §1, 14 Stat. 27, now codified in part as 42 U.S.C. §§1981 and 1982. The Civil Rights Act of 1871 is the Act of April 20, 1871, ch. 22, §1 and §2, 17 Stat. 13, now codified in part as 42 U.S.C. §§1983 and 1985, and as 28 U.S.C. §1343(3). The Civil Rights Act of 1875 is found at 18 Stat. 335.

THE RIGHTS OF RACIAL MINORITIES

24. The Civil Rights Cases, 109 U.S. 3 (1883). A nearly identical statute, Title II of the Civil Rights Act of 1964, similarly prohibiting discrimination in public and private accommodations, was upheld as constitutional in Heart of Atlanta Motel v. United States, 379 U.S. 241 (1964). See Chapter VI, Public Accommodations.
25. 392 U.S. 409 (1968). See also Runyon v. McCrary, 427 U.S. 160 (1976); Johnson v. Railway Express Agency, 421 U.S. 454 (1975); Tillman v. Wheaton-Haven Recreational Ass'n, 410 U.S. 431 (1973); Sullivan v. Little Hunting Park, 396 U.S. 229 (1969).
26. See note 23, *supra*.
27. The issue of whether proof of discriminatory intent is necessary under 42 U.S.C. §1981 could have been but was not decided by the Supreme Court in 1979 in the case of Los Angeles v. Davis, 99 S. Ct. 1379 (1979), 596 Ed. 2d 642, *vacating* 556 F.2d 1334 (9th Cir. 1978).
28. 42 U.S.C. §1981.
29. See Johnson v. Railway Express Agency, 421 U.S. 454 (1975), and cases cited therein at 459 n.6.
30. Tillman v. Wheaton-Haven Recreational Ass'n, 410 U.S. 431 (1973); Scott v. Young, 421 F.2d 143 (4th Cir.), *cert. denied*, 398 U.S. 929 (1970).
31. Runyon v. McCrary, 427 U.S. 160 (1976).
32. 42 U.S.C. §1982.
33. Sullivan v. Little Hunting Park, 396 U.S. 229 (1969); Jones v. Alfred H. Mayer Co., 392 U.S. 409 (1968); *cf.* Tillman v. Wheaton-Haven Recreational Ass'n, 410 U.S. 431 (1973).
34. See cases cited in note 25, *supra*.
35. 42 U.S.C. §1988, as amended by The Civil Rights Attorney Fees Awards Act of 1976, Pub.L.No. 94-559 (Oct. 19, 1976), 90 Stat. 2641.
36. Johnson v. Railway Express Agency, 421 U.S. 454 (1975).
37. *Id*.
38. 42 U.S.C. §1983. See note 23, *supra*.
39. *Id*.
40. See notes 10 and 11, *supra*, and accompanying text.
41. Monell v. Department of Social Services, 436 U.S. 658 (1978).

42. *See* notes 12 and 13, *supra*, and accompanying text.
43. *Id.*
44. *See* note 16, *supra.*
45. *See* note 35, *supra.*
46. *See* note 17, *supra.*
47. *See* note 18, *supra.*
48. 42 U.S.C. §1985(3). *See* note 23, *supra.*
49. Griffin v. Breckenridge, 403 U.S. 88 (1971).
50. Richardson v. Miller, 446 F.2d 1247 (3d Cir. 1971); Pennsylvania v. Local 542, Operating Engineers, 347 F.Supp. 268, 290–97 (E.D. Pa. 1972).
51. *See* notes 49 and 50, *supra.*
52. *See* notes 16–18 and 44–47, *supra.*
53. *See* note 23, *supra*, and accompanying text.
54. The Civil Rights Cases, 109 U.S. 3 (1883).
55. 42 U.S.C. §§2000a, *et seq.*
56. Heart of Atlanta Motel v. United States, 379 U.S. 241 (1964).
57. 42 U.S.C. §2000a(a).
58. 42 U.S.C. §§2000a(b) (1), (2), & (3), respectively.
59. 42 U.S.C. §2000a(e). This exception has been interpreted very narrowly. *See, e.g.,* Tillman v. Wheaton-Haven Recreational Ass'n, 410 U.S. 431 (1973).
60. 42 U.S.C. §2000a-4.
61. 42 U.S.C. §2000a-5.
62. 42 U.S.C. §2000a-3.
63. 42 U.S.C. §2000a-3(c). *See* Harris v. Ericson, 457 F.2d 765 (10th Cir. 1972).
64. 42 U.S.C., §2000a-6.
65. 42 U.S.C. §2000a-3(a). *See* Newman v. Piggie Park Enterprises, 390 U.S. 400 (1968).
66. 42 U.S.C. §2000a-3(b). Newman v. Piggie Park Enterprises, 390 U.S. 400 (1968).
67. 42 U.S.C. §§2000e *et seq.*
68. 42 U.S.C. §§2000e(b) and (e), respectively.
69. 42 U.S.C. §§2000e-2((a)–(d).
70. Griggs v. Duke Power Co., 401 U.S. 424 (1971); *see also* Albemarle Paper Co. v. Moody, 422 U.S. 405 (1975).

71. Dothard v. Rawlinson, 433 U.S. 321 (1977).
72. 42 U.S.C. §2000e-4 and §2000e-5.
73. 42 U.S.C. §2000e-5 and §2000e-6.
74. 42 U.S.C. §2000e-5.
75. 42 U.S.C. §2000e-5. *See* McDonnell-Douglas Corp. v. Green, 411 U.S. 792, 798 (1973); Love v. Pullman Co., 404 U.S. 522, 523 (1972).
76. 42 U.S.C. §2000e-5(g). Back pay is awardable not only to the individuals bringing a lawsuit but to all minorities discriminated against. Albemarle Paper Co. v. Moody, 422 U.S. 405 (1975).
77. 42 U.S.C. §2000e-5(k). Prevailing plaintiffs are awarded fees as a matter of course whereas prevailing defendants may recover fees only if the lawsuit was frivolous. Christiansburg Garment Co. v. EEOC, 434 U.S. 412 (1978).
78. *See generally,* 42 U.S.C. §§1973 *et seq.*
79. 42 U.S.C. §1973aa.
80. 42 U.S.C. §1973c.
81. 42 U.S.C. §§1973d, 1973f, 1973cc, and 1973aa-1a.
82. South Carolina v. Katzenbach, 383 U.S. 301 (1966); Katzenbach v. Morgan, 384 U.S. 641 (1966).
83. 42 U.S.C. §1973c.
84. 42 U.S.C. §1973j(d); Allen v. State Board of Elections, 393 U.S. 544 (1969).
85. 42 U.S.C. §§1973j(a), (b), & (c).
86. 42 U.S.C. §1973j(f).
87. 42 U.S.C. §§1973j(d) and 1973 1(e).
88. 42 U.S.C. §§3601 *et seq.*
89. 42 U.S.C. §3606(b)(1).
90. 42 U.S.C. §3604(a).
91. 42 U.S.C. §3604(d).
92. 42 U.S.C. §3604(c).
93. Arlington Heights v. Metropolitan Hous. Dev. Corp., 429 U.S. 252 (1977).
94. Metropolitan Hous. Dev. Corp. v. Arlington Heights, 558 F.2d 1283, 1286–1290 (7th Cir. 1977), *cert. denied,* 434 U.S. 1025 (1978), *on remand from* 429 U.S. 252 (1977).
95. 42 U.S.C. §3610 and §3611.

96. 42 U.S.C. §3613.
97. 42 U.S.C. §3610 and §3612.
98. 42 U.S.C. §3610.
99. 42 U.S.C. §3612.
100. *Id.*
101. Albemarle Paper Co. v. Moody, 422 U.S. 405, 417–418 (1975).
102. Christiansburg Garment Co. v. EEOC, 434 U.S. 412 (1978); *cf.* Newman v. Piggie Park Enterprises, 390 U.S. 400 (1968).
103. United States v. Chicago, 549 F.2d 415, 447 (7th Cir. 1977) (Pell, J., dissenting), *cert. denied,* 434 U.S. 875 (1978).
104. *Id.* at 448.
105. 42 U.S.C. §2000d *et seq.*
106. 31 U.S.C. §1242–45.
107. 42 U.S.C. §3766(c).

II
Voting

During the early history of the United States, voting was typically limited to white male property owners over the age of twenty-one. After the Civil War, however, the Confederate states were required to guarantee universal male suffrage without regard to race as a condition for reentry into the Union. And, with the adoption in 1870 of the Fifteenth Amendment, the equal right to vote without regard to race was guaranteed, at least in theory, throughout the rest of the nation.[1]

What federal prohibitions against racial discrimination in voting exist today?

Aside from the Fifteenth Amendment, which guarantees the equal right to vote without regard to race, color, or previous condition of servitude, the basic federal prohibitions against discrimination in voting are: (1) the Fourteenth Amendment, which prohibits intentional discrimination by public officials; (2) Reconstruction-era statutes imposing civil and criminal penalties upon those who interfere with voting rights;[2] and (3) the modern Voting Rights Acts of 1957, 1960, 1964, and 1965 (amended in 1970 and 1975).[3] Of these prohibitions, by far the most important is the Voting Rights Act of 1965, which prohibits literacy tests, provides for the appointment of federal voter registrars and examiners, and requires federal approval of changes in voting in those jurisdictions that have a history of voting discrimination.

PROTECTION OF VOTING RIGHTS GENERALLY

What kind of discrimination in voting is prohibited by the Fifteenth Amendment?

The Fifteenth Amendment prohibits discrimination in voting at all levels of the political process by federal, state, and local officials on the basis of race, color, or previous condition of servitude. The amendment, in the words of the Supreme Court, "nullifies sophisticated as well as simple-minded modes of discrimination" and makes unlawful "onerous procedural requirements which effectively handicap exercise of the franchise by the colored race."[4] The Supreme Court has never held that a showing of *intentional* racial discrimination is required for a violation of the Fifteenth Amendment, although racial motive has been abundantly apparent in the voting cases it has decided.[5] While the Fifteenth Amendment was enacted as a limitation on public officials, the acts of private individuals have been held unconstitutional under it where they perpetuate or act as a substitute for official discrimination.[6]

Was the Fifteenth Amendment effectively enforced after its ratification in 1870?

Far from it. The good intentions of the Reconstruction Congress were nullified by the other branches of the federal government. By Section 2 of the Fifteenth Amendment, Congress was authorized to enact consistent legislation. In due course a variety of voting laws were enacted during Reconstruction, requiring election officials to give all citizens the same opportunity to vote,[7] and making it a federal crime to violate state laws governing the election of federal officials, to interfere privately or officially with a citizen's right to vote, or to commit fraudulent acts in connection with registering voters or counting ballots.[8] Congress also established a system of federal supervisors of elections.[9] None of these laws, however, were adequately enforced, and some of them were declared unconstitutional by the Supreme Court.[10] Then, in 1894, in the aftermath of the end of

Reconstruction, Congress itself repealed many of the post–Civil War voting laws, including those dealing with federal supervision of state elections.[11]

What was the consequence of the lack of enforcement?
Predictably, the consequence of nonenforcement of the Fifteenth Amendment was the disfranchisement of black voters. After the Civil War, blacks registered and voted in substantial numbers in the states where they had formerly been disfranchised, and many were elected to office. But minority participation in the elective process was generally possible only because of the presence of federal troops dispatched under various Reconstruction laws.

After Reconstruction ended in 1877, and federal troops were withdrawn from the South, the disfranchisement of blacks began in earnest and the promise of equal voting rights held out by the Fifteenth Amendment faded. A common method of discouraging Negroes from voting was to make the elective process more difficult and cumbersome. During this period, white legislators gave free rein to their imaginations in burdening the franchise with onerous requirements.

The main work of disfranchisement was accomplished through a series of state constitutional conventions, the first of which was held in Mississippi in 1890. The avowed purpose of these conventions, in the words of U.S. Senator "Pitchfork" Ben Tillman, who addressed the South Carolina Disfranchising Convention of 1895, was "to take from [the 'ignorant blacks'] every ballot that we can under the laws of our national government." [12] One generally adopted method of excluding minorities from voting was to impose a literacy test. Typically, the test required the voter to be able to read and write a portion of the Constitution as a condition to register to vote. The literacy test was racially neutral on its face, but it was administered in a way which excluded blacks, but not whites, from registering. To make sure that illiterate whites were not disfranchised, alternatives to literacy were provided if the registrant could "understand and interpret" the Constitution, owned property, or was "of good character." Many states also enacted "grandfather clauses" which excused persons registered on or prior to January 1, 1866, and their descendants, from having to comply with any literacy or property requirement for registration. By definition, few Negroes could qualify for registration under the grandfather clauses, since Negroes were generally not allowed to vote prior to January 1, 1866. The poll tax was another way of limiting the franchise. The tax was, in essence, a fee for the privilege of voting and fell with disproportionate impact upon poor blacks.

One of the most effective ways of denying political participation to minorities was through the use of the "all-white" primary, established either through political party rule or statute, which restricted party membership and voting to whites. Since political parties were groups of private individuals, not governmentally controlled groups, they appeared to be beyond the reach of the Fifteenth Amendment. And because nomination in the primary was tantamount to election to office in the states that used the all-white primary, Negroes, even those who were registered, were effectively shut out from the elective process.

Voter-registration figures reveal the effectiveness of post-Reconstruction disfranchisement. In Louisiana in 1896, there were 130,334 Negroes registered to vote. In 1900, there were only 5,320. In Mississippi, 70 percent of the black voting age population was registered to vote in 1867. By 1899, the figure had plummeted to 9%.[13] Registration statistics from other states are much the same. It is no exaggeration to say that at the turn of the century, after the end of Reconstruction and after judicial and legislative repeal of laws supporting the Fifteenth Amendment, blacks and other racial minorities no longer participated in a meaningful way in the political life of the United States.

Did any of the laws designed to implement the Fifteenth Amendment survive Reconstruction?

Yes. Some of the Reconstruction voting laws have survived, including a statute protecting the right to vote without regard to race or color;[14] two laws making those who interfere with protected rights (e.g., the right to vote) liable for civil damages;[15] and two statutes imposing criminal penalties on persons who hinder others in their attempts to vote.[16] Even these surviving laws were limited in their scope and, until recently, were infrequently used. The criminal provisions for denial of the equal right to vote were used to prevent election fraud but rarely to protect against racial discrimination in exercise of the franchise.[17] The surviving civil remedies were occasionally used effectively in banning all-white primaries,[18] but seldom to attack other forms of discrimination in the administration of voting laws.

Was the Fifteenth Amendment eventually revived?

Yes, but only gradually. It was not until 1915, forty-five years after its ratification, that the amendment was actually used by the Supreme Court to invalidate a discriminatory election procedure.[19] In the case of *Guinn v. United States,* the Court declared the grandfather clause unconstitutional on the ground that its only purpose was to exclude blacks from voting in violation of the Fifteenth Amendment's guarantee of the equal right to vote. But in the same case the Court approved the use of discriminatory literacy tests for voting, because, in the Court's view, the use of literacy tests was an "exercise of the state of a lawful power vested in it, not subject to our supervision." [20]

Has Congress taken any action since Reconstruction to protect the voting rights of minorities?

Yes. In 1957, Congress passed the first civil rights act since the Civil War.[21] The Act established the six-member bipartisan Commission on Civil Rights and gave it the duty of gathering information on discrimination in voting. It also prohibited interference with voting in federal elections, authorized the Attorney General to bring lawsuits to protect voting rights, and set out procedures for holding in criminal contempt those who disobeyed court orders ending discrimination. The act was amended in 1960 to authorize federal referees to investigate voting discrimination and to register qualified voters.[22] Four years later Congress enacted the Civil Rights Act of 1964. It provided, among other things, that black registration be based upon the same voter qualifications that traditionally had been applied to whites; that any literacy or other test for voting be given entirely in writing; that immaterial errors in answering test questions not be made the basis for denying registration; and that a sixth-grade education was rebuttable evidence of literacy.[23] These various statutes, although they were often used effectively to deal with particular voting rights infringements, did not result in the enfranchisement of any appreciable number of racial minorities.

Then in 1965, Congress adopted an entirely new approach to voter legislation. Instead of relying primarily on lawsuits to insure fair administration of state voting standards and procedures—as it had done in the 1957, 1960, and 1964 acts—Congress passed the Voting Rights Act of 1965, which suspended the standards responsible for the exclusion of minorities from registration and placed supervision of new procedures in the hands of federal officials.[24] Because of the importance of this act, it is discussed in more detail later.

Can political parties still discriminate or exclude racial minorities from membership or voting in primaries?

No. The Supreme Court, reflecting a thaw in racial attitudes in the country, began an assault on discrimination by political parties in 1924, when it struck down a Texas law declaring Negroes ineligible to participate in Democratic party elections.[25] Subsequently, some states, in an effort to remove the conduct of primary elections from federal judicial review, repealed state laws regulating primaries, thereby allowing political parties to make their own rules, including rules excluding blacks from voting or party membership. Such exclusionary schemes were eventually held unconstitutional.

First, in *Nixon* v. *Condon*,[26] after holding that racial discrimination in voting was not delegable, the Supreme Court struck down a Texas statute authorizing the state Democratic party to fix qualifications for voting in primaries. Then, in *Smith* v. *Allwright*, the Court held a rule of the Democratic party of Texas limiting membership to whites, passed without the aid or authorization of the legislature, unconstitutional for the reason that the equal right to vote "is not to be nullified by a state through casting its electoral process in a form which permits a private organization to practice racial discrimination in the election." [27]

The rule in *Smith* v. *Allwright* was later applied to prevent exclusion of blacks from voting in elections held by an ostensibly private club which duplicated the functions of primaries held by political parties. "It violates the Fifteenth Amendment," the Supreme Court said, "for a state, by such circumvention, to permit within its borders the use of any device that produces an equivalent of the prohibited elections." [28]

Other forms of discrimination by political parties, such as rules requiring members to take an oath supporting the "social and educational separation of races," have also been held unconstitutional.[29]

Can payment of a poll tax be required for voting in federal or state elections?

No. The poll tax was never regarded as a legitimate revenue measure, but, like the literacy test, was enacted as a "clog" upon the franchise to keep blacks from voting.[30] Nonetheless, the Supreme Court initially ruled in 1937 that the tax was an appropriate condition for suffrage within the power of states to impose.[31] Numerous attempts were subsequently made to abolish the poll tax through federal legislation. It was not until 1964, however, with ratification of the Twenty-fourth Amendment, that the tax was banned in federal elections. Two years later, the Supreme Court, reversing its earlier decision, declared use of the poll tax in state elections to be unconstitutional because "the affluence of the voter or payment of any fee" was not a proper "electoral standard." [32]

Are literacy or education tests for registering and voting constitutional?

Not if they are used to exclude racial minorities from voting. The Supreme Court, as well as numerous lower courts, have now ruled that "interpretation tests" which require registrants to read and explain the state or federal Constitution are unconstitutional where they grant unlimited discretion to local voter registrars and are used to exclude blacks from registration. Under the circumstances, the test is "not a test but a trap, sufficient to stop even the most brilliant man on his way to the voting booth," and is invalid under both the Fourteenth and Fifteenth Amendments.[33]

Literacy tests are also banned by the Voting Rights Act of 1965, of which more will be said later.

Is discrimination or intimidation by private individuals against racial minorities in registering and voting unlawful?

Yes. Although the Supreme Court has held that neither the Fourteenth nor Fifteenth Amendments prohibits private acts of discrimination,[34] it has held that Article I, Section 4 of the Constitution granting authority to Congress to regulate federal elections justifies Congressional prohibition of private discrimination in registering and voting for federal officials.[35] Physical assaults and threats against minority registrants have been enjoined, as have different forms of economic coercion.[36]

In one case from Tennessee, blacks who registered, and whites who assisted them, were "blacklisted" and denied credit and the right to buy necessities by local businessmen. Tenant farmers and sharecroppers who were blacklisted were also evicted by their white landowners. In a lawsuit filed to stop this intimidation, a court held that injunctions should issue against the businessmen and the landowners to end their interference with the rights of blacks to register and vote.[37]

What other kinds of discrimination have been struck down in recent years under federal voting laws?

Just about every kind imaginable. Racial discrimination in voting has taken many forms, and has included such crude measures as segregated polling places,[38] purges of blacks from registration lists,[39] the requirement that the race of every candidate for elective office appear on the ballot,[40] and the arrest and prosecution of blacks conducting voting registration drives.[41] More subtle practices have been "slowdowns" in processing minority registration applications[42] and resignation from office by state officials leaving plaintiffs in voting rights lawsuits with no one to sue.[43] All of these practices have been held unconstitutional.

A classic example of modern racial discrimination in voting, at once crude and ingenious, involved the City of Tuskegee, Alabama, which redrew its city limits from a square into a "strangely irregular twenty-eight-sided figure." [44] The result of the alteration was to remove from the electorate all but four or five of the city's Negro voters, while not removing a single white voter or resident. The Supreme Court had little trouble in finding that the reapportionment was discriminatory in violation of the Fifteenth Amendment.

The Voting Rights Act, as we shall see, is a further deterrent to such racial gerrymanders, since jurisdictions seeking to change voting lines now have the burden under section 5 of the act to prove the absence of discriminatory purpose or effect.

Can a person be made to disclose his or her race as a condition for registering to vote?

Yes, if state law requires it. Many states require persons to list their race on voter registration forms. If the forms are not fully completed, registration may be denied. None of these compulsory disclosure laws have been held unconstitutional in themselves by the Supreme Court,[45] but their discriminatory misuse, for example to deny registration only to noncomplying racial minorities,[46] or the misuse of the information itself, for example to segregate or purge blacks on voter lists, would be patently unlawful.[47] Although racial classification was used in the past to exclude minorities from the elective process, the modern justification for requiring disclosure of race, aside from the incidental value it may have in identifying registrants and minimizing voter fraud, is to assist government in formulating and evaluating legislative programs to assist minorities and the courts in fashioning remedies for past discrimination.

In a related context, the Voting Rights Act Amendments of 1975 authorize the Director of Census to conduct surveys and compile registration and voting statistics on the extent to which racial minorities are registered to vote and have voted in elections.[48] The main purpose of the surveys is to assist the Congress in evaluating the effectiveness of federal voting rights legislation and the need for additional remedial action. Some persons object to supplying the government with racial information, not only because of their fear of its misuse, but because of their beliefs that governmental concepts of race and ethnic origin are loose and unscientific, and constitute an invasion of privacy. To meet these concerns, the Voting Rights Act Amendments of 1975 provide that no person may be compelled to disclose race, color, or national origin in response to any census survey taken under the act and that no penalty may be imposed for failure to make such disclosures.[49]

To further insure privacy, the amendments also provide that the confidentiality and criminal penalties provisions which are normally applicable to processes used to collect census data are applicable to surveys under the act.[50]

Given the importance of racial information, if government is to legislate intelligently and courts are to fashion effective remedies for past discrimination, the balance between individual rights and the public need for accurate data seems best struck by requiring disclosure of racial information, but guaranteeing protection against its discriminatory misuse and insuring privacy by separating racial or ethnic information from personal identifying information such as name and address.

How is the Fifteenth Amendment enforced? What remedies are available for violations?

The traditional methods of enforcing the Fifteenth Amendment have been prosecutions by the federal government for violations of criminal statutes protecting voting rights,[51] lawsuits by victims of discrimination under the various statutes enacted by Congress to enforce the Fifteenth Amendment,[52] and suits by the Attorney General under the same statutes to remedy individual violations as well as patterns and practices of voting discrimination.[53] More recently, the Department of Justice and jurisdictions covered by the Voting Rights

Act of 1965 have been given administrative responsibilities in connection with the implementation of changes in voting procedures. These procedures, designed to protect Fifteenth Amendment rights, are discussed later in this chapter. There are no administrative requirements which must be complied with prior to filing a lawsuit in court.[54]

Remedies for violations of protected rights include court orders ending the discrimination, retroactive relief such as the setting aside of elections,[55] and awards of attorneys' fees [56] and damages.[57]

THE VOTING RIGHTS ACT OF 1965

What are the basic provisions of the Voting Rights Act of 1965?

The Voting Rights Act of 1965, amended in 1970 and 1975,[58] supended "tests or devices" for voting which had been used in the past to disfranchise racial minorities.[59] The term "test or device" includes literacy tests, educational requirements, good-character tests, and exclusively English language registration procedures or elections conducted solely in English where a single linguistic minority comprises more than 5 percent of the voting age population of the jurisdiction. A second provision of the act, section 5, requires "covered" jurisdictions to gain approval or preclearance from federal authorities before implementing changes in voting laws or procedures to make certain that they do not have the purpose or effect of abridging the right to vote on account of race, color, or membership in a language minority.[60] The act also provides for federal voter registrars and observers, absentee balloting in presidential elections, and bilingual ballots for language minorities.[61]

The basic provisions of the Voting Rights Act of 1965 were held to be constitutional by the Supreme Court in *South Carolina* v. *Katzenbach*,[62] and *Katzenbach* v. *Morgan*.[63]

Is the Voting Rights Act ban on literacy and education tests for voting nationwide?

Yes. Literacy or other tests as a condition for voting were banned by the Voting Rights Act of 1965 initially only in those states in which Congress found there had been pervasive discrimination against blacks in registration and in which literacy tests had been specifically designed to disfranchise racial minorities.[64] Later, the ban on literacy and other tests was made nationwide by amendments to the Voting Rights Act of 1965, which also extended the life of the act through 1982.[65] The Supreme Court held the nationwide ban constitutional after concluding that literacy tests had reduced voter participation in a discriminatory manner throughout the country, and not merely in those states originally covered by the act.[66]

Do the preclearance procedures of Section 5 also apply nationwide?

No. Only those states are covered by Section 5 in which less than half of eligible persons are actually registered or voted in either the 1964, 1968 or 1972 presidential elections, *and*, if a "test or device" was used for registering or voting. When this formula is not met in a state as a whole, coverage may apply in any "political subdivision" within the state that satisfies the formula.

The Attorney General and the Director of Census are responsible for determining whether the conditions for coverage are met in particular jurisdictions.

What is a "political subdivision" for the purposes of the Act?

"Political subdivision" is defined in the Act as any county or parish or subdivision of a state which conducts registration for voting.[67] A list of jurisdictions now covered by Section 5 is as follows: [68]

Alabama—whole state
Alaska—whole state
Arizona—whole state
California—4 counties: Kings, Merced, Monterrey, and Yuba

Colorado—1 county: El Paso
Connecticut—3 towns: Groton, Mansfield, and Southbury
Florida—5 counties: Collier, Hardee, Hendry, Hillsborough, and Monroe
Georgia—whole state
Hawaii—2 counties: Hawaii and Honolulu
Idaho—1 county: Elmore
Louisiana—whole state
Maine—18 towns: Beddington, Carroll, Plantation, Caswell Plantation, Charleston, Chelsea, Connor Unorganized Territory, Cutler, Limestone, Ludlow, Nashville Plantation, New Gloucester, Reed Plantation, Winter Harbor, and Woodland
Massachusetts—9 towns: Amherst, Ayer, Belchertown, Bourne, Harvard, Sandwich, Shirley, Sunderland, and Wrentham
Michigan—1 town: Buena Vista
Mississippi—whole state
New Hampshire—10 towns: Antrim, Benton, Boscawen, Millsfield Township, Newington, Pinkhams Grant, Rindge, Stewartstown, Stratford, and Unity
New York—3 counties: Bronx, Kings, and New York
North Carolina—41 counties: Anson, Beaufort, Bertie, Bladen, Camden, Caswell, Chowen, Cleveland, Craven, Cumberland, Edgecomb, Franklin, Gates, Gatson, Granville, Greene, Guilford, Halifax, Marnett, Hertford, Hoke, Jackson, Lee, Lenoir, Martin, Nash, Northampton, Orslow, Pasquotank, Perquamins, Person, Pitt, Robeson, Rockingham, Scotland, Union, Vance, Wake, Washington, Wayne, and Wilson
Oklahoma—2 counties: Choctaw and McCurtain
South Carolina—whole state
South Dakota—2 counties: Shannon and Todd
Texas—whole state
Virginia—whole state
Wyoming—1 county: Campbell

Are all political units within designated jurisdictions covered by Section 5?

Yes. Section 5 covers all entities or political units within designated jurisdictions that exercise power over any aspect of the electoral process, and without regard to whether such units actually register voters or conduct elections.

Thus, cities which do not register voters,[69] political parties,[70] and entities such as school boards which neither register voters nor conduct elections,[71] located within designated jurisdictions, are subject to Section 5 where they exercise control over some aspect of the elective process.

Can a covered jurisdiction remove itself from Section 5 coverage?

Yes. While the decision of the Attorney General and Director of Census that a given jurisdiction is covered is not reviewable,[72] a covered jurisdiction, pursuant to Section 4 (a) of the act, may "bail out" from Section 5 coverage by obtaining a ruling from the federal court in the District of Columbia that it has not administered a "test or device" within the preceding ten years for the purpose or effect of denying or abridging the right to vote on account of race, color, or membership in a language minority, or that the illiteracy rate of the applicable language-minority groups is equal to or less than the national average. Exemption under Section 4 (a) has proved difficult, but not impossible.[73]

Is coverage under Section 5 of any real significance?

Yes. Coverage under Section 5 is enormously significant, for it means that *no* change in voting procedures in a covered jurisdiction may be implemented unless the change has first been cleared to insure that it does not have the purpose or effect of denying or abridging the right to vote on account of race, color, or membership in a language minority. Section 5 thus provides an effective safeguard against enactment of new forms of discrimination, and it places the burden of litigation or administrative proceedings and delay upon the perpetrators and not the victims of possibly discriminatory practices.[74]

What kinds of changes in voting are covered by Section 5?

Any change in voting sought to be implemented after November 1, 1964, in a covered jurisdiction is subject to

Section 5, with the exception of changes formulated and ordered by federal courts.[75] It is immaterial whether the change is major or minor, or whether brought about by legislation, constitutional amendment, political party rule or custom and practice. The Supreme Court has given Section 5 the broadest possible construction to include such seemingly inconsequential changes in voting as the relocation of a polling place.[76] Other changes within the scope of Section 5 include annexations, staggering of terms of office, majority vote requirements, changes to single member or multi-member districts, abolition of elective or appointive offices, changing of precinct lines, redistricting, and changes in filing fees or other candidacy requirements.[77] The Supreme Court has most recently held that a rule adopted by a county school board that its employees must take unpaid leaves of absence while campaigning for elective political office was a change in voting for which preclearance was required.[78]

Is a change in voting enacted prior to November 1, 1964, but not implemented until after November 1, 1964, subject to Section 5?

Yes, so long as the change in voting alters the practice in effect on November 1, 1964, it is subject to the preclearance procedures of Section 5 regardless of when the change was actually enacted. For example, in 1962, the State of Mississippi enacted a law requiring the City of Canton to change from ward to at-large elections for aldermen. The city, however, ignored the law in its 1965 elections and, as in previous years, elected aldermen by wards. In 1969, the city for the first time implemented the change in the law and switched to at-large elections. It refused to comply with Section 5 on the ground that it had no choice but to conform to the 1962 state statute. The Supreme Court nonetheless enjoined use of at-large elections until the city complied with Section 5, since the procedure actually in force and effect on November 1, 1964, was voting by wards.[79]

How is preclearance obtained?

Preclearance of changes in voting may be obtained in two ways. The change may be submitted administratively to the Attorney General who has sixty days, from the date submission is deemed completed, within which to note any objection. If the Attorney General fails to object, the proposed change may be implemented. On the other hand, if the Attorney General notes an objection, the change is rendered null and void and preexisting law remains in effect.

The second method by which a covered jurisdiction may obtain preclearance, whether or not submission has been made to the Attorney General, is to bring a lawsuit in federal court in the District of Columbia. If the court rules that the change has neither the purpose nor the effect of denying or abridging the right to vote on account of race, color, or membership in a language minority, it may be implemented. If, however, the court fails to make such a ruling, the change may not take effect.

Because of the time and expense of legal proceedings, administrative submission to the Attorney General has been the usual method of obtaining clearance of proposed changes in voting.

Do persons affected by proposed changes in voting have the right to make their views known, either to the Attorney General or the federal court, before clearance is granted or denied?

Yes. The Attorney General has issued guidelines involving administrative submissions,[80] which allow interested persons or organizations to request and receive notice of submissions, and more importantly, to submit evidence and arguments in favor of or against proposed changes. Persons potentially affected by changes in voting laws are also permitted to intervene in court proceedings in the District of Columbia to assert any interests they might have. In this manner, those persons affected by changes in voting laws play an important role in enforcing the preclearance procedures of Section 5 of the Voting Rights Act. Persons wishing to receive notice of submissions, or who have questions about voting laws in their jurisdictions, should contact the Attorney General, Department of Justice, Washington, D.C. 20530.[81]

Can the decision of the Attorney General in objecting or failing to object to a change in voting be appealed?

No. The Supreme Court has ruled that the decision of the Attorney General to object or not to object to a change in voting is final and not appealable.[82] However, if the Attorney General makes an objection, a covered jurisdiction has the option of bringing a lawsuit seeking a favorable ruling from the federal court in the District of Columbia.[83] If the Attorney General fails to object to a change, persons affected also may seek to enjoin its enforcement, but only in traditional lawsuits attacking the change on constitutional grounds filed in the federal courts in the jurisdiction where the voting change was proposed.[84]

Can decisions of the federal court in the District of Columbia approving or disapproving changes in voting be appealed?

Yes. Decisions of the federal court in the District of Columbia approving or disapproving changes in voting may be appealed directly to the Supreme Court.[85]

Once submission is made, how does the Attorney General or the federal court determine whether to grant clearance?

The Attorney General, or the court, must deny clearance to any proposed change which will "deny or abridge" the right to vote. Some changes, for example those which expand access to registration or increase the hours during which polling places remain open, would be unobjectionable. Other changes, such as those which make registration and voting more difficult, would be denied clearance. If the Attorney General or the court cannot determine whether a change might have a prohibited effect, preclearance must still be denied, for in Section 5 proceedings, public officials must prove that their actions do not have the purpose or effect of denying or abridging the right to vote on account of race, color, or membership in a language minority.[86] If they fail to carry this burden, approval must be withheld.

Section 5's allocation of the burden of proof has

proved to be a substantial curb to the introduction of new, discriminatory voting procedures.

Does a change which increases minority participation in the elective process—but does so only partially—"deny or abridge" the right to vote?

No. In *Beer* v. *United States*,[87] the Supreme Court was asked to review a decision of the federal court in the District of Columbia denying clearance to a reapportionment plan for the City of New Orleans. The lower court had ruled that, although the new plan created two single member districts with a majority of black voters where before there had been none, the plan was objectionable because it failed to eliminate pre-Voting Rights Act at-large seats for the city council which restricted the opportunities of minorities for election. The Supreme Court reversed the ruling, concluding that an "ameliorative new legislative apportionment cannot violate Section 5 unless the new apportionment itself so discriminates on the basis of race or color as to violate the Constitution."[88] In other words, a change in election procedures which removes some, but not all, barriers to voting ordinarily will not violate Section 5.

Do annexations of territory that increase majority voting strength "deny or abridge" the rights of minorities under Section 5?

No, provided the purpose of the annexation was not to dilute minority voting strength and minorities are insured fair representation in government in proportion to their percent of the post-annexation population. In one Section 5 case, the Supreme Court approved annexations by the city of Richmond, Virginia, which reduced the black population from 55 to 45 percent of the electorate, because there had been no discriminatory purpose and blacks were insured fair representation in government of the enlarged city.[89] Nevertheless, the decision does sanction a change which had the net effect of watering down the political strength of minority voters. One of the justices implied that the decision was a limited one and created a special "municipal hardship" exception from Section 5 coverage in favor of annexations.

THE RIGHTS OF RACIAL MINORITIES

Is there anything to keep a covered jurisdiction from ignoring Section 5 and implementing changes in voting without having received preclearance?

Yes. The Attorney General, or any person affected by a proposed change in voting, may seek an injunction against enforcement by filing an action before a three-judge court in the covered jurisdictions.[90] In such a proceeding, the sole issues are whether the jurisdiction is covered, whether the change affects voting, and whether there has been preclearance. If both the jurisdiction and the changes are covered, and there has been no preclearance, the three-judge court *must* prohibit implementation of the change. The court has no jurisdiction to resolve whether the change has the purpose or effect of abridging the right to vote on account of race, color, or membership in a language minority, since these issues may be resolved only by the Attorney General or the federal court in the District of Columbia.[91]

The Voting Rights Act also makes it criminal to fail to comply with preclearance requirements,[92] although there have been no known prosecutions for the offense.[93]

If an uncleared change has been implemented, can the courts grant retroactive relief?

Yes. In the event an uncleared change has actually been implemented, the court must not only enjoin its future use, but fashion a remedy to undo the violation of the Voting Rights Act, such as shortening of terms of office or ordering new elections under the preexisting election laws.[94] The Supreme Court recently indicated, however, that in certain circumstances it is appropriate to enjoin further use of an uncleared change, but allow local officials an opportunity to seek federal approval. The Court may then order new elections if approval is denied.[95]

How are federal examiners and observers appointed under the Voting Rights Act? What do they do?

The Attorney General is authorized by the Voting Rights Act to direct that federal examiners and/or observers be sent to covered jurisdictions from which twenty or more meritorious, written complaints alleging voter

52

discrimination have been received, or if the Attorney General determines that appointment is necessary to protect the equal right to vote.[96]

Examiners may register or list qualified voters.[97] Those listed are issued registration certificates and may vote in all federal, state, and local elections. The list of persons registered is sent monthly to local officials who must enter their names on election rolls. Federal observers act as poll watchers and determine whether all the eligible persons are allowed to vote and that ballots are properly counted.

Persons wishing to have either examiners or observers appointed in their jurisdictions should make a request directly to the Attorney General, Department of Justice, Washington, D.C. 20530.

Have examiners and observers been used extensively?

No. Federal examiners have been used sparingly, and primarily during the first years of the Voting Rights Act. The mere threat of appointment of examiners has generally been sufficient to ensure registration of minority voters.

Federal observers have been more widely used than examiners. During the first ten years of the Voting Rights Act, more than 6,500 observers were sent to monitor elections in covered jurisdictions.[98] The use of federal observers in more recent times, however, has significantly declined.

Are language minorities entitled to special protection in voting?

Yes. The Voting Rights Act Amendments of 1975, aside from banning literacy tests nationwide through 1982, require covered jurisdictions in which a single language minority is more than 5 percent of eligible voters, as well as noncovered jurisdictions in which language minorities are more than 5 percent of eligible voters, and where the illiteracy rate within the language minority is higher than the national average, to conduct bilingual elections and registration campaigns.[99] More specifically, affected jurisdictions are required to provide registration or voting notices, forms, instructions, assistance, or other materials or information relating to the electoral process, including ballots, in the language of the applicable language minority group if such items and services are provided in English.

Many states also make statutory provision for assistance to illiterate voters or those who do not read or understand English, while several court decisions have held that the right to receive assistance in voting is protected by the Constitution.[100]

Which language minorities are entitled to the special bilingual election and registration provisions of the Voting Rights Act? Which jurisdictions are covered?

The Voting Rights Act Amendments of 1975 define language minorities as American Indians, Asian-Americans, Alaskan Natives, or those of Spanish heritage.[101] Jurisdictions required to provide bilingual election procedures include the entire states of Alaska, Arizona, and Texas and approximately 215 counties and townships, too numerous to list here, in California, Colorado, Connecticut, Florida, Hawaii, Idaho, Kansas, Louisiana, Maine, Michigan, Minnesota, Mississippi, Montana, Nebraska, Nevada, New Mexico, New York, North Carolina, North Dakota, Oklahoma, Oregon, South Dakota, Utah, Virginia, Washington, Wisconsin, and Wyoming. The current list of jurisdictions is set out in 28 C.F.R., Part 55.

Does the act make any special provision for minorities with no written languages?

Yes. The act specifically provides that where the language of the applicable minority group is oral or unwritten or, in the case of Alaskan natives, if the dominant language is historically unwritten, the affected jurisdiction is required to furnish oral instructions, assistance, or other information relating to registration and voting.[102]

How are the bilingual provisions of the act enforced?

Enforcement of the bilingual provisions of the act is the responsibility of the covered jurisdictions themselves, the Attorney General, and private citizens.

Affected jurisdictions have the initial duty of determining what actions by them are necessary for compliance with the act.

Then, the Attorney General, through Section 5 preclearance procedures and by his authority to bring litigation, has the duty to prevent or remedy discrimination based on the failure to use the applicable minority language in the electoral process.[103] The Attorney General also has the responsibility of defending suits brought for termination of Voting Rights Act coverage.

Finally, private individuals may file complaints with the Attorney General or institute litigation to force compliance with the Act.

ELECTION PROCEDURES

There are various election procedures, such as at-large voting, which are not unlawful in themselves, but which nevertheless have the potential for discriminating against minority voters. Some of the procedures will be discussed in the following pages.

What is the difference between at-large and district voting?

When voting is at large, all the voters in a jurisdiction elect *all* office holders. For example, if a five-member city council is elected at large, each city voter can vote for each of the five council candidates. If voting is by district, the city is divided into five districts of substantially equal population with the voters of each district electing only one council member.

Does at-large voting favor majority over minority candidates?

Yes. Where one race is in the minority, and where voting tends to be along racial lines, minority candidates are at a distinct disadvantage in at-large elections. The majority can simply outvote the minority, assuring that minority candidates never hold political office.

Is at-large voting unconstitutional?

It depends. At-large elections are not unlawful *per se,* but their use is unconstitutional where, in the context of the facts of a given jurisdiction, they effectively remove minorities from equal political participation by diluting their voting strength.[104]

How is dilution proved?

As a general matter, dilution is proved by showing that the political process leading to nomination and election is not equally open to minority participation and that minority members have less opportunity than other residents in the jurisdiction to elect legislators of their choice.[105] More specifically, dilution may be shown by proof of an aggregation of some of the following factors: a history of official racial discrimination, particularly in registering and voting; a disproportionately low number of minority-group members elected to office; a lack of responsiveness on the part of elected officials to the needs of the minority community; depressed socio-economic status of minorities; majority-vote requirements; tenuous policy favoring at-large voting; lack of access to candidate slating by minorities; large district size; lack of residential requirements for candidates and anti-single-shot voting laws.[106]

Are there other election procedures which make it more difficult for minority candidates to get elected to office?

Yes. Majority vote and runoff requirements, as opposed to election by a plurality, favor majority candidates. If one black and several whites were to run for a single elective office in a majority white district, and if voting were along racial lines, it is conceivable that the white votes would be so evenly distributed among the white candidates that the black candidate would receive the most, or a plurality, of the votes cast. However, if the black candidate fell short of a majority—which would be likely since blacks would be a minority of voters—he or she would be forced into a runoff election with the white candidate who had received the next highest number of votes. In the runoff, the white voters could regroup behind the sole white candidate and easily elect that person to office.

Other election procedures which favor majority candidates are staggering of terms, which restricts the number of offices filled at any one election; numbered posts, which require candidates to designate for a particular post, or seat, where several vacancies are to be filled; and anti-single-shot laws, which do not permit minority voters to vote only for minority candidates.

Are there any remedies for dilution of minority voting strength?

Yes. One generally accepted way of remedying the dilution effect of at-large voting is to reapportion the jurisdiction into single-member districts, a proportionate number of which contain a majority of minority group members.[107] Such a plan would insure, not that a minority candidate would win, but that a candidate would not automatically lose because of his or her race. The Supreme Court, noting the impact of at-large voting upon minorities, has expressed a preference for single-member districts, and has concluded that they are required in court-formulated reapportionment plans unless a special combination of circumstances justifies a different result.[108] Greater leeway is allowed for experimentation in legislatively adopted plans, however.[109]

Other remedies, depending upon the particular facts, might prove equally or more effective, such as spreading minority voters among several districts rather than concentrating them in only a few, or combining at-large with single-member districts. At-large voting, in the absence of redistricting, can be ameliorated by use of plurality vote for election, nonstaggered terms of office, single shot voting, requirements that candidates reside in various districts throughout the jurisdiction, and abolition of numbered posts.

Can voting lines thus be drawn to *increase* minority participation in elective government?

Yes. It is permissible, both under the Constitution and the Voting Rights Act, for a state or its political subdivisions to take race into account in drawing district voting lines to insure minority participation in politics or to remedy the continuing effects of past discrimination in voting. Thus, in a case from New York, the Supreme Court approved a reapportionment plan creating several majority black districts in Kings County over the objections of whites who had been included in those districts, for the reasons that the plan overall neither stigmatized nor fenced out any racial group, but promoted a fair allocation of political power.[110]

Are racial minorities entitled to elect minority candidates to office in proportion to their presence in the population?

No. But racial minorities are entitled to the opportunity, equal to that of the majority, to elect candidates of their choice to office. Experience has shown that where such opportunities are in fact equal, minority candidates have been successful at the polls.

NOTES

1. Universal suffrage was not granted to women until ratification of the Nineteenth Amendment in 1920.
2. *E.g.*, 42 U.S.C. §§1983 and 1985 and 18 U.S.C. §§241 and 242.
3. The various acts are codified in 42 U.S.C. §§1971 and 1973 *et seq.*
4. Lane v. Wilson, 307 U.S. 268, 275 (1939).
5. *See, e.g.*, Guinn v. United States, 238 U.S. 347 (1915); Gomillion v. Lightfoot, 364 U.S. 339 (1960); White v. Regester, 412 U.S. 755 (1973). *Cf.* Wright v. Rockefeller, 376 U.S. 52 (1964), in which the plaintiffs framed the issues claiming an intent to discriminate under the Fourteenth and Fifteenth Amendments. The Court held intent had not been proved.
6. Smith v. Allwright, 321 U.S. 649 (1944); Terry v. Adams, 345 U.S. 461 (1953).
7. 16 Stat. 140 (1870).
8. 16 Stat. 141–46 (1870).
9. 16 Stat. 433 (1871).
10. United States v. Reese, 92 U.S. 214 (1876), held two

key provisions of voting legislation enacted in 1870 unconstitutional because they did not, consistent with the Fifteenth Amendment, prohibit state interference with voting solely on the basis of race. Another portion of the legislation prohibiting bribery to prevent persons from voting was later struck down in James v. Bowman, 190 U.S. 127 (1903), on the ground that the Fifteenth Amendment prohibited official, not private, discrimination.
11. 28 Stat. 36.
12. South Carolina v. Katzenbach, 383 U.S. 301, 310 n. 9 (1966); and JOURNAL OF THE CONSTITUTIONAL CONVENTION OF THE STATE OF SOUTH CAROLINA 464, 469, 471 (1895).
13. Political Participation, A Report of the United States Commission on Civil Rights, Washington, D.C., May, 1968, p. 8 and n. 46.
14. 42 U.S.C. §1971(a)(1).
15. 42 U.S.C. §§1983 and 1985.
16. 18 U.S.C. §§241 and 242.
17. *See, e.g.,* United States v. Stone, 188 F. 836 (D.Md. 1911); and Christopher, *The Constitutionality of the Voting Rights Act of 1965,* 18 STAN.L.REV. 1 (1965).
18. *See, e.g.,* Smith v. Allwright, 321 U.S. 649 (1944), brought under 42 U.S.C. §1983, a provision of the Civil Rights Act of 1871.
19. Guinn v. United States, 238 U.S. 347 (1915) *noted in* Nevett v. Sides, 571 F.2d 209, 220 n. 14 (5th Cir. 1978).
20. *Id.,* 238 U.S. at 359.
21. 71 Stat. 637.
22. 74 Stat. 90.
23. 78 Stat. 241
24. 79 Stat. 445.
25. Nixon v. Herndon, 273 U.S. 536 (1927).
26. 286 U.S. 73 (1932).
27. 321 U.S. 649, 664 (1944).
28. Terry v. Adams, 345 U.S. 461, 469 (1953).
29. Brown v. Baskin, 78 F.Supp. 933, 937 (E.D.S.C. 1948); Brown v. Baskin, 80 F.Supp. 1017 (E.D.S.C. 1948), *aff'd* 174 F.2d 391 (4th Cir. 1949).
30. Ratliff v. Beale, 74 Miss. 247, 20 So. 865, 869 (1896).
31. Breedlove v. Suttles, 302 U.S. 277 (1937).
32. Harper v. Virginia State Board of Elections, 383 U.S. 663, 666 (1966).
33. Louisiana v. United States, 380 U.S. 145, 153 (1965).

See also Schnell v. Davis, 336 U.S. 933 (1949); United States v. Raines, 189 F.Supp. 121 (M.D.Ga. 1960).
34. James v. Bowman, 190 U.S. 127 (1903); United States v. Reese, 92 U.S. 214 (1876). *Cf.* Terry v. Adams, 345 U.S. 461, 484 (1953).
35. *Ex parte* Yarbrough, 110 U.S. 651 (1884), affirming convictions under the predecessor of 18 U.S.C. §241 for a private conspiracy to deprive a black of the right to vote; United States v. Classic, 313 U.S. 299 (1941).
36. United States v. Original Knights of the Ku Klux Klan, 250 F.Supp. 330 (E.D.La. 1965) (three-judge court), invoking the Civil Rights Act of 1957, 42 U.S.C. §1971(c).
37. United States v. Beaty, 288 F.2d 653 (6th Cir. 1961). *See also* United States v. Deal, 6 R.Rel.Law Rep. 474 (W.D.La. 1961).
38. Bell v. Southwell, 376 F.2d 659 (5th Cir. 1967).
39. Reddix v. Lucky, 252 F.2d 930 (5th Cir. 1958).
40. Anderson v. Martin, 375 U.S. 399 (1964).
41. United States v. McLeod, 385 F.2d 34 (5th Cir. 1967).
42. Alabama v. United States, 371 U.S. 37 (1962).
43. United States v. Mississippi, 380 U.S. 128 (1965).
44. Gomillion v. Lightfoot, 364 U.S. 339, 341 (1960).
45. *Cf.* United States v. Rickenbacker, 309 F.2d 462 (2d Cir. 1962), *cert. den.*, 83 S.Ct. 542 (1963); and United States v. Steele, 461 F.2d 1148 (9th Cir. 1972).
46. *Cf.* Yick Wo v. Hopkins, 118 U.S. 356 (1886).
47. Reddix v. Lucky, 252 F.2d 930 (5th Cir. 1958); and Bell v. Southwell, 376 F.2d 659 (5th Cir. 1967).
48. 42 U.S.C. §1973aa-5(a).
49. 42 U.S.C. §1973aa-5(b).
50. 42 U.S.C. §1973aa-5(d).
51. 18 U.S.C. §§241 and 242. For a general discussion of these statutes, see Chapter IX, *infra.*
52. 42 U.S.C. §§1971 and 1973 *et seq.*
53. *Id.*
54. Reddix v. Lucky, 252 F.2d 930 (5th Cir. 1958). *Also see* 42 U.S. §§1971(d) and 1973j(f).
55. Bell v. Southwell, 376 F.2d 659 (5th Cir. 1967).
56. 42 U.S.C. §1973*l*(e).
57. Lane v. Wilson, 307 U.S. 268 (1939).
58. 79 Stat. 437; 84 Stat. 315; 89 Stat. 402; codified as 42 U.S.C. §§1973 *et seq.*
59. 42 U.S.C. §1973aa.
60. 42 U.S.C. §1973c.

VOTING

61. 42 U.S.C. §§1973d, 1973f, 1973cc and 1973aa-1a.
62. 383 U.S. 301 (1966).
63. 384 U.S. 641 (1966).
64. *See* ns. 58 and 59, *supra*.
65. *Id.*
66. Oregon v. Mitchell, 400 U.S. 112 (1970).
67. 42 U.S.C. §1973*l*(c)(2).
68. 28 C.F.R. Part 55; and n. 81, *infra*.
69. United States v. Board of Commissioners, 435 U.S. 110 (1978).
70. MacGuire v. Amos, 343 F.Supp. 119 (M.D. Ala. 1972).
71. Dougherty County v. White, 439 U.S. 32 (1978).
72. Briscoe v. Bell, 432 U.S. 404 (1977).
73. *See, e.g.*, Gaston County v. United States, 395 U.S. 285 (1969).
74. South Carolina v. Katzenbach, 383 U.S. 301, 335 (1966).
75. Connor v. Johnson, 402 U.S. 690, 691 (1971); Wise v. Lipscomb, 437 U.S. 535 (1978).
76. Perkins v. Matthews, 400 U.S. 379 (1971).
77. *E.g.*, Berry v. Doles, 434 U.S. 811 (1978).
78. Dougherty County v. White, 439 U.S. 32 (1978).
79. Perkins v. Matthews, 400 U.S. 379 (1971).
80. 28 C.F.R., pt. 51 (1973).
81. Section 5 procedures are explained in detail in a handbook, *Federal Review of Voting Changes*, prepared by David H. Hunter and published by the Joint Center for Political Studies, et al., Washington, D.C., 1974.
82. Morris v. Gressette, 432 U.S. 491 (1977).
83. Beer v. United States, 425 U.S. 130 (1976).
84. Allen v. State Board of Elections, 393 U.S. 544 (1969).
85. Beer v. United States, 425 U.S. 130 (1976).
86. 36 Fed.Reg. 18,186 (Sept. 10, 1971), 28 C.F.R. pt. 51.
87. 425 U.S. 130 (1976).
88. *Id.* at 141.
89. Richmond v. United States, 422 U.S. 358 (1975).
90. Allen v. State Board of Elections, 393 U.S. 544 (1969).
91. Perkins v. Matthews, 400 U.S. 379 (1971).
92. 42 U.S.C. §§1973r and 1973j.
93. South Carolina v. Katzenbach, 383 U.S. 301, 317 (1966).
94. Perkins v. Matthews, 400 U.S. 379 (1971).
95. Berry v. Doles, 434 U.S. 811 (1978).
96. 42 U.S.C. §§1973d and 1973f.
97. 42 U.S.C. §1973e.
98. The Voting Rights Act: Ten Years After, A Report of the United States Commission on Civil Rights, Washington, D.C., January, 1975, p. 35.

99. 42 U.S.C. §1973b and §1973aa-1a.
100. *E.g.,* Puerto Rican Org. for Political Action v. Kusper, 490 F.2d 575 (7th Cir. 1973).
101. 42 U.S.C. §1973aa-2(e).
102. 42 U.S.C. §1973aa-2(c).
103. 42 U.S.C. §1973aa-2.
104. *Cf.* Whitcomb v. Chavis, 403 U.S. 124 (1971), and White v. Regester, 412 U.S. 755 (1973).
105. White v. Regester, 412 U.S. 755 (1973).
106. *See* Zimmer v. McKeithen, 485 F.2d 1297 (5th Cir. 1973) (*en banc*); Kirksey v. Board of Supervisors, 554 F.2d 139 (5th Cir. 1977) (*en banc*); Nevett v. Sides, 571 F.2d 209 (5th Cir. 1978).
107. United Jewish Orgs. v. Carey, 430 U.S. 144 (1977).
108. Connor v. Finch, 431 U.S. 407 (1977).
109. Wise v. Lipscomb, 437 U.S. 535 (1978).
110. United Jewish Orgs. v. Carey, 430 U.S. 144 (1977).

III

Employment

Employment discrimination is probably the most widely proscribed form of racial discrimination. It is prohibited by various provisions of the modern Civil Rights Acts (particularly by Title VII of the Civil Rights Act of 1964), by the Thirteenth and Fourteenth Amendments, and by several of the Reconstruction Civil Rights Acts. Although there are many prohibitions against employment discrimination, they do not apply uniformly to all employers, nor do they make all discriminatory practices unlawful.

What are the major federal prohibitions against employment discrimination?

There are two general categories of federal prohibitions against employment discrimination.

The first includes the modern Civil Rights Acts. The primary prohibition in this category is Title VII of the Civil Rights Act of 1964,[1] which specifically prohibits employment discrimination by large private employers; by most state, county, and municipal governments; by most labor unions; and by most agencies of the federal government.

The second category includes prohibitions that are more than a hundred years old: the Fourteenth Amendment and part of the Civil Rights Act of 1871,[2] which prohibit discrimination in state and local government employment; and, the Thirteenth Amendment and part of the Civil Rights Act of 1866,[3] which prohibit discrimination in public *and private* employment.

Are there important differences between Title VII of the Civil Rights Act of 1964 and the older Reconstruction-era prohibitions against employment discrimination?

Yes. There are three important differences.

First, although Title VII and the older federal prohibitions sometimes cover the same employers, very often they do not. These differences give more options to minority members seeking to challenge discrimination.

Second, Title VII is administered by a federal agency, the Equal Employment Opportunity Commission (EEOC), which means that there are federal agency regulations in which the EEOC has described the types of prohibited discrimination.[4] The EEOC is also an enforcement agency. This means that an administrative charge of discrimination must be filed with the EEOC by a person who has been discriminated against before the person can go to court; and also that the charge of discrimination might be resolved administratively without going to court. Under the older federal prohibitions, on the other hand, there is no administrative agency. Accordingly, there are no agency regulations, there are no administrative remedies, and there is little hope of stopping discrimination without going to court.

Third, Title VII prohibits a larger variety of discriminatory practices than do the older federal prohibitions. For example, Title VII generally prohibits not only intentionally discriminatory practices but also forbids practices which have a discriminatory effect;[5] the older prohibitions, on the other hand, prohibit only *intentionally* discriminatory practices.[6]

The third difference is very important and usually crucial. This is because it is very difficult in this modern age to prove intentional discrimination, especially since no employer will admit that it engages in intentional discrimination. For this reason, minority persons who believe that they have been discriminated against always should try to obtain their rights to nondiscrimination under Title VII rather than under the older Reconstruction-era laws.

Are most employers covered by Title VII of the Civil Rights Act of 1964, as amended?

Yes. Title VII covers and hence prohibits discrimination by all private, state, county, and municipal employers with fifteen or more employees,[7] and by federal agencies employing civil service schedule employees.[8] Title VII does *not* cover and hence does *not* prohibit employment discrimination by small employers with fewer than fifteen employees, or by parts of the federal government not employing civil-service employees, such as Congress.

Title VII also covers and thus prohibits employment discrimination by employment-referral agencies, labor unions with fifteen or more members, and labor-apprenticeship programs.[9]

Given Title VII's broad coverage, it again needs to be stressed that minority persons who believe that they have been discriminated against always should try to obtain their rights to nondiscrimination under Title VII. In order to obtain your rights, however, you have to comply with several administrative requirements under Title VII. These administrative requirements are discussed later in this chapter.

PROHIBITED DISCRIMINATORY PRACTICES

What are the basic prohibitions against employment discrimination under Title VII?

Title VII of the Civil Rights Act of 1964 makes it unlawful for an employer, on grounds of race, color, or national origin, among others, to refuse to hire, or to discharge, any individual, or to discriminate with respect to "compensation, terms, conditions, or privileges of employment," or to classify employees or applicants "in any way which would deprive or tend to deprive any individual of employment opportunities."[10]

Employment agencies are prohibited from engaging in racial discrimination in referrals for employment,[11] and labor organizations may not exclude from membership or segregate any individual because of race, color, or national origin, or refuse to make referrals "or otherwise adversely affect his status as an employee or as an applicant for employment."[12] Training and apprenticeship programs are also required to be conducted on a nondiscriminatory basis.[13]

What if an employer fires or retaliates against an employee for filing an EEOC complaint or speaking out against discriminatory employment practices?

Title VII specifically provides that it is illegal for an employer, labor organization, etc., to retaliate in any way against a person who files a charge of discrimination or cooperates with the EEOC.[14] Title VII has also been interpreted to prohibit the discharge of an employee for lawful civil-rights activities whether or not they involve the EEOC.[15]

What is the standard for knowing whether a practice is unlawful under Title VII?

Under Title VII, the general rule is that an employment practice is unlawful, without regard to intent, if it has a discriminatory effect and is not job-related. In a 1971 case, for example, *Griggs* v. *Duke Power Co.*,[16] a power company had a policy requiring employees seeking better jobs in the company to have either a high school diploma or make a certain score on an aptitude test. Because of the heritage of unequal educational opportunities, fewer blacks than whites finished high school and fewer blacks than whites made high scores on the aptitude tests. The power company's requirements thus denied better employment to a disproportionate number of minority members. The Supreme Court held the diploma and test requirements to violate Title VII because they had a discriminatory impact against racial minorities and the company had not shown them to be job-related. Job-relatedness might be shown, for example, if high scorers on the test performed better on the job than low scorers. The Supreme Court said that Title VII "proscribes not only overt discrimination but also practices that are fair in form, but discriminatory in operation. The touchstone is business necessity. If an employment practice which operates to exclude [racial minorities] cannot be shown

EMPLOYMENT

to be related to job performance, the practice is prohibited." [17]

How can a person know if an employment practice has a discriminatory impact and is not job-related, thus making the practice unlawful under Title VII?

There are three steps in this process under Title VII.

First, the person discriminated against must be able to show that the practice has a disproportionate impact against racial minorities. For example, a written test has a disproportionate impact if a higher percentage of minority members than whites fail the test, or if most of the minority members are on the bottom of the passing list with the whites on the top.

Second, once the practice is shown to be discriminatory, the employer then must have evidence that the practice, in the words of the Supreme Court in *Griggs* v. *Duke Power Co.*, is "related to job performance" [18]—related to actual "job capability." [19] For example, the employer must show that the high scorers on its written test perform better on the job than the low scorers.

Even if an employer shows a practice to be job-related, that is not the end of the inquiry. In 1975, the Supreme Court said that a challenged practice, even if it is job-related, will still be found unlawful if the discriminated-against person can "show that other tests or selection devices, without a similarly undesirable racial effect, would also serve the employer's legitimate interest in 'efficient and trusty workmanship.'" [20]

What types of employment practices have been found to have a discriminatory impact and not to be job-related, and are therefore unlawful under Title VII?

Following the steps just discussed, the Supreme Court has found a number of practices unlawful. In 1971, in *Griggs* v. *Duke Power Co.*, the Supreme Court held that an employer's use of a written test had a discriminatory impact, that the employer's requirement of a high school diploma had a discriminatory impact, and that the employer had no evidence of the job-relatedness of either practice; accordingly, both requirements were unlawful under Title VII.[21] In 1975, the Supreme Court reviewed another written test which had a discriminatory impact on minority applicants; the Court held that the employer's evidence of job-relatedness was insufficient, and that use of the test thus was unlawful under Title VII.[22] In 1977, the Court reviewed a minimum height requirement which had a discriminatory impact; since the employer had no evidence of job-relatedness, the Court held the minimum-height requirement unlawful under Title VII.[23]

Lower federal courts have found a number of other practices unlawful under Title VII. A few examples will indicate the breadth of the general rule against practices with a discriminatory effect. (1) An employer's practice of discharging employees whose wages have been garnished (for nonpayment of debts) has been found unlawful under Title VII.[24] (2) An employer's rejection of applicants with arrest records,[25] or even with conviction records,[26] has been found unlawful under Title VII. (3) An employer's use of word of mouth recruitment[27] or prior work experience requirements,[28] where the employer employs few minority members, has been found unlawful under Title VII.

Are there any discriminatory, non-job-related employment practices which are lawful under Title VII?

Yes. There is one major exception to the general rule against practices with a discriminatory effect. In 1977, the Supreme Court held that seniority systems, regardless of their discriminatory impact against minorities and regardless of their non-job-relatedness, are lawful under Title VII—unless they were formulated with an intent to discriminate.[29] This decision was based upon the legislative history of a specific section of the Title VII statute, which states that a "bona fide seniority . . . system" is not to be considered unlawful.[30] This decision thus does not seriously affect the general rule against actions or practices which have a discriminatory effect.

Can discrimination against an individual be shown under Title VII in the absence of proof of discriminatory effect against minorities as a group?

Yes. In *McDonnell-Douglas Corp.* v. *Green*,[31] the Supreme Court explained the nature of proof necessary to make out a case of discrimination against an individual applicant on the basis of unequal use of employment criteria. The minority applicant, the Court said, must show:

1. that he/she belongs to a racial minority;
2. that he/she applied and was qualified for a job for which the employer was seeking applicants;
3. that, despite his/her qualifications, he/she was rejected; and
4. that, after his/her rejection, the position remained open and the employer continued to seek applicants from persons with similar qualifications.[32]

Once the minority applicant makes this showing, the employer must "articulate some legitimate, nondiscriminatory reason for the employee's rejection."[33] If this is shown by the employer, the minority applicant then must "be afforded a fair opportunity to show that [the employer's] stated reason for [the] rejection was in fact pretext."[34] That the employer's reason was a pretext can be shown by its failure to apply a similar standard to nonminority applicants.

In cases involving disparate treatment of individuals, the crucial point usually is showing that the employer's reason is a pretext for discrimination. For example, in a recent lawsuit against the Jackson, Mississippi, Police Department, black officers dismissed for allegedly accepting bribes argued that they had been discriminated against. They satisfied their initial burden of proof; the employer argued that accepting bribes was a legitimate nondiscriminatory reason. The federal court of appeals held that the reason appeared pretextual because white officers accused at the same time of accepting bribes were never even investigated, much less dismissed.[35]

Are employers and other organizations which are not covered by Title VII covered by other federal prohibitions against employment discrimination?

Yes. Many employers and other organizations (including those covered by Title VII) are covered by the Reconstruction-era Constitutional amendments and Civil Rights Acts. For example, all private employers, and unions too, whatever their size, are prohibited from engaging in *intentional discrimination* by the Thirteenth Amendment and by the Civil Rights Act of 1866. Similarly, all state, county, and municipal employers are prohibited from engaging in *intentional discrimination* by the Thirteenth and Fourteenth Amendments and by the Civil Rights Acts of 1866 and 1871. Note that small employers and unions thus are covered only by the Reconstruction-era prohibitions, while large employers and unions also are covered by Title VII.

Are practices that have a discriminatory effect and are not job-related also unlawful under the older Reconstruction-era federal prohibitions against discrimination?

No. Practices that are neutral on their face are not unlawful under the Reconstruction-era prohibitions unless such practices are *intentionally* discriminatory. In 1976, in *Washington* v. *Davis*,[36] the Supreme Court held that an employer's use of a written aptitude test, which had a disproportionately discriminatory impact against racial minorities, was *not* unlawful under the older laws. The Supreme Court held that proof of racially discriminatory intent or purpose is required to show a violation of the Fourteenth Amendment. The Court found that the employer had a good record of hiring minority members in recent years and had established a special minority recruitment program. The Court thus concluded that there was insufficient proof of discriminatory intent. In the absence of these findings, the Court *might* have ruled the use of the test to be intentionally discriminatory. Undoubtedly, though, most practices that have a discriminatory impact and are unlawful under Title VII would be held *lawful* under the older prohibitions.

How can one know if a discriminatory employment practice is intentionally discriminatory?

Discriminated-against persons usually believe, and correctly so, that discriminatory action is intentional. The problem is *proving* that to be so, because few if any employers will admit to intentional discrimination. In 1977, the Supreme Court recognized this problem and said that it was not necessary to prove that the challenged practice "rested solely on racially discriminatory purposes" but only that "a discriminatory purpose has been *a* motivating factor." [37] The Court next stated that determining whether a "discriminatory purpose was a motivating factor demands a sensitive inquiry into such circumstantial and direct evidence of intent as may be available." [38] A "starting point" is the racial "impact" of the action or practice.[39] The "historical background of the decision" is another source of evidence.[40] "Departures from the normal procedural sequence also might afford evidence that improper purposes are playing a role." [41]

Overall, a lengthy investigation of all of the facts is necessary to develop the proof necessary to show intentional discrimination. Obtaining the necessary proof sometimes can be very difficult. For this reason, nearly all discriminated-against persons assert their rights under Title VII, where proof of discriminatory *impact* is sufficient proof of probable discrimination.

Given the Supreme Court's 1976 decision holding that only intentionally discriminatory practices are unlawful under the Reconstruction-era prohibitions, is it now likely that the Supreme Court will hold that Title VII prohibits only intentional discrimination?

No. In 1977, the Supreme Court reviewed a Title VII employment case involving a practice which had a discriminatory effect. The practice was use of a standard of a minimum height and weight—a practice which has a discriminatory impact upon some minorities (*e.g.*, Chicanos, Puerto Ricans, and Asian-Americans) and against women. The Supreme Court reaffirmed its 1971 decision in *Griggs* v. *Duke Power Co.*, and held the height-and-weight requirement unlawful under Title VII, without regard to the good or bad intent of the employer, simply because it had a discriminatory impact and had not been shown to be job-related.[42]

REMEDIES FOR EMPLOYMENT DISCRIMINATION

What types of remedies are available to persons who have been discriminated against in employment in violation of Title VII?

Title VII remedies may include the following: (1) termination of the discrimination; (2) hiring, reinstatement, or promotion; (3) awards of back pay and retroactive seniority; and sometimes (4) affirmative hiring steps such as goals and timetables. One of the purposes of Title VII, the Supreme Court has announced, is "to make persons whole for injuries suffered on account of unlawful employment discrimination." [43] In addition to these remedies, court awarded attorneys' fees are available for the "prevailing party" in a Title VII lawsuit.[44]

How much back pay is available to a person who has been discriminated against in violation of Title VII?

Pursuant to the "make whole" objective of Title VII, an award of back pay is determined by the amount of pay that normally would have been earned if there had been no discrimination. There are two important limitations.

First, back pay is calculated no further back than two years prior to the date upon which the administrative charge of discrimination was filed with the EEOC.[45] Thus, for example, even if you have been continuously and discriminatorily denied a promotion for ten years by a private employer, you are eligible under Title VII to receive back pay only starting two years before filing your charge of discrimination with the EEOC.

Second, the amount of back pay for which you are theoretically eligible is reduced by "interim earnings or amounts earnable with reasonable diligence by the person or persons discriminated against." [46] For example, if you earned $150 a week until January 3, 1980, when you were discriminatorily fired, and if you refused to look for any other work until July 3, 1980, when you immediately found work at $145 a week, you probably would be able to recover no more than $5 a week back pay for your six months of unemployment as well as thereafter.

Under Title VII, is retroactive seniority an available remedy for unlawful employment discrimination?

Yes. Although the Supreme Court held in 1977 that seniority systems which have a discriminatory effect are not unlawful *per se*,[47] the Court did not overrule its earlier decision in 1975 holding that persons discriminated against were entitled to the seniority they would have earned had they not been discriminated against.[48] This means that even though a seniority system may itself be lawful, a person who has been unlawfully discriminated against is entitled to full retroactive seniority.

Who is eligible for retroactive seniority under Title VII? How is it awarded?

Any person who has been unlawfully discriminated against is eligible for retroactive seniority. This includes a person denied a transfer to a more lucrative job for which he/she was qualified.[49] It also includes a person who was unlawfully denied employment in the first place, or was deterred from applying for employment.[50] The retroactive seniority is available from the date the initial discrimination occurred. Thus, as soon as the complainant is placed in the sought-after job, whether by a court order or otherwise, retroactive seniority is accumulated—thereby protecting the complainant against future layoffs.

Are other remedies, such as affirmative hiring and goals and timetables, available under Title VII to make up for extensive past discrimination?

Yes. Although the Supreme Court has consistently refused to review cases requiring goals and timetables as a remedy under Title VII or under the older civil rights prohibitions,[51] the Supreme Court has tacitly approved affirmative hiring orders as appropriate to remedy past discrimination.[52] Since the scope of the remedy depends upon the scope of the unlawful actions, an order requiring extensive goals and timetables will be imposed only if there has been extensive past discrimination.[53]

Are monetary damages, other than back pay, an available remedy under Title VII for unlawful employment discrimination?

No. Although the Supreme Court has never decided this question, other federal courts have determined that back pay is the only monetary remedy available under Title VII.[54] This is because back pay is the only monetary remedy mentioned as available in the Title VII statute,[55] and because pain-and-suffering damages and, even more so, punitive damages are not necessarily consonant with the "make whole" objective of Title VII.

Are remedies similar to those available under Title VII also available in lawsuits filed under the older Reconstruction amendments and Civil Rights Acts?

Yes. But remember that proof of discriminatory intent is necessary under the Reconstruction amendments and Civil Rights Acts. Once a person has proved intentional discrimination in court under these older laws, similar remedies are available. The back pay remedy operates the same way as under Title VII, except that the two administrative limitations on back pay in the Title VII statute are not directly applicable to lawsuits filed under the older prohibitions.[56]

Are monetary damages, other than back pay, available under the older civil rights prohibitions?

Yes. Once a court determines that an employer has engaged in intentional discrimination, persons discriminated against may receive not only back pay but also other out-of-pocket damages and possible pain-and-suffering damages.[57] Additionally, if the discrimination is found to have been malicious, persons discriminated against may receive punitive damages.[58] These remedies, however, are very difficult to obtain because it is hard to prove intentional discrimination, much less malicious discrimination.

Is it necessary to file a lawsuit under Title VII to obtain its remedies for employment discrimination?

No, but it is highly advisable to prepare as if a lawsuit were going to be filed. Some charges of discrimination are resolved informally between the individual and the employer. Other charges are resolved administratively. However, since many employers do not want to volunteer the appearance of wrongdoing, they will not settle a charge unless the individual has strong proof of discrimination and appears able and willing to file a lawsuit. Thus, to be in the best position, a person discriminated against should always file a timely administrative charge under Title VII and should comply with the other prerequisites to filing a Title VII lawsuit.

PROCEDURES UNDER TITLE VII OF THE CIVIL RIGHTS ACT OF 1964

In order to be protected by Title VII in nonfederal employment, are there any procedural steps which must be taken?

Yes. In order to be protected by Title VII in nonfederal employment (a private, state, county, or municipal employer, or an employment agency, labor union, or apprenticeship program), a person must file an administrative charge of discrimination[59] with any district or regional office of the EEOC, or with the main office of the EEOC (Columbia Plaza Building, 2401 E Street, N.W., Washington, D.C. 20506). The EEOC has a form for filing administrative charges. The official EEOC form has four carbon copies. A copy of the form is reproduced on the following page.

The administrative charge of discrimination *must* be filed with the EEOC within 180 days of the discriminatory action which is complained about,[60] unless the discrimination is of a continuing nature such as a continuing refusal to hire or promote.[61]

The charge must be signed and sworn to,[62] it must detail or at least summarize the nature of the discrimination,[63] and it must give the name of every employer and union involved in the discrimination.[64] Thereafter, the EEOC will refer the charge to the appropriate state or local human-rights agency, if one exists, for 60 days.[65] Thereafter, the EEOC may investigate the charge and attempt to resolve the charge on your behalf.[66]

THE RIGHTS OF RACIAL MINORITIES

(PLEASE PRINT OR TYPE)

APPROVED BY GAO	CHARGE OF DISCRIMINATION	CHARGE NUMBER(S) (AGENCY USE ONLY)
B—180541 (RO511) Expires 1-31-81	IMPORTANT: This form is affected by the Privacy Act of 1974; see Privacy Act Statement on reverse before completing it.	☐ STATE/LOCAL AGENCY ☐ EEOC

Equal Employment Opportunity Commission and
_____ (State or Local Agency)

NAME (Indicate Mr., Ms. or Mrs.)	HOME TELEPHONE NUMBER (Include area code)
STREET ADDRESS	
CITY, STATE, AND ZIP CODE	COUNTY

NAMED IS THE EMPLOYER, LABOR ORGANIZATION, EMPLOYMENT AGENCY, APPRENTICESHIP COMMITTEE, STATE OR LOCAL GOVERNMENT AGENCY WHO DISCRIMINATED AGAINST ME. (If more than one list below).

NAME	TELEPHONE NUMBER (Include area code)
STREET ADDRESS	CITY, STATE, AND ZIP CODE
NAME	TELEPHONE NUMBER (Include area code)
STREET ADDRESS	CITY, STATE, AND ZIP CODE

CAUSE OF DISCRIMINATION BASED ON MY (Check appropriate box(es))

☐ RACE ☐ COLOR ☐ SEX ☐ RELIGION ☐ NATIONAL ORIGIN ☐ OTHER (Specify)

DATE MOST RECENT OR CONTINUING DISCRIMINATION TOOK PLACE (Month, day, and year)

THE PARTICULARS ARE:

I will advise the agencies if I change my address or telephone number and I will cooperate fully with them in the processing of my charge in accordance with their procedures.	NOTARY — (When necessary to meet State and Local Requirements) I swear or affirm that I have read the above charge and that it is true to the best of my knowledge, information and belief. SIGNATURE OF COMPLAINANT
I declare under penalty of perjury that the foregoing is true and correct.	SUBSCRIBED AND SWORN TO BEFORE ME THIS DATE (Day, month, and year)
DATE: _____ CHARGING PARTY (Signature)	

EEOC FORM 5G JAN 78   PREVIOUS EDITIONS OF ALL EEOC FORM 5'S ARE OBSOLETE AND MUST NOT BE USED

Is there much chance that the EEOC will resolve and successfully conciliate the charge of discrimination?

No. Since the EEOC has a backlog of about 100,000 charges of discrimination, and since it has been unable to resolve very many charges, it is unlikely that your charge will be administratively resolved by the EEOC.

If the EEOC cannot or does not resolve a charge of discrimination, can a complainant go to court under Title VII to seek to remedy the discrimination?

Yes. A complainant may sue in court after 180 days have elapsed since the filing of the charge, *and* after receiving a "right-to-sue letter" from the EEOC (to sue private employers) or from the Justice Department (to sue state, county, and municipal employers). Alternatively, if the EEOC certifies that it will not investigate the charge within 180 days, an individual may ask for a right-to-sue letter and bring suit immediately. However, the individual must sue, if at all, within 90 days after receiving the right-to-sue letter.[67]

There is another hitch. The person suing, the plaintiff, can name as defendants in the lawsuit only the employers, unions, and individuals named in the administrative charge filed with the EEOC; and the person suing can raise as claims only those matters reasonably growing out of the administrative charge.[68] Thus, the administrative charge to the EEOC always should be as broad as possible.

Can a person who can't afford a lawyer still file a lawsuit under Title VII?

Yes. Under Title VII a poor person can file a lawsuit *in forma pauperis,* which means that a poor person can sue without paying court costs.[69] And one can always file a lawsuit *pro se,* which means that a person can represent oneself. But since the law is very complicated, and since, as the saying goes, a person who represents oneself has a fool for a client, it is best to try to find a lawyer. Anyone who has a problem finding a lawyer should contact the organizations listed in Appendix B at the end of this book. If this fails, the EEOC might be of assistance, or a court might be able to appoint a lawyer.[70]

If the administrative requirements discussed above are not met, can a lawsuit still be filed under Title VII?

Generally, if the complainant does not file a charge with the EEOC within 180 days, or does not file the lawsuit within 90 days after receiving the right-to-sue letter, no lawsuit can be filed. But there are two limited exceptions.

First, the 180-day requirement for filing your EEOC charge may not apply if the discriminatory action you complain of is deemed to be a "continuing" act.[71] A continuing refusal to hire or promote may be considered a continuing act of discrimination. Most other actions, however, would not be deemed continuing acts.

Second, a person can become a plaintiff in a Title VII lawsuit if another plaintiff has met all of the time requirements. The Supreme Court has held that only one Title VII plaintiff need comply with the time requirements.[72]

If a discriminated-against minority person cannot file a lawsuit under Title VII, are there other possible means of obtaining relief from a court?

Yes, there are several other possible means of obtaining relief. First, the EEOC can sue private employers and unions, and the Justice Department can sue state, county, and municipal employers.[73] Although they file very few lawsuits, it sometimes is worth contacting them to see if they will sue. Second, a person always can sue private employers under the Thirteenth Amendment and the Civil Rights Act of 1866, and state, county, and municipal employers under the Thirteenth and Fourteenth Amendments and under the Civil Rights Acts of 1866 and 1871. An individual can file such a lawsuit without complying with any of Title VII's procedural requirements, but the lawsuit must be filed within the period allowed by the applicable state statute of limitations.[74] In order to win, however, an individual must be able to prove that the discrimination was intentionally discriminatory, and this is very difficult to prove.[75]

In addition to the foregoing lawsuits, there are two other remedies that can and should be pursued wherever they are applicable.

Section 122 of the Fiscal Assistance to State and Local Governments Act of 1972, as amended,[76] prohibits employment discrimination on grounds of race, color, and national origin by state and local governments receiving federal revenue-sharing funds. Since nearly every state and local government receives federal funding, this prohibition is broad indeed. It is enforced administratively by the federal Office of Revenue Sharing, and it also may be enforced through lawsuits brought by private individuals or by the Justice Department. Before it can be enforced through private lawsuits, however, the private individuals must file administrative charges of discrimination with the appropriate office (Civil Rights Division, Office of Revenue Sharing, United States Department of the Treasury, 2401 E Street, N.W., Washington, D.C. 20226). Because of the breadth and significance of this remedy, it is discussed separately in some detail in Chapter VII.

Section 518(c) of the Crime Control Act of 1968, as amended,[77] also prohibits employment discrimination on grounds of race, color, and national origin, but only by state and local law enforcement agencies receiving federal funds from the Law Enforcement Assistance Administration (LEAA). Since nearly all state and local law-enforcement agencies receive LEAA funding, all are covered by this prohibition. This prohibition is enforced administratively by LEAA, and it also may be enforced through lawsuits brought by private individuals or by the Justice Department. Before it can be enforced through private lawsuits, however, the private individuals must file administrative charges of discrimination with the appropriate office (Office of Civil Rights Compliance, Law Enforcement Assistance Administration, United States Department of Justice, 633 Indiana Avenue, N.W., Washington, D.C. 20531). Because of the importance of this remedy, it, too, is discussed separately in some detail in Chapter VII.

How about discrimination in federal agencies? Are the Title VII procedures the same?

No. Persons seeking the protection of Title VII against federal agency discrimination are governed by a separate set of complicated procedures that are even more difficult to follow than those applicable to discrimination by nonfederal employers. Furthermore, the initial steps must be undertaken not with the EEOC but instead with the federal agency itself.

1. Within thirty days of the discriminatory act, the individual must bring the matter to the attention of the federal agency's Equal Employment Opportunity Counselor.
2. After informal proceedings with the Counselor, and within only fifteen days of the final interview with the Counselor, the individual must file a formal written, signed complaint with the agency. Thereupon, the agency will investigate the complaint and attempt an informal "adjustment" of the matter.
3. If an informal adjustment is not reached, and if the individual desires an agency hearing on the complaint, the individual within fifteen days of the agency's proposed disposition must request a hearing. With or without the hearing, the agency will reach a "final" agency decision, which the individual may appeal to the EEOC.
4. If the individual wishes to sue the agency, the lawsuit must be filed within thirty days of notice of the final agency decision or of the EEOC decision.

Obviously, these time periods are very short, but they must be complied with if one is to be protected at all by Title VII in federal employment.[78]

Is there a good chance that the responsible federal agency will resolve the charge of discrimination?

No. Most federal agencies have reputations for being unable to resolve their own discrimination.

If the responsible agency or the EEOC does not satisfactorily resolve or "adjust" a complaint of discrimination, can an individual go to court under Title VII to seek to remedy the discrimination?

Yes, the individual can file a lawsuit against the federal agency. But there are two different time periods that apply. First, if there is a final decision by the responsible agency (and the individual elects not to appeal to the EEOC) or by the EEOC (after an appeal), the individual must file the lawsuit, if at all, within 30 days of that final decision. Second, if 180 days have elapsed since the filing of the administrative complaint and there has not yet been a final decision, the individual then may file a lawsuit even before there is a final administrative decision. Additionally, the administrative steps and time periods mentioned before also must be complied with.[79] If they are not met, the court will dismiss the lawsuit.[80]

If an individual gets to court under Title VII against a federal agency, may the court receive additional evidence about the discrimination, other than what was introduced in the administrative process?

Yes. Although federal agencies for many years argued that the court could do no more than review the administrative record, the Supreme Court in 1976 rejected that argument and held that the courts should admit all evidence relevant to the formal administrative complaint.[81] In other words, once in court, individuals can prove discrimination against federal employers just the same as against nonfederal employers.

Can you sue a federal agency under Title VII if you cannot afford an attorney?

Yes. The answer is the same with regard to a federal agency as it is with a nonfederal employer. Under Title VII, you may file free of cost in court and may represent yourself.[82] However, it is recommended that you try to find a lawyer.

If a person cannot file a lawsuit against a federal agency under Title VII because of noncompliance with the administrative steps and time requirements, are there other possible means of obtaining relief from a court?

No. Although there are three possible routes against nonfederal employers, none is available against federal agencies. (1) Neither the EEOC nor the Justice Department is authorized to sue federal agencies for employment discrimination. (2) Although the Fifth Amendment and the Civil Rights Act of 1866 arguably prohibit employment discrimination in the federal government, the Supreme Court in 1976 held that *Title VII is the exclusive remedy for suing federal employers covered by Title VII*.[83] Other prohibitions thus are irrelevant. (3) The revenue sharing and LEAA alternatives provide a potential remedy against the recipient, not against the federal government which is the grantor.

In other words, Title VII, with its short administrative time periods, is the only protection available against federal employers covered by Title VII. It thus is especially important to comply strictly with all applicable time periods.

What about federal employers such as Congress that are not covered by Title VII? Are they prohibited from engaging in employment discrimination by other federal prohibitions?

Yes and no. Federal employers not covered by Title VII technically are prohibited from engaging in *intentional discrimination* by the Fifth Amendment and by the Civil Rights Act of 1866. The problem is that it has been nearly impossible to sue them. Some courts have applied the ancient doctrine of sovereign immunity, holding that they cannot be sued without their consent.[84] The Supreme Court nonetheless has held that it is possible to sue a member of Congress directly under the Fifth Amendment.[85] In general the Fifth Amendment and the Civil Rights Act of 1866 are difficult to enforce against Congress and the federal judiciary.

EMPLOYMENT

AFFIRMATIVE ACTION

What is affirmative action in employment?

Affirmative action in employment is a device that helps employers to stop their discrimination against racial minorities.

When employers say that they do not discriminate against minorities and even promise to hire and to promote more minority members, they have not necessarily stopped their discrimination. There are two reasons for this. First, past discriminatory practices tend to perpetuate themselves. For example, employers who used discriminatory practices in the past not only have few minority employees to promote into higher positions, but they also have discriminatory reputations in minority communities—both of which often deter minorities from applying for jobs with these employers. Second, most employers, despite current protestations of nondiscrimination, continue to recruit potential employees by word of mouth. This practice continues to work to the advantage of the friends and acquaintances of most employers' predominantly white workforces, and thus to the disadvantage of minorities who are not yet inside this word of mouth system. Affirmative action is designed to overcome both of these problems, among others.

Affirmative action in employment embodies two closely-related practices. First, affirmative action requires the recruitment of minority applicants. This means that employers cannot rely on word of mouth recruitment and other forms of recruitment which work to the disadvantage of minorities. Instead, employers must advertise in minority newspapers and other media, and must affirmatively seek minority applicants. Second, affirmative action requires employers to set goals and timetables for actually hiring and promoting minority employees in positions where they are underrepresented. Goals and timetables are necessary to make certain that affirmative recruitment is not a sham; they are necessary to make certain that employers are not continuing to discriminate against minorities; and they are useful for employers to determine whether the employers actually are making progress in hiring and promoting minorities.

Some affirmative action plans are mostly on paper and are not very well implemented. Other plans, however, have teeth and thus are well implemented. For example, some plans include affirmative action performance by supervisors as a criterion for evaluating supervisory performance—leading to a demotion or reduction in pay for poor performance or to a promotion or raise for good performance. Other plans go even further by tying affirmative action performance directly to supervisors' salaries and job retention. Employers who add these types of incentives to their affirmative action plan prove their commitment to ending past discriminatory practices against minorities. Unfortunately, many affirmative action plans do not have such incentives and therefore are not well implemented. Worse, most employers do not even have affirmative action plans.

Does affirmative action require unqualified minority persons to be employed or promoted?

No. Affirmative action has never meant that a minority person who is not qualified for a job must be given that job. Instead, affirmative action means that qualified minority persons must be recruited and be fully considered for employment and promotion.

At the same time, affirmative action does require employers to look at how "qualifications" are used and what the word means. First, employers have been forced to realize that, regardless of the advent of affirmative action, many persons have been hired or promoted not on the basis of job qualifications but on the basis of appearance, personality, mutual club membership, and even friendship. Since the applicant who is theoretically best qualified is not necessarily the one who wins the job or the promotion, affirmative action simply requires that minority applicants too be fully considered even though they are not the best friends of the employers. Second, and more importantly, employers also have been forced to realize that many of their so-called qualifications are simply discriminatory devices unrelated to job performance. For example, many employers use culturally biased written tests which not only are discriminatory but also are unable to predict job performance. Affirmative action thus simply requires employers to reexamine their required qualifications, to recognize that many minority members who do not possess the so-called qualifications are in fact qualified for employment and promotion, and thereby to include minority persons in the pool of qualified applicants.

Do minority persons have a right to affirmative action?
Generally, no. Although affirmative action is only a device for ending past and current discrimination, affirmative action by employers generally is not required except in some situations where there is proven past discrimination or where there is substantial underrepresentation of minority employees. In these situations, affirmative action sometimes has been required by courts, by administrative agencies, and by legislative bodies. In other instances, affirmative action sometimes has been voluntarily adopted. But, in general, there is no right to affirmative action.

Is affirmative action involving the use of goals, timetables and other numerical measures lawful and constitutional?
In most instances, yes. But the permissibility of affirmative action in all instances is not yet definitively known.

In 1978, in *Regents of the University of California* v. *Bakke*,[86] the Supreme Court addressed the legality and constitutionality of a voluntarily adopted, race-conscious, medical school admissions plan which set aside 16 percent of the places in each entering class for disadvantaged minority applicants. In a confusing 4–1–4 vote, the Supreme Court held this rigid numerical plan unlawful but nonetheless also held that any race-conscious plan which merely gave minority applicants extra points would be both lawful and constitutional. Although *Bakke* was not an employment case, it does provide some guidelines for determining the permissibility of numerically based affirmative action in employment.

A year later, in 1979, the Supreme Court decided *United Steelworkers of America* v. *Weber*.[87] At issue in *Weber* was the legality under Title VII of a voluntarily adopted, race-conscious affirmative action plan which set aside 50 percent of the openings in an on-the-job training program for minority workers. This rigid numerical plan was upheld by the Court as lawful.

As a result of *Bakke* and *Weber*, race-conscious numerical measures are permissible in most instances. (1) They are lawful and constitutional when used to remedy identified past discrimination. (2) They are lawful without regard to past discrimination when implemented voluntarily by private employers. (3) And they probably are lawful and constitutional without regard to past discrimination when adopted voluntarily by government employers.

Can numerical affirmative action be imposed on employers to remedy judicially, legislatively or administratively identified past discriminaton against racial minorities?

Yes. Although the issue in both *Bakke* and *Weber* involved the permissibility of voluntary affirmative action, the Supreme Court nonetheless had an opportunity to address the appropriateness of numerical measures to remedy past discrimination. In *Bakke* the Court seized the opportunity and approved such affirmative remedies as both lawful and constitutional.

Four Justices in *Bakke* (Justices Brennan, White, Marshall and Blackmun) voted to approve voluntarily adopted, race conscious numerical measures as lawful and constitutional. In the course of their opinion, they also approved the use of numerical measures to remedy past discrimination in employment.[88]

Justice Powell wrote a separate opinion in *Bakke* in which he too approved the use of numerical measures to remedy past discrimination in employment, at least where those remedies are based on judicial,[89] administrative,[90] or legislative [91] findings of past discrimination.

The five-vote majority on this issue is virtually conclusive. Subsequent to *Bakke*, the lower federal courts have uniformly approved race-conscious numerical measures premised upon judicial,[92] administrative,[93] or legislative [94] findings of past discrimination.

Can race-conscious numerical measures be adopted voluntarily by *private* employers without regard to past discrimination?

Yes. This is precisely what was addressed and approved by the Supreme Court in *Weber*.

At issue in *Weber* was a race-conscious on-the-job training program for skilled craft workers. In order to increase minority representation in its workforce, the private company voluntarily set a goal of 39 percent minority representation (the minority representation in the surrounding labor force), adopted a hiring ratio of one minority for every white (so that 50 percent of the new skilled craft employees would be minority workers), and estimated that its goal would be reached under a 30-year timetable (meaning that the program would be in effect past the year 2000). A white employee challenged this numerically based program as discriminatory under Title VII of the Civil Rights Act of 1964. The Supreme Court rejected the challenge. In its view, the spirit and intent of Title VII was to open job opportunities for minority workers. Since the company's race-conscious numerical plan served that purpose without excluding whites, the plan was held lawful under Title VII.[95]

Are voluntarily adopted numerical measures also permissible in government employment?

Probably, but this is not yet definitively known.

For race-conscious numerical measures to be permissible when used in government employment, they must be lawful under Title VII, and they also must be constitutional under the Fourteenth or Fifth Amendment. As a result of *Weber*, they are lawful under Title VII. But we don't yet know whether they also are constitutional. For guidelines, we have to look back to *Bakke*.

In *Bakke*, the race-conscious plan set aside 16 percent of the available openings for disadvantaged minority applicants. As noted earlier, and as discussed more extensively in Chapter IV, Education, only five members of the Court in *Bakke* expressed their views on the constitutionality of the numerical plan. Justices Brennan, White, Marshall and Blackmun held that the 16 percent plan, or any similar numerical plan, is constitutional in order to remedy societal discrimination against minorities.[96] Justice Powell disagreed, held that rigid numerical plans were unconstitutional, but stated that flexible plans which merely take race into account are constitutional.[97] The other four members of the Court—Justices Stevens, Stewart and Rehnquist, and Chief Justice Burger—expressed no views about the constitutionality of numerical plans.[98]

Because of the votes in *Bakke,* the constitutionality of voluntarily adopted numerical measures depends upon the future votes of the four Justices who expressed no views on the constitutional issue in *Bakke.* If only one of the four Justices joins the position of Justices Brennan, White, Marshall and Blackmun, there then will be a majority on the Supreme Court favoring the constitutionality of voluntarily adopted numerical measures in government employment. It is likely that Justice Stevens will cast that fifth vote. It also is probable that Justice Stewart, who voted with the majority in *Weber* to uphold voluntary numerical measures in private employment, will similarly approve such measures in government employment.

Although this issue is not yet resolved, it undoubtedly will be resolved within the next few years in cases currently pending in the Supreme Court or winding their way up to the Court for a definitive decision.[99]

NOTES

1. 42 U.S.C. §§2000e *et seq.*
2. 42 U.S.C. §1983.
3. 42 U.S.C. §1981.
4. 29 C.F.R. §1606 and §1607.
5. Griggs v. Duke Power Co., 401 U.S. 424 (1971).
6. Washington v. Davis, 426 U.S. 229 (1976).
7. 42 U.S.C. §2000e(b) and §2000e-2(a).
8. 42 U.S.C. §2000e-16.
9. 42 U.S.C. §§2000e(c)–(e) and §§2000e-2(b)–(d).
10. 42 U.S.C. §2000e-2(a).
11. 42 U.S.C. §2000e-2(b).

EMPLOYMENT

12. 42 U.S.C. §2000e-2(c).
13. 42 U.S.C. §2000e-2(d).
14. 42 U.S.C. §2000e-3(a). *See* Rutherford v. American Bank of Commerce, 565 F.2d 1162 (10th Cir. 1977); Drew v. Liberty Mut. Ins. Co., 480 F.2d 69 (5th Cir. 1973), *cert. denied,* 417 U.S. 935 (1974).
15. McDonnell-Douglas Corp. v. Green, 411 U.S. 792 (1973).
16. 401 U.S. 424 (1971).
17. 401 U.S. 424, 431 (1971).
18. 401 U.S. 424, 431 (1971).
19. 401 U.S. 424, 432 (1971).
20. Albemarle Paper Co. v. Moody, 422 U.S. 405, 425 (1975).
21. 401 U.S. 424 (1971).
22. Albemarle Paper Co. v. Moody, 422 U.S. 405 (1975).
23. Dothard v. Rawlinson, 433 U.S. 321 (1977).
24. Wallace v. Debron Corp., 494 F.2d 674 (8th Cir. 1974).
25. Gregory v. Litton Systems, 472 F.2d 631 (9th Cir. 1972); Carter v. Gallagher, 452 F.2d 315 (8th Cir. 1971), *modified on other grounds, en banc,* 452 F.2d 327 (8th Cir.), *cert. denied,* 406 U.S. 950 (1972).
26. Green v. Missouri Pac. R.R., 523 F.2d 1290 (8th Cir. 1975).
27. *E.g.,* Reed v. Arlington Hotel Co., 476 F.2d 721 (8th Cir.), *cert. denied,* 414 U.S. 854 (1973); United States v. Georgia Power Co., 474 F.2d 906 (5th Cir. 1973).
28. Sabol v. Snyder, 524 F.2d 1009 (5th Cir. 1975); Rowe v. General Motors Corp., 457 F.2d 348 (5th Cir. 1972).
29. International Bhd. of Teamsters v. United States, 431 U.S. 324 (1977). *See also* Acha v. Beame, 570 F.2d 57, 64–65 (2d Cir. 1978).
30. 42 U.S.C. §2000e-2(h).
31. 411 U.S. 792 (1973).
32. 411 U.S. at 802.
33. 411 U.S. at 802.
34. 411 U.S. at 804.
35. Corley v. Jackson Police Dep't, 566 F.2d 994 (5th Cir. 1978). *See also* Turner v. Texas Instruments, Inc., 555 F.2d 1251 (5th Cir. 1977); *cf.* McDonald v. Santa Fe Trail Transp. Co., 427 U.S. 273, 283 (1976).
36. 426 U.S. 229 (1976). The reasoning of the Supreme Court in Washington v. Davis, requiring proof of intent

THE RIGHTS OF RACIAL MINORITIES

to discriminate under the Fourteenth Amendment and the Civil Rights Act of 1871, may require proof of intent to discriminate also under the Thirteenth Amendment and the Civil Rights Act of 1866. This latter issue was presented to but not decided by the Supreme Court in 1979 in the case of Los Angeles v. Davis, 99 S.Ct. 1379, 59 L.Ed. 2d 642 (1979), *vacating* 556 F.2d 1334 (9th Cir. 1978).

37. Arlington Heights v. Metropolitan Hous. Dev. Corp., 429 U.S. 252 (1977).
38. 429 U.S. 252, 266 (1977).
39. *Id.*
40. 429 U.S. 252, 267 (1977).
41. *Id.*
42. Dothard v. Rawlinson, 433 U.S. 321 (1977).
43. Albemarle Paper Co. v. Moody, 422 U.S. 405, 418 (1975).
44. 42 U.S.C. §2000e-5(k). A prevailing plaintiff will ordinarily receive attorneys' fees, whereas a prevailing defendant can be awarded attorneys' fees only if the plaintiff's lawsuit was plainly frivolous. *See* Christiansburg Garment Co. v. EEOC, 434 U.S. 412 (1978).
45. 42 U.S.C. §2000e-5(g).
46. *Id. See, generally,* Albemarle Paper Co. v. Moody, 422 U.S. 405 (1975).
47. International Bhd. of Teamsters v. United States, 431 U.S. 324 (1977).
48. Franks v. Bowan Transp. Co., 424 U.S. 747 (1975).
49. *Id.*
50. International Bhd. of Teamsters v. United States, 431 U.S. 324 (1977).
51. *E.g.,* Boston Chapter NAACP v. Beecher, 504 F.2d 1017 (1st Cir. 1974), *cert. denied,* 421 U.S. 910 (1975); Carter v. Gallagher, 452 F.2d 327 (8th Cir.) (*en banc*), *cert. denied,* 406 U.S. 950 (1972); United States v. Local 86, Ironworkers, 443 F.2d 544 (9th Cir), *cert. denied,* 404 U.S. 984 (1971).
52. *See* United Steelworkers of America v. Weber, 99 S.Ct. 2721, 61 L.Ed.2d 480 (1979); *see also* Regents of the University of California v. Bakke, 438 U.S. 265, 300–310 (opinion of Powell, J.), 438 U.S. at 355–387 (opinion of Brennan, J., with White, Marshall and Blackmun, JJ., concurring).

Subsequent to Bakke, the lower federal courts have

EMPLOYMENT

held that affirmative hiring orders to remedy past discrimination may be imposed by the courts, *e.g.,* Firefighters Institute for Racial Equality v. St. Louis, 588 F.2d 235 (8th Cir. 1978); Morrow v. Dillard, 580 F.2d 1284 (5th Cir. 1978); as well as by the EEOC, *e.g.,* EEOC v. Contour Chair Lounge Co., 596 F.2d 809 (8th Cir. 1979), *aff'g* 457 F.Supp. 393 (E.D. Mo. 1978).

53. *Compare* Kirkland v. New York State Department of Correctional Services, 520 F.2d 420 (2d Cir. 1975), *with* Rios v. Steamfitters Local 638, 501 F.2d 622 (2d Cir. 1974).
54. Richerson v. Jones, 551 F.2d 918, 926–28 (3d Cir. 1977); Pearson v. Western Electric Co., 542 F.2d 1150 (10th Cir. 1976); EEOC v. Detroit Edison Co., 515 F.2d 301, 308–10 (6th Cir. 1975), *vac'd & rem'd on other grounds,* 431 U.S. 951 (1977).
55. 42 U.S.C. §2000e-5(g).
56. Brown v. Gaston County Dyeing Mach. Co., 457 F.2d 1377 (4th Cir.), *cert. denied,* 409 U.S. 982 (1972).
57. *Cf.* Sullivan v. Little Hunting Park, 396 U.S. 229 (1969).
58. *Id.*
59. *See, generally,* 42 U.S.C. §§2000e-5(c) and (e).
60. 42 U.S.C. §2000e-5(e).
61. If the disrimination is alleged to be "continuing," this may extend the time period indefinitely. *See, e.g.,* Bethel v. Jendoco Const. Corp., 570 F.2d 1168, 1173–75 (3d Cir. 1978); Clark v. Olinkraft, Inc., 556 F.2d 1219 (5th Cir. 1977), *cert. denied,* 434 U.S. 1069 (1978); Williams v. Norfolk & W. Ry., 530 F.2d 539 (4th Cir. 1975). *But see* United Air Lines v. Evans, 431 U.S. 553 (1977). Many acts of discrimination, however, have been held not to be "continuing." *See* Smith v. American President Lines, 571 F.2d 102 (2d Cir. 1978); Smith v. Arkansas State OEO, 538 F.2d 226 (8th Cir. 1976).
62. 42 U.S.C. §2000e-5(b). Failure to swear to the charge deprives the EEOC of administrative jurisdiction and may result in the dismissal of your subsequent lawsuit. EEOC v. Appalachian Power Co., 568 F.2d 354 (4th Cir. 1978).
63. Any subsequent lawsuit is limited only to those issues which are "reasonably related to the allegations in the administrative charge." Jenkins v. Blue Cross Mut.

Hosp. Ins., 538 F.2d 164 (7th Cir. 1976); Smith v. Delta Air Lines, 486 F.2d 512 (5th Cir. 1973).
64. Persons or parties not named in the administrative charge will be dismissed from any subsequent lawsuit. *E.g.,* Williams v. General Foods Corp., 492 F.2d 399, 404–05 (7th Cir. 1974).
65. See 42 U.S.C. §§2000e-5(c) and (e), and Love v. Pullman Co., 404 U.S. 522 (1972).
66. 42 U.S.C. §2000e-5(b).
67. 42 U.S.C. §2000e-5(f). Bradshaw v. Zoological Soc'y of San Diego, 569 F.2d 1066 (9th Cir. 1978); Page v. U.S. Industries, 556 F.2d 346 (5th Cir. 1977), *cert. denied,* 434 U.S. 1045 (1978). *But see* Zambuto v. American Tel. & Tel., 544 F.2d 1333 (5th Cir. 1977), *and* DeMatteis v. Eastman Kodak Co., 520 F.2d 409 (2d Cir. 1975), both holding that the ninety-day period to file suit begins to run not upon receipt of the right-to-sue notice but upon receipt of a notice that the EEOC charge has been dismissed.
68. See notes 63 and 64, *supra.*
69. 42 U.S.C. §2000e-5(f)(1).
70. Pursuant to 42 U.S.C. §2000e-5(f), the courts are authorized to appoint an attorney for a claimant. The appointment, however, is discretionary, and the court will require you to show that you have tried to find an attorney or are financially unable to afford one. Spanos v. Penn Cent. Transp. Co., 470 F.2d 806 (3d Cir. 1972).
71. See note 61 *supra.*
72. Albemarle Paper Co. v. Moody, 422 U.S. 405 (1975).
73. 42 U.S.C. §2000e-5(f).
74. *See* Johnson v. Railway Express Agency, 421 U.S. 454 (1975), and the cases cited therein at 459 n.6.
75. *E.g.,* Washington v. Davis, 426 U.S. 229 (1976).
76. 31 U.S.C. §§1242 *et seq.*
77. 42 U.S.C. §3766(c).
78. 42 U.S.C. §2000e-16, and 5 C.F.R. §§713 *et seq.,* modified by Presidential Reorganization Plan No. 1, 43 Fed. Reg. 19807 (May 9, 1978), and implemented by Executive Order 12106, 44 Fed. Reg. 1053 (Jan. 3, 1979).
79. *Id.*
80. Richardson v. Wiley, 569 F.2d 140 (D.C. Cir. 1977).
81. Chandler v. Roudebush, 425 U.S. 840 (1976).
82. 42 U.S.C. §2000e-16(d) incorporates 42 U.S.C. §§2000e-5(f)–(k). *See notes* 69 and 70, *supra.*

EMPLOYMENT

83. Brown v. General Serv. Admin., 425 U.S. 820 (1976).
84. *Cf.* Penn v. Schlesinger, 497 F.2d 970 (5th Cir. 1974) (*en banc*).
85. Davis v. Passman, 60 L.Ed.2d 846 (1979).
86. 438 U.S. 265 (1978).
87. 99 S.Ct. 2721, 61 L.Ed.2d 480 (1979).
88. 438 U.S. 265, 355–379 (1978) (opinion of Brennan, J., with White, Marshall and Blackmun, JJ.).
89. 438 U.S. 265, 301–310 (1978) (opinion of Powell, J.). Justice Powell supported this proposition by relying on such cases as Bridgeport Guardians, Inc. v. Members of Bridgeport Civil Serv. Comm'n, 482 F.2d 1333 (2d Cir. 1973) (50 percent of new hires must be minority persons to overcome past discrimination), and Carter v. Gallagher, 452 F.2d 315 (8th Cir. 1971), *modified en banc*, 452 F.2d 327 (8th Cir.), *cert. denied*, 406 U.S. 950 (1972) (33 percent of new hires must be minority persons to overcome past discrimination).
90. 438 U.S. 265, 301–310 (1978) (opinion of Powell, J.). To support this proposition, Justice Powell cited with approval such cases as Associated Gen. Contractors of Massachusetts v. Altshuler, 490 F.2d 9 (1st Cir. 1973), *cert. denied*, 416 U.S. 957 (1974), and Contractors Ass'n of E. Pennsylvania v. Secretary of Labor, 442 F.2d 159 (3d Cir.), *cert. denied*, 404 U.S. 954 (1971), neither of which actually relied on administrative findings of past discrimination but instead relied only on findings of minority underrepresentation.
91. 438 U.S. 265, 301–310 (1978) (opinion of Powell, J.). Here Justice Powell cited with approval such cases as Califano v. Webster, 430 U.S. 313 (1977); United Jewish Organizations v. Carey, 430 U.S. 144 (1977); Katzenbach v. Morgan, 384 U.S. 641 (1966); South Carolina v. Katzenbach, 383 U.S. 301 (1966).
92. *See* note 52, *supra*.
93. *Id.*
94. *E.g.*, Fullilove v. Kreps, 584 F.2d 600 (2d Cir. 1978), *cert. granted*, 60 L.Ed.2d 1064 (1979).
95. United Steelworkers of America v. Weber, 99 S.Ct. 2721, 61 L.Ed.2d 480 (1979).
96. 438 U.S. 265, 355–379 (1978) (opinion of Brennan, J., with White, Marshall and Blackmun, JJ.).
97. 438 U.S. 265, 287–320 (1978) (opinion of Powell, J.).
98. 438 U.S. 265, 408–421 (1978) (opinion of Stevens, J., with Burger, C.J., and Stewart and Rehnquist, JJ.).

Their opinion addressed only the legality of numerical plans under Title VI of the Civil Rights Act of 1964, 42 U.S.C. §2000d, a statute which does not apply to employment practices, 42 U.S.C. §2000d-3.

99. *See* note 94, *supra*. *See also* Detroit Police Officers Association v. Young, 446 F.Supp. 979 (E.D. Mich. 1978), *rev'd*, 48 U.S. L.W. 2277 (6th Cir. Oct. 12, 1979) (No. 78-1163).

IV

Education

The modern civil rights era in many respects was initiated by the Supreme Court's historic, unanimous decision in *Brown* v. *Board of Education*.[1] "Separate educational facilities," the Supreme Court declared, "are inherently unequal." [2]

Within several years, the *Brown* decision was widely applied by the Supreme Court to end segregation in numerous government facilities and services.[3] Segregation in public education, however, did not end with the Supreme Court's 1954 decision. Indeed, the Supreme Court did not even devise a remedy for unconstitutional segregation until the following year. In 1955, in *Brown II*,[4] the Supreme Court declined to impose a nationwide remedy but instead merely directed the school boards in the five consolidated cases that comprised *Brown* to replace their dual school systems with unitary systems with "all deliberate speed." [5]

For nearly twenty years after *Brown I* and *Brown II*, however, most school districts rejected deliberate speed and pursued numerous strategies to resist desegregation. The Supreme Court consistently rejected these tactics and delays.

In the Little Rock case, in 1958, the Court discounted white hostility to desegregaion, declaring that the "constitutional rights of [black children] are not to be sacrificed or yielded" because of white opposition to those rights.[6] In 1963, in another case, the Court rejected voluntary transfer plans that allowed white students to transfer out of desegregated schools.[7] That same year, the Court eliminated another delaying tactic—the requirement that

95

plaintiffs in a desegregation lawsuit exhaust state administrative remedies before seeking federal court relief—a tactic which had been urged successfully on several lower courts.[8] A year later, in 1964, the Court required the reopening of a school system which chose to close its schools rather than to desegregate, noting that "[t]he time for mere 'deliberate speed' had run out."[9] The following year the Court banned as too slow the use of a new delaying strategy: one-grade-per-year desegregation plans.[10] In 1968, the Court invalidated freedom-of-choice desegregation plans and ordered the elimination of all segregation "root and branch."[11] In 1969, the Court rejected delaying tactics attempted by the federal government and repeated the duty of all school districts to desegregate their schools and classrooms "at once."[12] Finally, in 1971, in the case of *Swann* v. *Charlotte-Mecklenburg Board of Education*,[13] the Court approved the reassignment of students and realignment of school transportation routes (busing) in order to desegregate school systems effectively.

Despite the resistance to desegregation, the right of racial minorities to a desegregated education was established as a fundamental tenet of civil rights law. In varying degrees, this tenet has been expanded in recent years to include the right to a desegregated interdistrict education (*i.e.*, transfers between and among school districts in a metropolitan area), the right to a bilingual education for non-English-speaking minority students, and the right to nondiscriminatory admissions procedures in private schools. These rights, however, are enforceable in most instances only through lawsuits filed by aggrieved minorities against offending school boards.

PUBLIC SCHOOL SEGREGATION

Is racial imbalance unconstitutional?

No, unless it results from intentional acts of discrimination. Although school districts have the power to require that "each school have a prescribed ratio of [minority] to white students reflecting the proportion for the district as a whole," there is *no* general requirement of racial balance in any schools in a school district.[14] On the other hand, the use of "mathematical ratios" to assign students to schools on the basis of race is an appropriate "starting point in the process of shaping a remedy" to overcome past practices of unconstitutional segregation.[15] In other words, racial balance and student reassignment on the basis of race are legally required only where school districts have engaged in segregation in violation of the equal-protection clause of the Fourteenth Amendment.

What forms of school segregation violate the Fourteenth Amendment's guarantee of equal protection of the laws?
The most basic form of unconstitutional segregation was the state-imposed dual school system formerly used throughout the South, which, in *Brown I*, was held to violate the Fourteenth Amendment.[16] Under a state-enforced dual school system, black students were required by state law to attend separate, all-black schools.

What is the remedy for an unconstitutional state-imposed dual school system?
Segregated school systems are required "to effectuate a transition to . . . racially nondiscriminatory school system[s],"[17] and affirmatively to eliminate all aspects of the dual systems "until it is clear that state-imposed segregation has been completely removed."[18]

Since many school districts in the South still have not complied with this mandate, they have to be forced to desegregate through lawsuits. In such lawsuits,

> where plaintiffs prove that a current condition of segregated schooling exists within a school district where a dual school system was compelled or authorized by statute at the time of *Brown I* in 1954, the school district and the state are under a continuing affirmative duty "to effectuate a transition to a racially nondiscriminatory school system," that is to eliminate from the public schools within their school system "all vestiges of state-imposed segregation."[19]

If a school district or a state fails to carry out this affirmative duty, a federal court may order appropriate remedies.[20]

Specific remedies for achieving this goal were spelled out in detail in *Swann* v. *Charlotte-Mecklenburg Board of Education*.[21] They include the reassignment of teachers and students according to mathematical ratios based upon race, the alteration of attendance zones and feeder patterns, and the realignment of bus transportation routes.[22] In another case, the Supreme Court held that such services as special reading programs for students and in-service human relations training for teachers were proper remedies for the continuing effects of past discrimination.[23]

Does school segregation in the North and West, which was not imposed by state law, also violate the Fourteenth Amendment?

Generally, yes. Most of the segregation in the North and West was caused by the intentional policies and practices of school authorities. This violates the Fourteenth Amendment as much as segregation imposed by state statutes in the South.

In *Keyes* v. *School District No. 1*, a 1973 decision involving Denver, Colorado, the Supreme Court outlined a number of the policies and practices that create a segregated school system and accordingly violate the Fourteenth Amendment:

> First, it is obvious that a practice of concentrating Negroes in certain schools by structuring attendance zones or designating "feeder" schools on the basis of race has the reciprocal effect of keeping other nearby schools predominantly white. Similarly, the practice of building a school . . . to a certain size and in a certain location, "with conscious knowledge that it would be a segregated school," has a substantial reciprocal effect on the racial composition of other nearby schools. So also, the use of mobile classrooms, the drafting of student transfer policies, the transportation of students, and the assignment of faculty and staff, on racially identifiable bases, have the clear effect of earmarking schools according to their racial composition, and . . . causing further racial concentration within the schools.[24]

If a school district claims that it has not engaged in intentional discrimination but has only followed a neighborhood assignment policy, is that school district thus absolved of any unconstitutional segregation?

No. School districts frequently argue that the existence of any school segregation is merely the result of residential segregation. Such bald claims, however, are closely examined by the courts, as was done by the Supreme Court in *Keyes*:

> the mere assertion of such a policy is not dispositive where, as in this case, the school authorities have been found to have practiced de jure segregation in a meaningful portion of the school system by techniques that indicate that the 'neighborhood school' concept has not been maintained free of manipulation.[25]

A close review of a purported neighborhood assignment policy usually will reveal that students are not in fact assigned to the nearest school but are racially assigned, and that school assignment patterns and feeder patterns have been changed to parallel racial residential changes.[26]

If only a portion of a school system is intentionally segregated, is the entire system required to desegregate and correct racial imbalance?

Yes, if the discrimination has been significant and has had a systemwide impact.[27] There is no requirement that segregation be practiced in every school before the entire system is made to desegregate. The Supreme Court has held that the existence of "intentionally segregative school board actions in a meaningful portion of a school system . . . creates a presumption that other segregated schooling within the system" similarly is intentionally segregative.[28] When there is a systemwide impact, meaning that the entire school system is segregated, the entire system is required to desegregate.

There is, however, an exception to the systemwide imposition of these appropriate remedies. This exception arises when only a very small portion of a school system is unconstitutionally segregated and the segregation has no significant impact on the system as a whole. In this situation, a federal court can impose remedies only in the unconstitutionally segregated portion of the school system in order to correct the "incremental segregative effect" of the unconstitutional segregation.[29]

Are the remedies for segregation caused by school authorities carrying out intentionally discriminatory policies and practices the same as those for segregation caused by state statutes?

Yes. When an entire school system is segregated, the appropriate remedies in the North and the West are identical to those in the South. When an entire school system is unconstitutionally segregated, the school system, the state, and in the last instance, a federal court must provide affirmative remedies desegregating the school district. These remedies, as noted, include reassignment of students and teachers, alteration of attendance zones and feeder patterns, and the realignment of bus routes (sometimes increasing the amount of transportation).[30] The remedies also include remedial education programs and additional teacher training.[31]

When a school district is unconstitutionally segregated and a court-ordered desegregation plan is imposed, will the plan stay in effect for many years? Can it be altered to correct increasing racial imbalance in the school district?

Once a desegregation plan is imposed, it usually will stay in effect for at least several years so as to insure that all vestiges of segregation are removed from the school district. Thereafter, however, as the Supreme Court in *Swann* observed, neither school districts nor the courts "are constitutionally required to make year-by-year adjustments of the racial composition of student bodies once the affirmative duty to desegregate has been accomplished and racial discrimination through official action is eliminated from the system." [32] The remedy similarly need not be changed to take into account changing residential patterns: "in the absence of a showing that either the school authorities or some other agency of the State has deliberately attempted to fix or alter demographic patterns to affect the racial composition of the schools, further intervention by a district court should not be necessary."[33]

In view of the flight of whites from desegregated schools, aren't desegregation remedies useless when applied to inner-city schools?

No. First, even in predominantly minority school districts, many whites do remain after desegregation. And there really is no difference between desegregating a school district with 70 percent minority and 30 percent white students and desegregating one with the reverse proportions. The objective in both situations is eliminating the intentional racial segregation caused by school authorities.

Second, white flight is not a recent phenomenon due solely to school desegregation but rather is an ongoing process that began with suburbanization after World War II. In fact, much of the white suburbanization and the concomitant concentration of minorities in the central cities had been caused by government action capitalized upon by school authorities.[34] This situation in many metropolitan areas may have been caused in violation of the Fourteenth Amendment, and thus may be remediable in court through desegregation plans which include city as well as suburban school districts.

When a central-city school district is predominantly minority and suburban districts are predominantly white, does this interdistrict segregation violate the Fourteenth Amendment?

Maybe, but only if the suburban districts as well as the central-city district have engaged in interdistrict constitutional violations (for example, when white students are transferred from city districts to suburban districts) or if government officials unconstitutionally contributed to segregated residential patterns.

In 1974, the Supreme Court reviewed an interdistrict case involving metropolitan Detroit. In that lawsuit, unconstitutional segregation was proven only against the Detroit school district, and the many suburban districts were brought into the lawsuit by the federal district court thereafter only for purposes of determining the scope of the interdistrict remedy.[35] On review, the Supreme Court, in a 5–4 decision, held that an interdistrict remedy in this situation was improper. The Court, however, said that "an interdistrict remedy might be in order" if it is shown "that there has been a constitutional violation within one district that produces a significant segregative effect in another district."[36] The Court also stated that "an interdistrict remedy" might be "proper, or even necessary" if it were shown "that state officials had contributed to the separation of the races by drawing or redrawing school district lines, or by purposeful, racially discriminatory use of state housing or zoning laws."[37]

Much of this evidence is available in metropolitan areas. But it was not sufficiently proven in the Detroit case.

Have any interdistrict school desegregation lawsuits been successful after the Supreme Court's decision in the Detroit case?

Yes. As a result of two successful lawsuits, interdistrict desegregation is now in effect in metropolitan Louisville, Kentucky, and in metropolitan Wilmington, Delaware. The Supreme Court, however, did not review either case.

In Louisville, the interdistrict remedy was based primarily upon the past existence of interdistrict school segregation whereby the city and suburbs had assigned their minority students to all-black schools in the city, and had never fully desegregated their separate school systems.[38]

In Wilmington, the interdistrict school remedy was premised primarily on the unconstitutional government contributions to segregated residential patterns.[39] For example: nearly all low-cost public housing in the metropolitan area had been placed in Wilmington; deeds containing racially restrictive covenants had been accepted by government officials; and the state real-estate commission handbook had encouraged racially homogeneous neighborhoods, as had the federal mortgage underwriting manual. These constitutional violations, among others, were deemed sufficient for an interdistrict school-desegregation remedy.

EDUCATION

If minority students believe that they are unconstitutionally segregated, how can they enforce their rights to nondiscrimination in public schools?

Virtually the only way to eliminate discrimination in public education is through a lawsuit filed by students and their parents or guardians under the Fourteenth Amendment and under part of the Civil Rights Act of 1871.[40]

The main remedies available in desegregation lawsuits are the desegregation remedies already discussed. Monetary damages have rarely if ever been recovered. Attorneys' fees, however, are awarded to plaintiffs whose lawsuits against school districts "bring about compliance" with the law.[41]

Aside from lawsuits brought by individuals, are there any other ways to remedy discrimination in public schools?

Yes, there are two other possibilities. First, the Department of Justice is authorized by two civil rights statutes to file discrimination lawsuits against school districts. Under one section of Title IV of the Civil Rights Act of 1964, the Department of Justice may file a lawsuit if it receives a written charge from parents alleging discrimination and if the Department certifies that the complainants are unable to bring a lawsuit on their own behalf.[42] Similarly, under several sections of the Equal Education Opportunities Act of 1974, the Department of Justice may file a lawsuit on behalf of any "individual denied an equal educational opportunity."[43] Although the Department of Justice files very few such lawsuits, it is worth sending an administrative charge of discrimination to the Department of Justice, Washington, D.C. 20530.

The second possibility involves desegregation enforcement by the Department of Health, Education, and Welfare (HEW). Under Title VI of the Civil Rights Act of 1964, HEW is required to terminate its federal funding to discriminatory school districts.[44] This powerful potential remedy for unconstitutional discrimination is initiated by the filing of an administrative charge of discrimination with any regional office of HEW or with its main office

(HEW, Office for Civil Rights, 330 Independence Avenue, S.W., Washington, D.C. 20201).

Because of the importance of this latter remedy with HEW, it is discussed in detail in Chapter VII.

SCHOOL FINANCING AND BILINGUAL EDUCATION

In addition to the right of racial minorities to a desegregated education, do they enjoy other educational rights such as a right to equal school financing and a right to bilingual education?

No and yes. Although enforcement of the right to a desegregated education has exposed many educational inequities besides segregation, those inequities have not been uniformly addressed. Two of the biggest areas of educational inequities other than segregation are disparities in school financing and the absence of bilingual education. As to the former, the Supreme Court has held that there is no enforceable right under the Fourteenth Amendment to equitable school financing. On the other hand, there is a right to a bilingual education for non and limited English speaking minorities.

What are the inequities in school financing?

Public school districts in nearly every state are supported primarily by a combination of (1) state funds awarded fairly equally to each district based upon the number of students attending schools in the district, and (2) local property taxes. Local property taxes not only provide the greatest monetary support for school districts but also are very inequitable. For example, a poor, predominantly minority urban school district may tax its residents heavily but raise relatively little revenue for its schools, whereas a rich, predominantly white suburban school district may tax its residents only slightly but still raise much greater revenues for its schools. These inequities in school financing are particularly harsh to low income minorities because of the high taxation imposed and the low revenues raised for schools.

If school financing inequities are so patent, why are they not unconstitutional under the Fourteenth Amendment?

In 1972, in *San Antonio School District* v. *Rodriguez*,[45] the Supreme Court, in a 5-4 decision, held that school financing inequities do not violate the Fourteenth Amendment's guarantee of equal protection of the laws.

The inequities in San Antonio were typical. The poorest school district, which was 96 percent minority, had an average property value for taxation per student of $6,000; at a property tax rate of $1.05 per $100 of property, the school district raised only $26 for the education of each student. The wealthiest school district, which was 19 percent minority, had an average property value for taxation per student of $49,000; at a lower property tax rate of only $0.85 per $100 of property, this wealthy school district raised $333 for the education of each student. With the addition of state and federal funds (more federal funds usually go to poor districts than to wealthy districts), the poor district could spend only $356 per student as compared to $594 per student in the wealthy district. Based upon these financing disparities, poor and minority parents alleged that the use of local property taxes was discriminatory and unconstitutional under the Fourteenth Amendment.

Not so, replied the Supreme Court. Although the Court conceded that "substantial disparities exist," [46] it held that it could not review the case under the strict standard of review usually applied to distinctions which disadvantage minorities, because the disparities were not intentionally discriminatory on grounds of race. Applying the more lenient rational-basis standard of review, the Supreme Court held that the disparities were rational primarily in view of this country's long tradition of local control of schools, and that "some inequality" was not a sufficient basis for striking down the financing system.[47]

Can school financing inequities be challenged in any way other than through a lawsuit filed under the Fourteenth Amendment?

Sometimes. Because of the Supreme Court's decision in *Rodriguez,* a number of school financing challenges have been brought in state courts alleging discrimination in violation of the equal-protection clauses of state constitutions. Since state-court interpretations of their own state constitutions are not reviewable by the Supreme Court, state courts need not interpret state equal-protection clauses in the same way that the Supreme Court interpreted the Fourteenth Amendment in *Rodriguez*. Only a few state courts, however, notably those in California,[48] Connecticut,[49] and New Jersey,[50] have interpreted their state constitutions to prohibit property-tax school-financing inequalities. Thus, at least in several states, there is a right to equal school financing.

What is bilingual education?

Bilingual education generally means the effective education of students who do not speak English or who have limited English-speaking ability who come from environments where the dominant language is other than English. In order to provide an effective bilingual education, schools teach the students English but they teach all other subjects in the students' dominant language—such as Spanish—until the students are able to learn the other subjects in English.

Bilingual education in recent years has been heralded as an educational priority in the United States. Congress, in enacting the Bilingual Education Act, recognized "the special educational needs of the large numbers of children of limited English-speaking ability in the United States" and declared "it to be the policy of the United States to provide financial assistance to local educational agencies to develop and carry out" bilingual educational programs.[51]

Do non or limited English-speaking students have a right to a bilingual education?

Yes, said the Supreme Court in *Lau* v. *Nichols*,[52] at leeast when there are a substantial number of non or limited English-speaking students who speak the same dominant language.

Lau was a lawsuit filed on behalf of 1,800 Chinese-speaking students who were being taught only in English by the San Francisco school district. They argued that they were being discriminated against in violation of the Fourteenth Amendment and of Title VI of the Civil Rights Act of 1964 [53] which bans discrimination "based on the ground of race, color, or national origin" in "any program or activity receiving Federal financial assistance." [54] The Supreme Court agreed that they had been discriminated against in violation of Title VI: "There is no equality of treatment merely by providing students with the same facilities, textbooks, teachers, and curriculum; for students who do not understand English are effectively foreclosed from any meaningful education." [55]

The Supreme Court's decision in *Lau*, although it was brought on behalf of Chinese-speaking students, has its greatest impact in requiring bilingual education for Spanish-speaking students, members of the largest language minority in the country.

How do non or limited English-speaking students enforce their right to a bilingual education?

The primary way, which was used in *Lau*, is to file suit against the school district alleging a violation of Title VI.[56] Before such a lawsuit can be filed, however, an administrative charge of discrimination must be filed with the federal agency which administers Title VI with regard to schools, the Department of Health, Education, and Welfare (HEW). The charge may be resolved administratively by HEW without ever having to file a lawsuit. Complaints should be sent to any HEW regional office or to the main office (HEW, Office for Civil Rights, 330 Independence Avenue, S.W., Washington D.C. 20201).

Because of the importance of this administrative remedy under Title VI, it is discussed in some detail in Chapter VII.

DISCRIMINATION IN PRIVATE SCHOOLS

Are there any prohibitions against discrimination in *private*, as opposed to public, schools?

Yes. As we have seen, the constitutional prohibition against discrimination in public education is the Four-

THE RIGHTS OF RACIAL MINORITIES

teenth Amendment's guarantee of equal protection of the laws. The Fourteenth Amendment, however, applies only to state and local governments and their officials and not to entities that are primarily private.

But this does not mean that discrimination is permitted in private schools: there are federal statutes that do prohibit private-school discrimination. The two basic laws which have been used to date are one part of the Civil Rights Act of 1866,[57] which protects minority contract rights; and Title VI of the Civil Rights Act of 1964, which prohibits discrimination in programs or activities receiving federal financial assistance. Both of these laws, at least in some ways, prohibit discrimination in private schools.

If a private school intentionally denies admission to a minority student, is that an unlawful denial of the right to contract in violation of the Civil Rights Act of 1866?

Yes. As noted, part of the Civil Rights Act of 1866 guarantees all persons the same right "to make and enforce contracts . . . as is enjoyed by white citizens." This law, the Supreme Court has held, prohibits private schools from intentionally denying admission to minority students, and makes the private schools liable for court-awarded damages.[58]

Enforcement of the Civil Rights Act of 1866 is accomplished only through litigation, and the lawsuits must be timely filed within the applicable state statute of limitations.[59]

What types of discrimination in private schools are prohibited by Title VI? How is the law enforced?

Title VI, as noted, generally prohibits all forms of discrimination based "on the ground of race, color, or national origin" in "any program or activity receiving federal financial assistance."[60] So long as a private school receives federal financial assistance, it generally is prohibited from engaging in discrimination.

Title VI is enforced through administrative procedures and sometimes through lawsuits—both of which are discussed in Chapter VII.

AFFIRMATIVE ACTION IN ADMISSIONS

What is affirmative action in educational admissions?

Affirmative action in admissions embodies two closely related concepts. First, affirmative action requires special recruitment of minority students. This allows colleges and universities which are predominantly white, which may have used or may still use admissions criteria that discriminate against minority applicants, and which may have discriminatory reputations in minority communities, to expand their pool of applicants to include minority applicants. Second, affirmative action requires that the minority race of an applicant be considered as a positive factor in admissions. This allows colleges and universities to overcome their past and current admissions practices which discriminate against minorities and to increase the admission of minorities to their schools.

Why is affirmative action used in higher education? And is it widely used?

Prior to the late 1960s, there was no affirmative action in education. At that time, although racial minorities constituted approximately 19 percent of the population of the United States, they were vastly underrepresented in higher education and thereby in professional life. For example, less than 2 percent of all doctors, lawyers, medical students, and law students were minority persons. In fact, as of 1970, two black medical schools, Howard and Meharry, had trained more than 75 percent of all of the minority doctors in the country.

During the late 1960s and early 1970s, colleges, universities, and graduate schools (especially medical and law schools) began to expand their student enrollments substantially. Some but hardly most of these institutions of higher education at the same time began to adopt and to implement affirmative-action admissions programs. The affirmative-action programs were adopted for three reasons.

First, some institutions of higher education sought to overcome their past and current practices that discriminated against minorities. They felt not only that such discrimination was wrong but also that they (especially the public institutions) had an obligation to serve all segments of the community, not just the white portions of the community. And because they were expanding their enrollments, they resolved to give some of their expanded enrollment admissions to minority applicants.

Second, some institutions also realized that the grade-point averages and written aptitude tests used as admissions criteria not only discriminated against minority applicants (because of the segregated and inferior public education given to minorities for so long) but also were not very useful in making admissions decisions about applicants. Additionally, some institutions evaluated applicants by discriminatory subjective criteria such as their parents' wealth, and whether their parents were alumni. Since these subjective criteria have a discriminatory impact upon minority applicants, some of the institutions resolved to overcome this pattern by also giving extra weight to the minority status of the qualified applicants.

Finally, some of the institutions also simply believed that the admission of more than a token number of minority students was necessary to provide a genuinely diverse student body in which all of the students would learn from each other and would benefit from a robust exchange of ideas.

Accordingly, many but not most institutions of higher education did adopt and implement affirmative-action programs during the late 1960s and early 1970s. Some of those programs set aside a minimum number of admissions for minority applicants. Most of the programs simply added race as another of the many positive factors which were used to make admissions decisions.

What effect does the *Bakke* case have? Is it lawful to use an affirmative-action admissions program which sets aside a minimum number of admissions for disadvantaged minority applicants and which considers disadvantaged minority applicants separately from all other applicants?

Probably not. In *Regents of the University of California* v. *Bakke*,[61] the Supreme Court reviewed a medical school's affirmative-action admissions program which set aside sixteen out of one hundred places in the medical school for disadvantaged minority students, which used separate admissions criteria for the disadvantaged minority applicants different from the criteria used for all other applicants, and which thus considered the disadvantaged minority applicants separately from all other applicants. In a close and confusing vote, the Supreme Court held that this program, on the facts in the case, was unlawful.

Four of the nine members of the Supreme Court, led by Justice Stevens, voted to strike down this dual admissions program, and implicitly other race-conscious programs, as unlawful under Title VI of the Civil Rights Act of 1964. Four other members of the Supreme Court, led by Justice Brennan, voted to uphold this program, and thus virtually any other race-conscious program, as lawful under Title VI and as constitutional under the Fourteenth Amendment. The ninth member of the Court, Justice Powell, voted to hold the rigid program in *Bakke* unlawful and unconstitutional, but also voted to uphold flexible race consciousness under Title VI and the Fourteenth Amendment. Accordingly, a majority of the Supreme Court in *Bakke* held the rigid program there unlawful.

The program, however, would not necessarily have been unlawful in all circumstances. For example, Justice Powell, whose crucial vote made a majority in *Bakke*, stated that the program would have been lawful if there had been findings of past discrimination against the medical school, which there were not.

Significantly, Justice Powell stated that a race-conscious admissions program is lawful and constitutional to provide a diverse student body in which all of the students would benefit from a robust exchange of ideas. But he held that the rigid program in *Bakke* was not lawful because it used race as a sole criterion rather than as one of many criteria for admissions.

As a result of Bakke, is it now lawful and constitutional to use an affirmative-action admissions program which uses race as a positive factor in admitting minority applicants?

Yes. As discussed, four of the nine judges on the Supreme Court, led by Justice Brennan, voted to uphold the rigid affirmative-action admissions program in *Bakke* as both lawful and constitutional, and thereby voted to uphold more flexible programs which merely take race into account. Another judge, Justice Powell, voted to uphold as lawful and constitutional only flexible programs which take race into account. In such programs, educational institutions may seek to create educational diversity by giving positive consideration to such factors "as geographic origin or life spent on a farm," [62] and similarly, "race or ethnic background may be deemed a 'plus' in a particular applicant's file." [63]

To emphasize the legality and constitutionality of race-conscious affirmative-action programs, Justice Powell gave specific approval to the Harvard College admissions program, a race-conscious admissions program which seeks to increase minority enrollment by giving additional positive consideration to applicants who are minority members. Since nearly all educational institutions with affirmative-action admissions programs use a flexible program similar to Harvard's rather than a rigid program similar to the University of California's, the Supreme Court in *Bakke* did sanction affirmative-action admissions programs in higher education.

NOTES

1. 347 U.S. 483 (1954).
2. *Id.* at 495
3. *See* cases cited in the footnotes to Chapter VI, Public Accommodations.
4. 349 U.S. 294 (1955).
5. *Id.* at 301.
6. Cooper v. Aaron, 358 U.S. 1 (1958); *see also* Brown II, 349 U.S. 294, 300 (1955).
7. Goss v. Board of Educ., 373 U.S. 683, 689 (1963).
8. McNeese v. Board of Educ., 373 U.S. 668, 676 (1963), *disapproving, e.g.*, Parham v. Dove, 271 F.2d 132, 138 (8th Cir. 1959); Covington v. Edwards, 264 F.2d 780, 783 (4th Cir. 1959).
9. Griffin v. County School Bd., 377 U.S. 218, 234 (1964).
10. Rogers v. Paul, 382 U.S. 198, 199 (1965).

EDUCATION

11. Green v. County School Bd., 391 U.S. 430, 439–41 (1968).
12. Alexander v. Holmes County Bd. of Educ., 396 U.S. 19, 20 (1969); *see also*, Carter v. West Feliciana Parish School Bd., 396 U.S. 290, 291–93 (1970).
13. 402 U.S. 1 (1971).
14. *See* Swann v. Charlotte-Mecklenburg Bd. of Educ., 402 U.S. 1, 15–19 (1971), interpreting several sections of Title IV of the Civil Rights Act of 1964, as amended, 42 U.S.C. §2000c(b) and §2000c-6, which prohibits reassignment of students merely to overcome racial imbalance. *See also* Keyes v. School Dist. No. 1, 413 U.S. 189 (1973); North Carolina Bd. of Educ. v. Swann, 402 U.S. 43 (1971); McDaniel v. Barresi, 402 U.S. 39 (1971).
15. Swann v. Charlotte-Mecklenburg Bd. of Educ., 402 U.S. 1, 25 (1971).
16. 347 U.S. 483 (1954).
17. Brown v. Board of Educ., 349 U.S. 294, 301 (1955).
18. Green v. County School Bd., 391 U.S. 430, 439 (1968).
19. Keyes v. School Dist. No. 1, 413 U.S. 189, 200 (1973) (citations omitted), quoting from, respectively, Brown II, 349 U.S. 294, 301 (1955), and Swann v. Charlotte-Mecklenburg Bd. of Educ., 402 U.S. 1, 15 (1971).
20. *See* Swann v. Charlotte-Mecklenburg Bd. of Educ., 402 U.S. 1 (1971), and cases cited therein.
21. 402 U.S. 1 (1971).
22. *Id.* at 1, 22–31 (1971). *See also* Davis v. Board of School Commr's, 402 U.S. 33 (1971).
23. Milliken v. Bradley, 433 U.S. 267 (1977).
24. 413 U.S. 189, 201–02 (1973) (footnotes and citations omitted).
25. *Id.* at 189, 212.
26. *E.g.*, NAACP v. Lansing Board of Education, 559 F.2d 1042 (6th Cir.), *cert. denied*, 434 U.S. 997 (1977).
27. Keyes v. School Dist. No. 1, 413 U.S. 189 (1973). *See also* Dayton Board of Education v. Brinkman, 99 S.Ct. 2971, 61 L.Ed.2d 720 (1979); Columbus Board of Education v. Penick, 61 L.Ed.2d 666, 99 S.Ct. 294.
28. Keyes at 189, 208.
29. Dayton Bd. of Educ. v. Brinkman, 433 U.S. 406, 420 (1977). Compare cases in note 27, *supra*.
30. *See* notes 22 and 27, *supra*.
31. *See* note 23, *supra*.

32. Swann v. Charlotte-Mecklenburg Bd. of Educ., 402 U.S. 1, 32 (1971).
33. *Id. See also* Pasadena Bd. of Educ. v. Spangler, 427 U.S. 424 (1976).
34. *See* Chapter V, Housing.
35. Milliken v. Bradley, 418 U.S. 717, 724–34, 745 (1974) (plurality opinion of Burger, C.J.), *rev'g* 484 F.2d 215 (6th Cir. 1973).
36. 418 U.S. 717, 745 (1974) (plurality opinion of Burger, C.J.).
37. 418 U.S. 717, 755 (1974) (concurring opinion of Stewart, J.).
38. Newburg Area Council v. Board of Educ. of Jefferson County, 510 F.2d 1358 (6th Cir. 1974), *cert. denied*, 421 U.S. 931 (1975).
39. Evans v. Buchanan, 393 F.Supp. 428 (D. Del.), *sum. aff'd*, 423 U.S. 963 (1975), *guidelines for an interdistrict remedy imposed*, 416 F.Supp. 328 (D. Del.), *appeal dismissed*, 429 U.S. 973 (1976), *guidelines aff'd, en banc*, 555 F.2d 373 (3d Cir.), *cert. denied*, 434 U.S. 944 (1977).
40. 42 U.S.C. §1983. *See also* §207 of the Equal Educational Opportunities Act of 1974, 20 U.S.C. §1706, which authorizes the filing of a lawsuit by any "individual denied an equal educational opportunity."
41. Section 718 of the Emergency School Aid Act, as amended by the Education Amendments of 1972, 20 U.S.C. §1617. *See* Bradley v. School Bd. of Richmond, 416 U.S. 696 (1974). Attorneys' fees also are authorized for the "prevailing party" in §1983 actions by the Civil Rights Attorneys' Fees Awards Act of 1976, 42 U.S.C. §1988.
42. Section 407 of the Civil Rights Act of 1964, as amended, 42 U.S.C. §2000c-6.
43. Sections 207 and 211 of the Equal Educational Opportunities Act of 1974, 20 U.S.C. §1706 and §1710, respectively.
44. Title VI of the Civil Rights Act of 1964, as amended, 42 U.S.C. §§2000d *et seq*.
45. 411 U.S. 1 (1972).
46. 411 U.S. 1, 11 (1972).
47. 411 U.S. 1, 51 (1972).
48. Serrano v. Priest, 5 Cal.3d 584, 96 Cal.Rptr. 601, 487 P.2d 1241 (Cal.Sup.Ct. 1971); *subsequent opinion*, 18

EDUCATION

Cal. 3d 728, 135 Cal.Rptr. 345, 557 P.2d 929 (Cal.Sup. Ct. 1976).
49. Horton v. Meskill, 172 Conn. 615, 376 A.2d 359 (Conn.Sup.Ct. 1977), *aff'g,* 31 Conn.Supp. 377, 332 A.2d 813 (Hartford Sup. Ct. 1974).
50. Robinson v. Cahill, 62 N.J. 473, 303 A.2d 273 (N.J. Sup. Ct. 1973).
51. 20 U.S.C. §880b. The Bilingual Education Act, as amended, is codified at 20 U.S.C. §§880b, *et seq. See also* the Equal Educational Opportunities Act of 1974, as amended, 20 U.S.C. §1703.
52. 414 U.S. 563 (1974).
53. 42 U.S.C. §§2000d *et seq.*
54. 42 U.S.C. §2000d.
55. Lau v. Nichols, 414 U.S. 563, 566 (1974).
56. *See also* Serna v. Portales Mun. Schools, 499 F.2d 1147 (10th Cir. 1974), *aff'g,* 351 F.Supp. 1279 (D.N.M. 1972); Rios v. Read, 73 F.R.D. 589 (E.D.N.Y. 1977); ASPIRA of New York, Inc. v. Board of Educ. of New York, 58 F.R.D. 62 (S.D.N.Y. 1973).
57. 42 U.S.C. §1981.
58. Runyon v. McCrary, 427 U.S. 160 (1976).
59. *Id. See also* the discussion of the Thirteenth Amendment and of the Civil Rights Act of 1866 in Chapter I, Introduction, and Overview, *supra.*
60. 42 U.S.C. §2000d.
61. 438 U.S. 265 (1978).
62. 438 U.S. 265, 316 (1978) (Powell, J.).
63. 438 U.S. 265, 317 (1978) (Powell, J.).

V

Housing

Of all the forms of racial discrimination discussed in this book, housing discrimination undoubtedly is the most widely practiced today. As a result, our residential patterns reflect apartheid.

Modern discriminatory housing practices in many respects are products of our past history of official segregation:[1] racially restrictive covenants (an agreement by which the purchaser was bound not to sell the property to a minority person of another race) in deeds and land contracts for the sale of housing were legally enforceable until 1948;[2] mortgage-insurance practices under FHA and VA policies officially encouraged the development and preservation of racially "homogeneous" neighborhoods until the 1950s; public housing programs until the early 1960s provided housing for both blacks and whites but on a segregated basis; etc. Not surprisingly, discriminatory practices by private realtors were pervasive.

In the early 1960s, overt federal encouragement of residential segregation was declared terminated by presidential executive order.[3] Several years later, in 1968, two events increased the hope that it might be possible to curb private discrimination as well. First, Congress passed Title VIII of the Civil Rights Act of 1968[4] (also known as the Fair Housing Act), specifically prohibiting racial discrimination in most private housing transactions. Second, the Supreme Court in *Jones* v. *Alfred H. Mayer Co.*[5] revived the Civil Rights Act of 1866,[6] by deciding that it too prohibits racial discrimination not only in the public arena but also in the sale or rental of property by private individuals

The "sweeping promise of Civil Rights Acts, particularly of Title VIII of the Civil Rights Act of 1968, that racial discrimination in housing would be permanently ended, has not been realized."[7] The Civil Rights Acts, however, remain the primary basis for the right of racial minorities to nondiscrimination in housing.

What are the major federal prohibitions against discrimination in housing?

There are three major prohibitions against housing discrimination. (1) The first is Title VIII of the Civil Rights Act of 1968,[8] which prohibits discriminatory real estate practices by government agencies or by private individuals. Second, the Civil Rights Act of 1866,[9] revived by the Supreme Court in 1968,[10] also prohibits discriminatory real estate practices by public officials and by private individuals. Finally the Fourteenth Amendment prohibits all forms of intentional housing discrimination practiced by state and local government agencies.

Are there differences in coverage and enforcement among Title VIII, the Civil Rights Act of 1866, and the Fourteenth Amendment?

Yes, there are very important differences among the three federal prohibitions. Those differences are discussed at some length later in this chapter. Briefly:

1. Title VIII broadly prohibits real estate discrimination but it contains several coverage exemptions generally considered to be privacy exceptions. Procedurally, Title VIII may be enforced by discriminated-against persons who may proceed by either or both of two alternative procedural routes.
2. The Civil Rights Act of 1866 is the most sweeping prohibition against real estate discrimination; it contains no coverage exceptions. It is enforced only through lawsuits filed by individuals.
3. The Fourteenth Amendment prohibits only inten-

tional discrimination by government agencies. It too is enforced only through lawsuits.

PROHIBITED REAL ESTATE PRACTICES

Whta types of discriminatory real estate practices are prohibited by Title VIII?

Title VIII, enacted in 1968 with the hopes that it would assist in replacing segregated housing with "truly integrated and balanced living patterns," [11] prohibits a number of specific discriminatory practices on grounds of race, color, or national origin,[12] including:

a. refusal "to sell or rent," refusal "to negotiate for the sale or rental," or simply to make "unavailable" any dwelling; [13]
b. discrimination in "the terms, conditions or privileges" or in "the provision of services or facilities" in connection with the sale or rental of a dwelling; [14]
c. publication of "any notice, statement, or advertisement" with respect to sale or rental indicating a racial limitation or preference; [15]
d. representation to any person "that any dwelling is not available for inspection, sale or rental when such dwelling is in fact so available"; [16]
e. any "attempt to induce," for profit, any person to sell or rent a dwelling based upon representations about the probability of minority persons moving into the neighborhood (blockbusting).[17]

The prohibitions enumerated above give nondiscrimination rights primarily to prospective buyers and renters. Another section of Title VIII protects minority brokers and agents from the denial of access to "membership or participation" in any multiple-listing service or real estate organization.[18]

Are any real estate transactions specifically exempted from compliance with the foregoing nondiscrimination requirements of Title VIII?

Yes, two major types of transactions are exempt from compliance with the Title VIII prohibitions. First, Title

VIII exempts the sale or rental of a single-family dwelling sold or rented by its owner so long as no real estate sales or rental services are used and so long as the owner does not own more than three such single-family houses.[19] The second exemption, often referred to as the "Mrs. Murphy rooming house" exemption, permits discrimination in the rental of rooms or units in a dwelling containing living quarters for no more than four famiies so long as the owner actually occupies one of the living quarters.[20] Even those sellers and renters exempted from the above coverage, however, are prohibited from publishing or causing to be published any notice, statement, or advertisement indicating a racial limitation or preference.

Despite the two major exceptions, "it is estimated that 80 percent of America's housing is covered by Title VIII." [21]

Are any other discriminatory real estate practices prohibited by Title VIII?

Yes. Title VIII also applies to banks, building-and-loan associations, insurance companies, and other businesses that make real-estate loans; and it specifically prohibits them from engaging in any discriminatory loan denials (for "purchasing, contracting, improving, repairing, or maintaining a dwelling") and any discrimination "in the fixing of the amount, interest rate, duration, or other terms or conditions of such loan or other financial assistance." [22]

Finally, Title VIII contains a catch-all provision making it unlawful to "intimidate" or to "interfere with" any person in connection with the exercise of rights protected by Title VIII.[23] This provision, for example, protects employees from being fired for having rented apartments to minority persons.[24]

Does Title VIII prohibit unintentional as well as intentional discrimination in real estate transactions?

Yes. Practices which have a discriminatory *effect* are unlawful under Title VIII, regardless of whether their use was intentionally discriminatory.[25]

THE RIGHTS OF RACIAL MINORITIES

How does one prove discrimination in the sale of a lot or of a dwelling?

Proof of discrimination follows two basic principles. First, as a federal court recently summarized, where a prospective minority buyer or renter

> meets the objective requirements of a real estate developer [seller or agent] so that a sale [or rental] would in all likelihood have been consummated were he white, and where statistics show that all of a substantial number of lots [or dwellings] in the development have been sold [or rented] only to white, a prima facie inference of discrimination arises as a matter of law if his offer to purchase [or to rent] is refused.[26]

Second, after prima facie discrimination is shown, the "burden shifts" to the developer, seller, or agent "to articulate some legitimate nondiscriminatory reason" for rejecting the offer; he or she also must "demonstrate the absence of any acceptable alternative that will accomplish the same business goal with less discrimination."[27]

For example, in a recent case, prospective minority buyers proved that they had offered to purchase a lot from a developer, that similar offers were accepted from white buyers, that a substantial number of other lots had been sold to whites, and that the minority buyers' offer had been refused. This evidence shifted the burden of proving nondiscrimination onto the developer. The developer asserted that it did not sell lots to buyers but only to approved builders. This assertion, however, did not excuse the discrimination because the developer failed to give the minority buyer a list of approved builders, and in any event the approved builders were all white. The minority buyers were thus found to have been discriminated against in violation of Title VIII.[28]

In order to establish a violation of Title VIII, must a person prove that race was the *sole* basis for a refusal to rent or sell?

No. A minority person does not need to prove that the refusal to sell or rent a dwelling was solely because of race. Instead, it need be shown only that race was a "significant factor" in the refusal.[29]

In proving discrimination under Title VIII, is it useful to have evidence of discrimination from testers?

Yes. Testers are minority persons and white persons, carefully matched in age, income, education, etc., who do not seek housing for themselves but who apply for a dwelling to "test" its availability. In proving a case of discrimination under Title VIII it is very helpful to have evidence from testers.[30] Additionally, testers themselves have a right to sue under Title VIII.[31]

Proof of discrimination against testers, although helpful, is not necessarily essential. Discrimination, as previously indicated, can be proved in part through the use of statistics showing few or no sales or rentals to minorities.

What is the scope of the Civil Rights Act of 1866?

The Civil Rights Act of 1866, as opposed to Title VIII, is short and straightforward. One section of the older act, Section 1982, states in one sentence that all citizens "shall have the same right . . . as is enjoyed by white citizens . . . to inherit, purchase, lease, sell, hold and convey real and personal property." [32] Section 1981 states that all persons "shall have the same right . . . to make and enforce contracts . . . as is enjoyed by white citizens." [33] Despite the breadth of its language, the 1866 act for a hundred years was presumed to apply only to government and not to private discrimination. However, two months after Title VIII was enacted by Congress, the Supreme Court in *Jones* v. *Alfred H. Mayer Co.* held for the first time that the act, specifically Section 1982, also prohibits private discrimination.[34] In fact, the Court ruled that it "bars *all* racial discrimination, private as well as public, in the sale or rental of property." [35]

Does the Civil Rights Act of 1866 have exemptions similar to those in Title VIII?

No. While Title VIII exempts the sale or rental of certain single-family homes and it exempts certain small rooming houses, the 1866 act, by contrast, has no exemptions. Thus some practices permitted by Title VIII are prohibited by the 1866 act, and hence are unlawful.[36]

If the prohibitions against discrimination in the 1866 act are broader than in Title VIII, is Title VIII unnecessary?

No. Although it is ironic that the Supreme Court in *Jones* v. *Alfred H. Mayer Co.* revived the 1866 act only two months after Congress enacted Title VIII, the newer law does provide several advantages to discriminated-against persons that are not provided by the 1866 act. For example, Title VIII, unlike the 1866 act, prohibits discriminatory advertising,[37] authorizes an administrative remedy through the Department of Housing and Urban Development,[38] authorizes lawsuits by the Department of Justice,[39] and prohibits housing practices which have a discriminatory effect regardless of whether they were intentionally racially discriminatory.[40] Because of these differences, it is important to examine the methods of enforcement both of Title VIII and of the 1866 act.

REMEDIES AND PROCEDURES UNDER TITLE VIII AND UNDER THE CIVIL RIGHTS ACT OF 1866

Are there any enforcement procedures which must be complied with under Title VIII or under the Civil Rights Act of 1866 in order to obtain the rights guaranteed by those federal statutes?

Yes. Although Title VIII and the 1866 act together "prohibit all forms of discrimination, sophisticated as well as simpleminded," [41] the federal guarantees usually are realized only through enforcement lawsuits. As stated by the Supreme Court in a Title VIII case entitled *Trafficante* v. *Metropolitan Life Ins. Co.*, federal court "complaints by private persons are the primary method of obtaining compliance" with Title VIII.[42]

Enforcement under Title VIII requires a private complainant to strictly follow a number of procedures within short time limitations. Enforcement under the 1866 act, on the other hand, simply requires that you sue in court as soon as possible. Although it is sometimes tricky, the best enforcement is to sue in court under both Title VIII alternatives and under the 1866 act.

Who is authorized to enforce the guarantees of Title VIII?

Private individuals are authorized to enforce Title VIII. Also, the Department of Justice can enforce Title VIII in cases "of general public importance" or where a "pattern or practice" of discrimination is shown to exist.[43] Of these two methods, lawsuits by private persons have proved to be the most important means of obtaining compliance with Title VIII. Although housing lawsuits by the Department of Justice are rare, individuals should make their grievances known to the Department of Justice and urge that legal action be taken.

How does a private person proceed under Title VIII?

There are two separate methods of private enforcement under Title VIII; each is authorized by a separate section of the statute providing different remedies. The first method, under Section 3610, "contemplates the resolution of disputes in the slower, less adversary context of administrative reconciliation and mediation."[44] Certain administrative requirements must be met under Section 3610 before suing in federal court. The second method of enforcement, under Section 3612, has relatively few preconditions to meet before filing suit. "Those entitled to bring an action under this section have immediate access to a federal forum."[45] Because of the different procedures (and remedies) under Sections 3610 and 3612, they will be examined separately.

What are the remedies and procedures under the slow, administrative method of enforcement authorized by Section 3610 of Title VIII?

The remedies under the slow method of enforcement authorized by Section 3610 are quite limited. In fact, the only remedy is an injunction ordering an end to the discrimination.[46] There is no statutory authorization under

Section 3610 for a court to award monetary damages or attorneys' fees to the complainant.[47]

The procedures one must follow under the slow method are fairly complicated, at least if the complainant desires to preserve the option of eventually suing under Section 3612 in federal court:

1. The complainant must file a signed and sworn administrative charge of discrimination with the Department of Housing and Urban Development (HUD) within 180 days after the allegedly discriminatory housing practice occurred.[48] The attached government form for filing a charge of discrimination with HUD is reproduced on the following pages.
2. Thereafter, HUD must investigate the charge and may attempt to resolve the matter by "informal methods of conference, conciliation, and persuasion."[49] HUD, however, may take no administrative action if there is a state or local law which is substantially equivalent to Title VIII and if a state or local official, upon notice from HUD, has commenced state or local proceedings in the matter.[50]
3. If HUD fails to obtain voluntary compliance from the discriminator, the complainant may file a lawsuit in federal court, if at all, within 30 days of the expiration of any of the foregoing periods of acting or nonacting;[51] *but* no lawsuit may be filed in federal court if there is a remedy under state or local law substantially equivalent to Title VIII.[52]

If voluntary compliance is not achieved under this slow method, and if all the procedures have been complied with, the complainant may then file a lawsuit in federal court under Section 3610 against the alleged discriminator.

What about suing under Section 3612 of Title VIII?

The possible remedies in a Title VIII lawsuit filed under Section 3612 include not only an injunction to end the discriminaion but also an award of "actual damages and not more than $1000 punitive damages,"[53] and attorneys' fees for a "prevailing plaintiff" not financially able to pay fees.[54]

The award of actual damages allows recovery of out-of-pocket expenses, and damages for humiliation and emotional distress.[55] Punitive damages can be awarded only if intentional or willful discrimination is proven.[56] Because awards of damages are possible, either party can demand a jury trial.[57]

Under Section 3612, not only are the remedies broader than under Section 3610, but the procedures are easier. Under Section 3612, there are no administrative enforcement efforts contemplated and hence no administrative prerequisites. There is, however, one requirement: the lawsuit must be filed within 180 days after the allegedly discriminatory housing practice occurred.[58]

Since Section 3612 has simple procedures and broad remedies are there any advantages to proceeding administratively under Section 3610 of Title VIII?

The major advantage to proceeding administratively under Section 3610, and not suing within 180 days of the discriminatory act under Section 3612 (and earlier under Section 3610 if necessary), is the possibility that HUD might obtain an administrative compliance agreement. Unfortunately, there is only a slight possibility of that, because, as the Supreme Court has remarked, "HUD has no power of enforcement." [59]

Are Sections 3610 and 3612 wholly separate, or can a complainant proceed under both provisions at the same time?

A person who has been discriminated against in housing may proceed under both alternatives simultaneously because, as many courts have held: "Sections 3610 and 3612 provide complementary enforcement procedures under the Fair Housing Act." [60]

The wisest course is to proceed under both sections—file a lawsuit under Section 3612 within 180 days of the discrimination while proceeding administratively under Section 3610. In other words, since there is such a slight possibility that HUD will be able to obtain voluntary

THE RIGHTS OF RACIAL MINORITIES

Form Approved OMB No. 63-R1226

U.S. DEPARTMENT OF HOUSING AND URBAN DEVELOPMENT
HOUSING DISCRIMINATION COMPLAINT

FOR HUD USE ONLY

Number _____
Date _____
Filing Date _____
STATE OR LOCAL _____
FEDERAL COVERAGE _____
PRIOR ACTION _____
PRELIMINARY DETERMINATION _____

INSTRUCTIONS: Read this form and the instructions on reverse carefully before completing. All questions should be answered. However, if you do not know the answer or if a question is not applicable, leave the question unanswered and fill out as much of the form as you can. Your complaint should be signed and dated and, if possible, notarized. Where more than one individual or organization is filing the same complaint, each additional individual or organization should complete boxes 1 and 7 of a separate complaint form and attach it to the original form, but the other boxes need not be completed if the information is the same as in the original. Complaints may be (1) mailed to the Regional Office covering the State where the complaint arose _____ or to an Area Office, or to Fair Housing, HUD, Washington, D.C. 20410, or (2) filed or presented in person at HUD in Washington, D.C. or at any HUD Regional or Area Office.

PLEASE TYPE OR PRINT

1. Name of aggrieved person or organization *(Last Name – First Name – Middle Initial) (Mr. Mrs. Miss)*

Telephone Number

Street Address, City, County, State and ZIP Code

2. Whom is this complaint against?
Name *(Last Name – First Name – Middle Initial)* | Street Address, City, County, State and ZIP Code | Telephone Number

Is the party named above a: *(Check applicable box or boxes)*
☐ Builder ☐ Owner ☐ Broker ☐ Salesman ☐ Supt. or Manager ☐ Bank or Other Lender ☐ Other

If you have named an individual above and you know that he was acting for a company in this case, check this box ☐ and write the name and address *(Street, City, County, State and ZIP Code)* of the company in this space.

Name and identify Others *(if any)* you believe violated the law in this case

126

HOUSING

3. What did the person you are complaining against do? (Check applicable box or boxes)
- [ ] Refused to rent, sell, or deal with you
- [ ] Discriminate in the conditions or terms of sale, rental, occupancy, or in services or facilities
- [ ] Advertise in a discriminatory way
- [ ] Falsely deny housing was available
- [ ] Engage in blockbusting
- [ ] Discriminate in financing
- [ ] Discriminate in broker's services
- [ ] Other (Explain in box 6 below)

When did act or acts occur? (Be sure to include most recent date, if several dates are involved)

4. Do you believe there was discrimination because of? (Check applicable box and write your race, color, religion, sex or national origin on the line below the box checked)
- [ ] Race or Color
- [ ] Religion
- [ ] Sex
- [ ] National Origin

5. What kind of house or property was involved?
- [ ] Single family house
- [ ] A house or building for 2, 3, or 4 families
- [ ] A building for 5 families or more
- [ ] Other, including vacant land held for residential use (Explain in box 6 below)

Did the owner live there?
- [ ] Yes [ ] No [ ] Unknown

Is the house or property (Check applicable box)
- [ ] Being sold [ ] Being rented

What is the address of the house or property?
Street _____
City _____
County _____ State _____

6. Summarize in your own words what happened. Use this space for a brief and concise statement of the facts. Additional details of what happened may be provided on an attachment.

NOTE: HUD will furnish copy of complaint (including any attachments) to the person or organization against whom complaint is made.

7. I swear or affirm that I have read this complaint and that it is true to the best of my knowledge, information, and belief.

_____   _____
(Date)   (Sign your name)

8. Subscribed and sworn to before me this _____ day of _____ 19___

NOTARIZATION:

_____   _____
(Name)   (Title)

IF IT IS DIFFICULT FOR YOU TO GET A NOTARY PUBLIC TO SIGN THIS, SIGN YOUR OWN NAME AND MAIL IT WITHOUT NOTARIZATION. HUD WILL HELP YOU GET YOUR COMPLAINT SWORN TO.

HUD-903 (2-72) PREVIOUS EDITION IS OBSOLETE

THE RIGHTS OF RACIAL MINORITIES

compliance, it is best to preserve the right to sue under Section 3612.

The right to sue under Section 3612 is not affected by the administrative requirements of Section 3610.[61] But the individual's lawsuit under Section 3612 still must be filed within 180 days of the discriminatory act.

Is the court authorized to appoint an attorney for a complainant who cannot afford a lawyer but who wishes to file suit under Title VIII?

Yes. The court is authorized to appoint an attorney upon "application by the plaintiff and in such circumstances as the court may deem just." [62] There is no provision, however, for payment of attorneys' fees unless the plaintiff is deemed the prevailing party at the end of the lawsuit. This restriction on payment as a practical matter makes the courts hesitant to appoint an attorney for an indigent party and also makes it unlikely that attorneys will volunteer their services. Complainants, of course, may always act as their own counsel.

What remedies are available to persons who have been discriminated against in housing in violation of the Civil Rights Act of 1866?

The remedies are very broad—probably even broader than the remedies authorized under Section 3612 of Title VIII. For example, although the 1866 act itself specifies no remedies, the Supreme Court has held that court orders terminating the discrimination as well as awarding damages (including unlimited punitive damages) are available.[63] Courts also may award attorneys' fees to the prevailing party.[64]

Does a person have to choose whether to bring a housing discrimination lawsuit under Title VIII or under the Civil Rights Act of 1866?

No. Title VIII and the Civil Rights Act of 1866 provide independent remedies for discrimination in housing.[65] Any aggrieved person who files a lawsuit should claim violations of both statutes.

If a complainant fails to follow the procedural and time limitation requirements of Title VIII, can he or she still bring a lawsuit under the Civil Rights Act of 1866?

Yes. Failure to comply with the procedural requirements under either or both Title VIII alternatives does not affect a complainant's right to sue under the 1866 act to remedy housing discrimination.[66]

Are there any procedural requirements which must be complied with before suing a housing discriminator under the Civil Rights Act of 1866?

The 1866 act itself contains no procedural requirements. However, the courts have uniformly held that a lawsuit under the 1866 act must be filed within the time period established by state law—periods which vary, depending upon the state, from one year to five or more years, and which are unaffected by any administrative filings under Title VIII or any other procedure.[67] Therefore, a complainant ordinarily should file a lawsuit under the 1866 act (and under Title VIII's direct litigation method) as soon as possible after the discriminatory action, because the time is not extended for the period during which the administrative proceeding was pending.

EXCLUSIONARY ZONING AND OTHER GOVERNMENTAL DISCRIMINATION

Is discrimination still practiced in the public sector by state and local governments?

Unfortunately and quite obviously, yes. As noted at the outset of this chapter, our currently segregated residential patterns were created in part by federal, state, and local governments. Although most of the overtly segregative policies have disappeared, many have been replaced by more subtle policies of discrimination. Primary among the latter are exclusionary zoning policies which keep many suburban communities virtually all white.

What forms of overt discrimination in the public sector have been held unconstitutional or otherwise unlawful?

Generally, all forms of overt discrimination are prohibited. Probably the most blatant form of housing segregation ever confronted by the Supreme Court involved local ordinances which strictly prohibited blacks from living in white neighborhoods. As early as 1917, the Supreme Court in a case entitled *Buchanan* v. *Warley* [68] held such ordinances to be intentionally discriminatory, violating the Fourteenth Amendment.

Another form of overt segregation involved enforcement by state courts of racially restrictive covenants (which require successive white purchasers of homes to sell ultimately only to other white purchasers). Believing these racially restrictive covenants to be an entirely private matter, the Supreme Court at first refused to find their state-court enforcement unconstitutional.[69] However, in *Shelley* v. *Kraemer*,[70] a case decided in 1948, the Court did decide that state judicial enforcement of racially restrictive covenants violated the Fourteenth Amendment. This decision, while it banned the enforcement, did not of itself ban restrictive covenants. In 1972, however, a federal court held that it was a violation of Title VIII for a local government even to file a deed with a racially restrictive covenant.[71]

Another form of overt segregation has been racial designation or "siting" of public housing: *i.e.*, formally designating a public housing project as a black project or placing a housing project in the center of a black community. These practices have been held unlawful whether implemented by local housing authorities [72] or encouraged by the federal government.[73] In *Hills* v. *Gautreaux*,[74] where the federal government had been shown to have participated in the segregated siting of public housing in minority areas only within the city of Chicago, the Supreme Court held that HUD and the Chicago Housing Authority properly could be ordered to place public housing projects in white communities inside and outside of the city.

Have these various forms of overt housing segregation been reduced?

Yes. Overt segregation by government agencies has been reduced for a number of reasons. First, the Supreme Court has held several forms of overt discrimination unconstitutional.[75] Second, federally assisted discrimination was declared at an end in Executive Order 11063, issued by President Kennedy in 1962.[76] Third, HUD has been required by Title VIII [77] and by *Gautreaux* to seek affirmative integration.[78]

This is not to say that the days of overt segregation are past. (As late as 1977, a federal appeals court held that the City of Philadelphia had intentionally refused on grounds of racial discrimination to site a public housing project in a virtually all-white part of town.[79]) It is only to say, as one court has concluded, that "overtly bigoted behavior has become more unfashionable . . . not . . . that racial discrimination has disappeared." [80]

What is racially exclusionary zoning?

Zoning by its very nature has an exclusionary effect. For example, land which is zoned residential cannot be used for commercial development. In civil rights, exclusionary zoning refers to the use of low-density residential zoning (large expansive lots with big houses and few residents) to the almost total exclusion of other types of residential zoning (*e.g.*, small-lot, multi-dwelling, multi-family zoning). The use of such exclusionary zoning, especially by a virtually all-white community, has a discriminatory effect upon minorities since most minority members are poorer than whites and less able to buy or rent low-density housing.

Does racially exclusionary zoning deny minorities equal protection of the law in violation of the Fourteenth Amendment?

Yes, but it is almost impossible to prove it in court. Three major obstacles make proof of unconstitutional discrimination difficult.

1. The Supreme Court has been extremely deferential to local zoning under the Fourteenth Amend-

ment. In a seminal decision on zoning, the Court in 1926 upheld local zoning as a valid exercise of the police power unless it were clearly arbitrary and had no substantial relation to the public welfare.[81] The Court has adhered to this standard.[82]

2. The Supreme Court has narrowly defined those people who have "standing" to challenge exclusionary zoning under the Fourteenth Amendment. Thus, for example, the Court has held that a minority person who is poor and who simply desires to live anywhere in a virtually all-white suburban community is not specifically harmed by that suburb's exclusionary zoning, and hence has no "standing" to challenge it.[83] Instead, only a minority person who desires to live in a specific suburban housing development which has been prevented from being built because of suburban zoning practices—only that person has sufficient "standing" to challenge the community's exclusionary zoning.[84]

3. And, as if the above two obstacles weren't enough, the Supreme Court in *Arlington Heights* v. *Metropolitan Housing Development Corp.*,[85] a 1977 case, held that: "Proof of racially discriminatory intent or purpose is required to show a violation of the Equal Protection Clause." [86] Since there was no proof that the exclusionary zoning undertaken by the village of Arlington Heights was intentionally discriminatory, the zoning was upheld as constitutional despite its discriminatory effect.[87] Similarly, in a 1971 case, the Supreme Court upheld a state requirement that all low-rent public housing had to be approved in a community referendum before the housing could be built; the referendum provision, the Court held, reflected devotion to democracy, not deference to discrimination.[88]

Is racially exclusionary zoning, regardless of the Fourteenth Amendment, prohibited by Title VIII of the Civil Rights Act of 1968?

Yes. Although the Supreme Court has not yet decided this issue, it has declined to review a number of lower-

HOUSING

court cases which have held that exclusionary zoning is prohibited by Title VIII.[89] The conclusion reached by the lower courts is warranted for a number of reasons.

1. Title VIII applies not just to private entities but also to government.[90]
2. Title VIII's prohibitions against making a dwelling unit "unavailable" on grounds of race and against interfering with Title VIII rights cover exclusionary zoning.[91]
3. Title VIII prohibits practices which have a discriminatory effect regardless of intent.[92]
4. The Supreme Court has been more liberal in conferring "standing" upon minorities and others affected by discriminatory housing practices prohibited by Title VIII.[93]

As we have seen, the Supreme Court in *Arlington Heights* v. *Metropolitan Housing Development Corp.*[94] held that Arlington Heights' exclusionary zoning did not violate the Fourteenth Amendment. However, the Court sent the case back to the court of appeals for a decision on whether the exclusionary zoning violated Title VIII. The court of appeals decided that the zoning was unlawful under Title VIII because of its discriminatory effect, and the Supreme Court declined review.[95] As a federal court recently stated, "we suspect that Title VIII will undoubtedly appear as a more attractive route to non-discriminatory housing, as litigants become increasingly aware that Title VIII rights may be enforced even without direct evidence of discriminatory intent." [96]

Must the procedural requirements of Title VIII be complied with when filing a lawsuit under Title VIII to stop exclusionary zoning?

Yes. Under Section 3612 a person must file a lawsuit, if at all, within 180 days of the discriminatory zoning action (usually a refusal to rezone). Under Section 3610 there are even more procedural prerequisites. These various procedural problems were discussed earlier. One court has indicated, however, that these time limitations and procedures might not be applicable to lawsuits challenging exclusionary zoning.[97]

Are there any other possible remedies for racially exclusionary zoning?

Yes. In several states, state courts have held racially exclusionary zoning to be unconstitutional under state constitutions on the grounds that it does not promote the general welfare of the state.[98] However, state courts generally cannot be expected to be more receptive to claims of discrimination in housing than are the federal courts.

NOTES

1. Our history of official housing segregation is summarized in U.S. COMMISSION ON CIVIL RIGHTS, TWENTY YEARS AFTER BROWN: EQUAL OPPORTUNITY IN HOUSING (Government Printing Office, 1975). *See also* D. FALK and H. FRANKLIN, EQUAL HOUSING OPPORTUNITY: THE UNFINISHED FEDERAL AGENDA 9–13, 46 n.1 (Potomac Institute, 1976).
2. In Shelley v. Kraemer, 334 U.S. 1 (1948), the Supreme Court held that state judicial enforcement of racially restrictive covenants unconstitutionally involved the state in discrimination in violation of the Fourteenth Amendment.
3. Overt segregation was barred from federal programs by President Kennedy's Executive Order 11,063, entitled Equal Opportunity in Housing, 27 Fed.Reg. 11,527 (Nov., 1962).
4. 42 U.S.C. §§3601 *et seq.*
5. 392 U.S. 409 (1968).
6. Now codified in part as 42 U.S.C. §1982 and 42 U.S.C. §1981.
7. D. FALK and H. FRANKLIN, *supra* note 1, at 161.
8. 42 U.S.C. §§3601 *et seq.*
9. Codified in part as 42 U.S.C. §1982 and 42 U.S.C. §1981.
10. Jones v. Alfred H. Mayer Co., 392 U.S. 409 (1968).

11. 114 CONG.REC. 3422 (1968) (remarks of Senator Walter F. Mondale, author of one of the enforcement sections of Title VIII).
12. Title VIII also prohibits discrimination on grounds of religion and sex. 42 U.S.C. §§3604–6.
13. 42 U.S.C. §3604(a). *See* Dillon v. AFBIC Development Corp., 597 F.2d 556 (5th Cir. 1979).
14. 42 U.S.C. §3604(b). *See* United States v. Pelzer Realty Co., 484 F.2d 438 (5th Cir. 1973), *cert. denied*, 416 U.S. 936 (1974).
15. 42 U.S.C. §3604(c). *See* United States v. Hunter, 459 F.2d 205 (4th Cir. 1972), *cert. denied*, 409 U.S. 934 (1972).
16. 42 U.S.C. §3604(d). This section gives a valid discrimination claim to a "tester" (a person who does not seek housing for oneself but who tests the availability of or restrictions on a dwelling on grounds of race). *See* Bellwood v. Gladstone Realtors, 569 F.2d 1013 (7th Cir. 1978), *aff'd* 99 S.Ct. 1601 60 L.Ed.2d 66 (1979), and cases cited therein; *cf.*, Evers v. Dwyer, 358 U.S. 202 (1958).
17. 42 U.S.C. §3604(e). *See* United States v. Bob Lawrence Realty, Inc., 474 F.2d 115 (5th Cir. 1973).
18. 42 U.S.C. §3606.
19. 42 U.S.C. §3603(b)(1). *See* Singleton v. Gendason, 545 F.2d 1224 (9th Cir. 1976) (exemption is not available when commercial rental services are used).
20. 42 U.S.C. §3603(b)(2).
21. D. FALK and H. FRANKLIN, *supra* note 1, at 57.
22. 42 U.S.C. §3605. *See* Laufman v. Oakley Bldg. & Loan Co., 408 F.Supp. 489 (S.D. Ohio 1976) (redlining prohibited by this section).
23. 42 U.S.C. §3617. *See* Laufman v. Oakley Bldg. & Loan Co., 408 F.Supp. 489, 497–98 (S.D. Ohio 1976); *cf.* Metropolitan Hous. Dev. Corp. v. Arlington Heights, 558 F.2d 1283 (7th Cir. 1977), *cert. denied*, 434 U.S. 1025 (1978).
24. Smith v. Stechel, 510 F.2d 1162 (9th Cir. 1975).
25. *See* Resident Advisory Bd. v. Rizzo, 564 F.2d 126, 146–48 (3d Cir. 1977), *cert. denied*, 435 U.S. 908 (1978); Metropolitan Hous. Dev. Corp. v. Arlington Heights, 558 F.2d 1283, 1286–90 (7th Cir. 1977), *cert.*

denied, 434 U.S. 1025 (1978); Smith v. Anchor Building Corp., 536 F.2d 231, 233 (8th Cir. 1976); United States v. Black Jack, 508 F.2d 1179, 1185 (8th Cir. 1974), *cert. denied*, 422 U.S. 1042 (1975); United States v. Pelzer Realty Co., 484 F.2d 438, 443 (5th Cir. 1973), *cert. denied*, 416 U.S. 936 (1974).

These decisions are in accord with Supreme Court decisions interpreting Title VII of the Civil Rights Act of 1964, Dothard v. Rawlinson, 433 U.S. 321 (1977); Griggs v. Duke Power Co., 401 U.S. 424 (1971); and interpreting Title VI of the Civil Rights Act of 1964, Lau v. Nichols, 414 U.S. 563 (1974).

26. Williams v. Mathews Co., 499 F.2d 819, 826 (8th Cir), *cert. denied*, 419 U.S. 1021 (1974). These principles are borrowed from the employment-discrimination principles set forth in McDonnell-Douglas Corp. v. Green, 411 U.S. 792, 802 (1973).

27. Williams v. Mathews Co., 499 F.2d at 827-28. *See also* Resident Advisory Bd. v. Rizzo, 564 F.2d 126, 149 (3d Cir. 1977), *cert. denied*, 435 U.S. 908 (1978); United States v. West Peachtree Tenth Corp., 437 F.2d 221 (5th Cir. 1971).

28. Williams v. Mathews Co., *supra*.

29. Burris v. Wilkins, 544 F.2d 891 (5th Cir. 1977); *cf.* Smith v. Sol D. Adler Realty Co., 436 F.2d 344 (7th Cir. 1970) (same standard under Civil Rights Act of 1866).

30. *E.g.*, United States v. Youritan Construction Co., 509 F.2d 623 (9th Cir. 1975), *aff'g*, 370 F.2d 643 (N.D. Cal. 1973); Johnson v. Jerry Pals Real Estate, 485 F.2d 528 (7th Cir. 1973); Hamilton v. Miller, 477 F.2d 908 (10th Cir. 1973); state laws which prohibit "testing" are themselves unlawful under Title VIII. United States v. Wisconsin, 395 F.Supp. 732 (W.D. Wis. 1975).

31. *See* note 16, *supra*.

32. 42 U.S.C. §1982. *See* Smith v. Sol D. Adler Realty Co., 436 F.2d 344 (7th Cir. 1970).

33. 42 U.S.C. §1981.

34. 392 U.S. 409, 420 (1968).

35. 392 U.S. at 413 (emphasis in original).

36. *E.g.*, Morris v. Cizek, 503 F.2d 1303 (7th Cir. 1974) (the 1866 Act prohibits discrimination in the lease of an

apartment in a small apartment house exempted from Title VIII). *Compare* 42 U.S.C. §3603(b)(2).

37. 42 U.S.C. §3604(c). *See* note 15, *supra*.
38. 42 U.S.C. §§3608-11.
39. 42 U.S.C. §3613.
40. *See* cases cited in note 25, *supra*, supporting the proposition that Title VIII prohibits practices with a discriminatory effect. It is unclear whether proof of discriminatory intent is necessary to prove a violation of the 1866 Act.
41. Williams v. Mathews Co., 499 F.2d 819, 826 (8th Cir.), *cert. denied*, 419 U.S. 1021 (1974), and cases cited therein.
42. 409 U.S. 205, 209 (1972).
43. 42 U.S.C. §3613.
44. TOPIC v. Circle Realty, 532 F.2d 1273, 1276 (9th Cir. 1976), *cert. denied*, 429 U.S. 859 (1977).
45. *Id.*
46. 42 U.S.C. §3610(d).
47. *Id. See, e.g.*, Brown v. Ballas, 331 F.Supp. 1033 (N.D. Tex. 1971).
48. 42 U.S.C. §3610(b). *See* Howard v. W.P. Bill Atkinson Enterprises, 412 F.Supp. 610 (W.D. Okla. 1975).
49. 42 U.S.C. §3610(a). For a discussion of HUD investigation and enforcement procedures, *see* 42 U.S.C. §3611 and 24 C.F.R. §§105 *et seq.*
50. 42 U.S.C. §3610(c). HUD has recognized half of the states and many localities as having laws substantially equivalent to Title VIII. They are listed in 24 C.F.R. §115.12.
51. 42 U.S.C. §3610(d). There is considerable disagreement among the lower federal courts about what "period of reference" initiates the thirty-day period within which the complainant must sue, if at all, in federal court. *Compare*, Logan v. Carmack & Assoc., 368 F.Supp. 121 (E.D. Tenn. 1973), *with* Sumlin v. Brown, 420 F.Supp. 78 (N.D. Fla. 1976), *and* Brown v. Blake & Bane, Inc., 402 F.Supp. 621 (E.D. Va. 1975).
52. 42 U.S.C. §3610(d). *See* McLaurin v. Brusturis, 320 F.Supp. 190 (E.D. Wis. 1970) (claim under §3610 dismissed because of substantially equivalent rights and remedies under state law).

53. 42 U.S.C. §3612(c).

54. *Id. See* Smith v. Anchor Bldg. Corp., 536 F.2d 231, 236 (8th Cir. 1976) (determination of financial ability does not include speculative consideration of future earnings); Hairston v. R&R Apartments, 510 F.2d 1090, 1091–92 (7th Cir. 1975) (attorneys' fees are not limited only to indigents).

55. *See, e.g.,* William v. Mathews Co., 499 F.2d 819 (8th Cir. 1974), *cert. denied,* 419 U.S. 1021 (1975); Jeanty v. McKey & Poague, Inc., 496 F.2d 1119 (7th Cir. 1974); Steele v. Title Realty Co., 478 F.2d 380 (10th Cir. 1973). Humiliation and emotional distress, however, are not presumed to flow from a violation of Title VIII; instead, there must be proof that humiliation or emotional stress in fact did occur. Fort v. White, 530 F.2d 1113 (2d Cir. 1976).

56. Marr v. Rife, 503 F.2d 735 (6th Cir. 1974) (punitive damages not awarded); Seaton v. Sky Realty Co., 491 F.2d 634 (7th Cir. 1974) (punitive damages awarded).

57. Curtis v. Loether, 415 U.S. 189 (1974).

58. 42 U.S.C. §3612(a). *See,* Meyers v. Pennypack Woods Home Ownership Ass'n, 559 F.2d 894, 899 (3d Cir. 1977) (§3612 claim dismissed for failure to sue within 180 days of the discrimination); Hickman v. Fincher, 483 F.2d 855, 856 (4th Cir. 1973) (same).

59. Trafficante v. Metropolitan Life Ins. Co., 409 U.S. 205, 210 (1972). HUD, however, may refer the matter to the Department of Justice for litigation, 42 U.S.C. §3612(g) and §3613.

60. TOPIC v. Circle Realty, 532 F.2d 1273, 1275 (9th Cir. 1976); *see also,* Bellwood v. Gladstone Realtors, 569 F.2d 1013, 1018–20 (7th Cir. 1978), *aff'd,* 99 S.Ct. 1601, 60 L.Ed.2d 66 (1979), U.S. (1978), and cases cited therein.

61. *See also,* Miller v. Poretsky, 409 F.Supp. 837 (D.D.C. 1976); Johnson v. Decker, 333 F.Supp. 88 (N.D. Cal. 1971).

62. 42 U.S.C. §3612(b) authorizes the courts to "appoint an attorney for the plaintiff" upon "application by the plaintiff and in such circumstances as the court may deem just."

63. Sullivan v. Little Hunting Park, 396 U.S. 229, 239

HOUSING

(1969); Jones v. Alfred H. Mayer Co., 392 U.S. 409 (1968). *See also* Gore v. Turner, 563 F.2d 159, 164 (5th Cir. 1977); Bishop v. Pecsok, 431 F.Supp. 34 (N.D. Ohio 1976) ($1500 compensatory damages and $5000 punitive damages); Parker v. Shonfeld, 409 F.Supp. 876 (N.D. Cal. 1976) ($10,000 compensatory damages and $10,000 punitive damages).

64. 42 U.S.C. §1988, as amended by the Civil Rights Attorneys Fees Awards Act of 1976. *See* Gore v. Turner, 563 F.2d 159, 163 (5th Cir. 1977).

65. Jones v. Alfred H. Mayer Co., 392 U.S. 409 (1968). *See* Dillon v. AFBIC Development Corp., 597 F.2d 556 (5th Cir. 1979).

66. Meyers v. Pennypack Woods Home Ownership Ass'n, 559 F.2d 894, 899–900 (3d Cir. 1977); Warren v. Norman Realty Co., 513 F.2d 730, 732–33 (8th Cir.), *cert. denied*, 423 U.S. 855 (1975); Hickman v. Fincher, 483 F.2d 855, 856–57 (4th Cir. 1973); *cf.*, Johnson v. Railway Express Agency, Inc., 421 U.S. 454 (1975).

67. *Id.*

68. 245 U.S. 60 (1917).

69. Corrigan v. Buckley, 271 U.S. 323 (1926).

70. 334 U.S. 1 (1948).

71. Mayers v. Ridley, 465 F.2d 630 (D.C. Cir. 1972).

72. Gautreaux v. Chicago Hous. Auth., 265 F.Supp. 582 (N.D. Ill. 1967), 296 F.Supp. 907 (N.D. Ill. 1969), and 304 F.Supp. 736 (N.D. Ill. 1969), *aff'd*, 436 F.2d 306 (7th Cir. 1970), *cert. denied*, 402 U.S. 922 (1971); *cf.*, Otero v. New York City Hous. Auth., 484 F.2d 1122 (2d Cir. 1973), and cases cited therein.

73. *See* Gautreaux v. Romney, 448 F.2d 731 (7th Cir. 1971); Shannon v. HUD, 436 F.2d 809 (3d Cir. 1970).

74. 425 U.S. 284 (1976).

75. *See* notes 68 and 70, *supra*.

76. *See* note 3, *supra*.

77. 42 U.S.C. §§3608(c) and (d)(5) require HUD to administer its housing programs "affirmatively" to further the purposes and policies of Title VIII. *See* Otero v. New York City Hous. Auth., 484 F.2d 1122, 1133–34 (2d Cir. 1973), and cases therein.

78. *See, generally*, 24 C.F.R. Part 1.

79. Resident Advisory Bd. v. Rizzo, 564 F.2d 126 (3d Cir. 1977), *cert. denied*, 435 U.S. 908 (1978).
80. Metropolitan Hous. Dev. Corp. v. Arlington Heights, 558 F.2d 1283, 1290 (7th Cir. 1977), *cert. denied*, 434 U.S. 1025 (1978).
81. Euclid v. Ambler Realty Co., 272 U.S. 365 (1926).
82. *Compare* Belle Terre v. Boraas, 416 U.S. 1 (1974), *with* Moore v. East Cleveland, 431 U.S. 494 (1977).
83. Warth v. Seldin, 422 U.S. 490 (1975); *see also* Hartford v. Glastonbury, 561 F.2d 1032 (2d Cir. 1977) (*en banc*), *cert. denied*, 434 U.S. 1034 (1978); Evans v. Lynn, 537 F.2d 571 (2d Cir. 1976).
84. Arlington Heights v. Metropolitan Hous. Dev. Corp., 429 U.S. 252 (1977).
85. *Id.*
86. 429 U.S. at 265.
87. Earlier lower court decisions holding that proof of discriminatory intent was unnecessary to show that exclusionary zoning violated the equal-protection clause of the Fourteenth Amendment were overruled by the Supreme Court not just in Arlington Heights but also in Washington v. Davis, 426 U.S. 229, 244 n.12 (1976).
88. James v. Valtierra, 402 U.S. 137 (1971); *compare* Hunter v. Erickson, 393 U.S. 385 (1969).
89. Resident Advisory Bd. v. Rizzo, 564 F.2d 126 (3d Cir. 1977), *cert. denied*, 435 U.S. 908 (1978); Metropolitan Hous. Dev. Corp. v. Arlington Heights, 558 F.2d 1283 (7th Cir. 1977), *cert. denied*, 434 U.S. 1025 (1978); United States v. Black Jack, 508 F.2d 1179 (8th Cir. 1974), *cert. denied*, 422 U.S. 1042 (1975).
90. *Id. See also* Mayers v. Ridley, 465 F.2d 630, 635 (D.D.C. 1972) (Wright, J., concurring).
91. 42 U.S.C. §3604(a) and §3617. *See* cases cited in note 89, *supra*.
92. *See* note 25, *supra*.
93. Gladstone Realtors v. Bellwood, 99 S.Ct. 1601, 60 L.Ed. 2d 66 (1979). Trafficante v. Metropolitan Life Ins. Co., 409 U.S. 205 (1972); *but see* TOPIC v. Circle Realty, 532 F.2d 1273 (9th Cir. 1976), *cert. denied*, 429 U.S. 859 (1977).
94. 429 U.S. 252 (1977).

HOUSING

95. Metropolitan Hous. Dev. Corp. v. Arlington Heights, 558 F.2d 1283, 1290–94 (7th Cir. 1977), *cert. denied,* 434 U.S. 1025 (1978).

96. Resident Advisory Bd. v. Rizzo, 564 F.2d 126, 146 (3d Cir. 1977), *cert. denied,* 435 U.S. 908 (1978).

97. *Compare* Metropolitan Hous. Dev. Corp. v. Arlington Heights, 558 F.2d 1283, 1288 (7th Cir. 1977), *cert. denied,* 434 U.S. 1025 (1978) (an exclusionary-zoning challenge based in part upon §3617), *with* Smith v. Stechel, 510 F.2d 1162, 1164 (9th Cir. 1975) (holding that there is no time limitation for filing a lawsuit based upon §3617).

98. *E.g.,* Southern Burlington County NAACP v. Mount Laurel, 67 N.J. 151, 336 A.2d 713 (N.J. Sup.Ct., 1975), *appeal dismissed,* 423 U.S. 808 (1975) (requiring every developing municipality in New Jersey to accommodate its fair share of the regional housing needs of low- and moderate-income families). *See generally,* D. FALK and H. FRANKLIN, *supra* note 1, at 104–21.

VI

Public Accommodations

The modern civil rights movement, which toppled the more overt forms of racial discrimination, had its beginning in an effort to integrate public accommodations—city buses in Montgomery, Alabama. On December 1, 1955, Mrs. Rosa Parks, a black woman, refused to yield her seat on a city bus to a white passenger. Following her arrest for violating an ordinance requiring segregation in public transportation, a citywide boycott of buses was organized by a twenty-seven-year-old minister named Martin Luther King, Jr. In the years that followed, his tactic of direct, nonviolent action was replicated in countless lunch counter sit-ins, freedom rides, marches, boycotts, and demonstrations, and helped change the laws and customs of a nation.

What federal laws protect against racial discrimination in public accommodations?

Racial discrimination in public accommodations is prohibited by the Thirteenth Amendment, which bars the imposition of "badges and incidents of slavery" and protects the equal right to contract; the Fourteenth Amendment, which prohibits official discrimination; statutes implementing the Thirteenth and Fourteenth Amendments and imposing civil and criminal penalties upon those who interfere with access and use of public accommodations;[1] the Interstate Commerce Act of 1887, which forbids common carriers from imposing "unreasonable discrimination" upon their patrons;[2] and

Title II of the Civil Rights Act of 1964, the modern public accommodations law protecting the equal enjoyment of most business establishments without regard to race, color, religion, or historical origin.[8]

THE THIRTEENTH AND FOURTEENTH AMENDMENTS AND THE CIVIL RIGHTS ACT OF 1866

What kinds of discrimination in public accommodations are prohibited by the Thirteenth and Fourteenth Amendments?

The Fourteenth Amendment prohibits all forms of state imposed or sanctioned racial segregation in places of public accommodation regardless of whether the facilities are actually owned or operated by the state.[4] Purely private acts of segregation, however, in which there has been no significant state involvement, do not violate the equal protection clause of the Fourteenth Amendment.

The Thirteenth Amendment, unlike the Fourteenth, applies to private as well as official acts. Although it was initially construed as banning only slavery and physical restraint, the Supreme Court more recently has ruled that the Thirteenth Amendment prohibits the imposition of "badges and incidents of slavery" such as the refusal of private realtors to sell or lease real estate to blacks,[5] and protects the equal right to contract for services and accommodations.[6]

Were the Thirteenth and Fourteenth Amendments effectively enforced after their enactment to prohibit discrimination in public accommodations?

No. Both the Thirteenth and Fourteenth Amendments contain provisions authorizing congressional implementation through appropriate legislation.[7] Under this constitutional authority, Congress enacted in 1875 the nation's first public accommodations law,[8] intended to guarantee to all persons, without regard to race or color, the full and equal enjoyment of the accommodations, advantages, facilities, and privileges of inns, public conveyances, theaters, and other places of public amusement. Eight years later, in a decision known as *The Civil Rights Cases*,[9] the Supreme Court declared the act unconstitutional. The Court had before it five cases involving the denial to blacks of the use of privately owned hotels, theaters, and the ladies' car of a railroad company. A majority of justices concluded that the Thirteenth Amendment prohibited slavery, not racial discrimination, and that the Fourteenth Amendment was a limitation on state, not private, action. The discrimination involved in the facilities, although perhaps a "civil injury" under state law, was not prohibited by the Constitution. The decision thus denied Congress the authority to implement the Thirteenth and Fourteenth Amendments to ban segregation in privately owned places of public accommodations.

Was there any response by the states to The Civil Rights Cases?

Yes. Partially in response to *The Civil Rights Cases*, but more importantly as part of the "redemption" of white rule after Reconstruction, many of the states adopted so-called Jim Crow statutes *requiring* segregation of the races in places of public accommodation. No detail of life was too small to fall under the regulation of Jim Crow. Jim Crow laws required segregation in schools, churches, housing, transportation, jobs, prisons, cemeteries, and public buildings. Courts in Atlanta used a Jim Crow Bible to swear in Negro witnesses, and Birmingham had an ordinance making it a crime "for a Negro and a white person to play together or be in company of each other" at checkers or dominoes.[10]

Was Jim Crow ever tested in court?

Yes. In 1896, the Supreme Court decided *Plessy* v. *Ferguson*,[11] a case involving a Jim Crow law from the State of Louisiana. Plessy, who was seven-eighths white and one-eighth Negro, was a passenger in June, 1892, on the East Louisiana Railway from New Orleans to Covington. He purchased a first class ticket and took a seat in the car reserved for white passengers. The conductor, however, directed that Plessy take a seat in the Jim Crow car, which by state law was required to be "equal but separate." Plessy refused to move. He was arrested and charged with the crime of going "into a coach or compartment to which by race he does not belong." Plessy argued that the law was unconstitutional and that in any event "the mixture of colored blood was not discernible in him." His arguments were rejected and the Court, adhering to the narrow interpretation of the Constitution it had set down in *The Civil Rights Cases*, held that "separate but equal" accommodations for blacks on railway cars, even though required by state law, were constitutional because they existed for the "preservation of the public peace and good order." [12] The Court thus approved official racial segregation in places of public accommodation and allowed the states the right to adopt Jim Crow as the law of their land.

Plessy v. *Ferguson*, was not, however, to be the last word spoken by the Court on the constitutionality of Jim Crow. In 1954, in *Brown* v. *Board of Education*,[13] a case as dramatic for race relations as *Plessy* v. *Ferguson*, the Supreme Court effectively reversed itself and laid Jim Crow to rest.

Brown was the culmination of a line of cases in which the Court had found the maintenance of separate educational facilities and programs for blacks to be unconstitutional because they were in fact *unequal*.[14] The Court did not expressly overrule *Plessy* v. *Ferguson*, but it held categorically that "in the field of public education the doctrine of 'separate but equal' has no place." [15]

What specific practices have been held unconstitutional under *Brown* and the Fourteenth Amendment?

Brown marked the beginning of the end of the formal aspects of Jim Crow. Over the next twenty years the decision was used to ban officially sanctioned racial segregation in such places of public accommodation as buses,[16] parks,[17] hospitals,[18] swimming pools and bath houses,[19] city golf courses,[20] airport restaurants,[21] courtroom seating,[22] municipal auditoriums,[23] prisons and jails,[24] and in virtually every other form in which it came before the courts.

Is it always easy to draw a line between state imposed or sanctioned discrimination in public accommodations prohibited by the Fourteenth Amendment and purely private discrimination beyond its reach?

No. There is no specific formula for determining state action.[25] Instead, the courts sift and weigh all the facts involved, including whether the operation of a facility is essentially a public function,[26] and whether the state has any obligation or responsibility or confers or receives any benefit in its operation. If there is a "sufficient" degree of state involvement, the facility, even if privately owned, is subject to the prohibition against racial discrimination contained in the Fourteenth Amendment.

In one case, for example, the Supreme Court held that a privately operated coffee shop located in a parking building owned by the City of Wilmington, Delaware, was in partnership with the state so that the coffee shop's refusal to serve blacks was state action prohibited by the Fourteenth Amendment.[27] The Court based its conclusion upon the facts that the building was publicly owned and maintained, the parking lot was dedicated to public use, while operation of the cafe conferred mutual benefits to the city, patrons of the parking lot, and the operators of the cafe. Under the circumstances, there was sufficient state involvement to trigger the Fourteenth Amendment. In a later case, however, the Court held that the refusal of a Moose Lodge in Harrisburg, Pennsylvania, to serve a Negro was not prohibited by the Constitution.[28] The complainant, Leroy Irvis, contended that because the Pennsylvania liquor board had issued the lodge a license to serve alcohol that the refusal to serve him was state action, prohibited by the equal-protection clause of the Fourteenth Amendment. The Court disagreed. It found the lodge to be private because it was a member of a national fraternal organization, the building in which its activities were conducted was owned by it, there were well-defined requirements for membership, and only members and their guests were permitted in any lodge of the order. Even though the lodge had a license from the state to serve alcoholic beverages, that fact did not constitute sufficient state involvement or support in the operation of the lodge to make its racially exclusive membership policies unconstitutional.

Racial discrimination in the operation of privately owned facilities, however, is always unconstitutional under *Brown* v. *Board of Education* and the Fourteenth Amendment if it is carried out under state or local Jim Crow laws, or as part of official policy.[29] Under such circumstances, the state may be said to have compelled the discrimination. The Supreme Court has even held that a Florida Board of Health Regulation requiring separate toilet and lavatory rooms for the races in privately owned restaurants involved the state in the promotion of segregation to such an extent that the trespass convictions of civil rights demonstrators who had protested a local restaurant's segregationist policies violated the Fourteenth Amendment.[30]

Can a state or municipality close down a place of public accommodation rather than operate it on a desegregated basis?

Yes and no. The Supreme Court has held that a state may not close public schools and meanwhile contribute to the support of private, segregated white schools.[31] Such a course merely continues segregation in violation of the Fourteenth Amendment. However, in another case, the Court held it to be no violation of the Fourteenth Amendment for the City of Jackson, Mississippi, to close its municipal swimming pools rather than operate them on a desegregated basis.[32] The Court reasoned that the closing of the pools to all citizens, black and white, did not deny to either group equal treatment under the Constitution. The decision has been severely criticized on the grounds that the Fourteenth Amendment prohibits all forms of purposeful discriminatory state action, including opposition to the desegregation of public facilities, which was admittedly present in the case.

Aside from the public accommodations law of 1875, was there any other Reconstruction era legislation barring private discrimination in public accommodations?

Yes. The Civil Rights Act of 1866 contained two provisions, now known as Sections 1981 and 1982, barring, among other things, discrimination in public accommodations. Section 1982 provides that all citizens "shall have the same right . . . as is enjoyed by white citizens . . . to inherit, purchase, lease, sell, hold and convey real and personal property." [33] Section 1981 states that all persons "shall have the same right . . . to make and enforce contracts . . . as is enjoyed by white citizens." [34]

Have Sections 1981 and 1982 been used extensively to remedy discrimination in public accommodations?

No, but the law is changing, and the use of the two statutes will certainly increase. Both Sections 1981 and 1982 were presumed for more than a hundred years to apply only to state action, while Jim Crow, as we have seen, was long regarded as constitutional. The statutes thus had no impact on private discrimination in public accommodations. In 1968, however, the Supreme Court ruled that Section 1982, based in part upon the Thirteenth Amendment, prohibited private discrimination in real estate transactions,[35] and in 1975, that Section 1981 prohibited private discrimination in the making of contracts.[36] The effect of these decisions has thus been to allow use of the Reconstruction era statutes to prohibit owners and managers from discriminating in contracting with minorities for the use of privately owned public accommodations.

Do Sections 1981 and 1982 contain any express or implied limitations excluding certain kinds of discriminatory practices from coverage?

Neither statute contains any express limitations in coverage, while the Supreme Court has never ruled whether the statutes are limited by implication. The argument has been raised in several cases in the Supreme Court that the scope of Sections 1981 and 1982 is impliedly limited by the right of privacy, so that certain discriminatory practices, such as those in the home or a similar intimate setting, are simply beyond the power of the government to regulate. In those cases, however, the Court concluded that the setting in which the discrimination was practiced was not in fact private, and thus had no occasion to rule on implied privacy limitations that might be contained in the statutes. In one of the cases the Court held that the refusal of a community corporation, which operated a park and playground, to approve assignment of a membership share to a black was unlawful under Section 1982 since membership was generally open to all persons—except blacks—living within a certain geographic area.[37] The corporation was not in fact a private social club, only a racially exclusive club. The Court reached the same result under Section 1982 in a similar case decided four years later involving a community swimming pool association.[38] In one of the most recent Section 1981 cases, the Supreme Court held that the statute prohibited a private, commercially operated, nonsectarian school from refusing to contract with and admit blacks.[39] The decision of the Court was said to be limited to its facts, however, and the extent to which Sections 1981 and 1982 may subsequently be found to contain narrow privacy exceptions remains to be seen.[40]

How are the Thirteenth and Fourteenth Amendments and Sections 1981 and 1982 enforced to end discrimination in places of public accommodation? What remedies do they provide?

The Thirteenth and Fourteenth Amendments are enforced primarily through lawsuits brought by private individuals pursuant to implementing legislation, such as Sections 1981 and 1982, enacted by Congress.[41] Remedies include orders terminating discrimination and awarding damages[42] and attorneys' fees.[43] The federal government also has authority to prosecute violations of criminal statutes protecting Thirteenth and Fourteenth Amendment rights,[44] including equal access to public accommodations.

Are there any procedural requirements which must be complied with before suing to enforce Thirteenth and Fourteenth Amendment equal accommodation rights?

No. However, the courts have held that a lawsuit must be filed within the time period established by state law[45]—periods which vary, depending upon the state, from one year to five or more. Therefore, a complainant ordinarily should file a lawsuit as soon as possible after the discriminatory action.

THE INTERSTATE COMMERCE ACT

What is the Interstate Commerce Act? Does it prohibit racial discrimination?

Congress enacted the Interstate Commerce Act[46] in 1887 in order to regulate interstate commerce under the interstate commerce clause of the Constitution.[47] The act established the Interstate Commerce Commission (ICC) whose duty it is to license and regulate rail and bus carriers. The act specifically prohibits common carriers engaged in interstate commerce from giving undue preference to any person or subjecting any person to unjust or unreasonable discrimination, prejudice, or disadvantage.[48]

Is discrimination affecting only transportation within a state also prohibited by the act?

No. Discrimination which is purely local and has no impact upon commerce between the states, or with foreign countries, is not subject to regulation by the Interstate Commerce Act.[49]

Is state action a requirement for a violation of the act?

No. The act prohibits discrimination in interstate commerce by private as well as public carriers, and whether or not the discrimination is caused by state or local laws or the carrier's own practices.

What kinds of practices have been found discriminatory under the Interstate Commerce Act?

As might be expected, during the early years of its existence the Interstate Commerce Act was held to permit Jim Crow facilities for the races in interstate commerce, whether required by state statute or carrier rule.[50] In 1941, however, the Supreme Court ushered in a new era in interstate transportation in a case involving a black Congressman from Chicago, Arthur W. Mitchell.[51] Mitchell, who held a first class ticket, was required to accept second class accommodations pursuant to state Jim Crow laws when the train on which he was a passenger crossed over the state line from Tennessee into Arkansas. The ICC dismissed the Congressman's complaint, but the Supreme Court reversed.[52] The Court refused to decide whether Arkansas's segregation statutes were lawful, but held that the denial to Mitchell of equality of accommodations because of his race was a violation of the Interstate Commerce Act.[53]

Following the *Mitchell* case, the Court in 1946 confronted Jim Crow in interstate commerce head on and struck down a Virginia statute requiring separate but equal facilities for the races on motor buses. Mr. Justice Frankfurter in a concurring opinion observed that "imposition upon national systems of transportation of a crazy-quilt of state laws would operate to burden commerce unreasonably, whether such contradictory and confusing state laws concern racial commingling or racial segregation." [54]

As for the ICC, it issued rulings in two major cases on November 7, 1955, terminating segregation in interstate rail travel[55] and on buses.[56] As a consequence of the various decisions of the courts and the ICC, the Interstate Commerce Act is now regarded as imposing the same standard as far as race is concerned as the Fourteenth Amendment, and as barring "discriminations of all kinds." [57]

Do the nondiscrimination provisions of the act apply to such facilities as restaurants and terminals that cater to interstate passengers?

Yes. The act bans discrimination in terminals and restaurants that are an integral part of the carrier's service for interstate passengers, and it is immaterial whether such facilities are actually owned or operated by the carrier itself. The Supreme Court has held that a carrier cannot escape its statutory duty to treat all interstate passengers alike either through segregation in facilities it owns or use of the facilities of others who practice segregation.[58]

How are the antidiscrimination provisions of the act enforced?

The antidiscrimination provisions of the act are enforced administratively in proceedings before the ICC, and by lawsuits brought in the federal district courts. Any person, organization, or governmental entity adversely affected by a carrier practice may file a discrimination complaint with the Secretary of the ICC in Washington, D.C.[59] The ICC is required to investigate, and if it finds a violation, it is required to take action to correct it. Damages, costs, and attorneys' fees are authorized,[60] while those who disobey ICC orders are subject to a fine of $5000 for each day of disobedience.[61]

As an alternative to filing an administrative complaint, those discriminated against, as well as the Attorney General and the ICC itself, may file a suit in federal district court for injunctive relief and damages.[62]

There is no requirement that administrative remedies be exhausted before filing a lawsuit, but if a complaint is filed with the ICC, then the federal courts have jurisdiction only to review the action taken by the ICC, as opposed to hearing the matter from the beginning on its merits.[63]

Is the Interstate Commerce Act frequently used today to remedy discrimination in interstate commerce?

No. The importance of the Act has diminished with the decline of discrimination in interstate travel and, as we shall see, with enactment of Title II of the Civil Rights Act of 1964.

TITLE II OF THE CIVIL RIGHTS ACT OF 1964

What is Title II of the Civil Rights Act of 1964 and what does it provide?

Title II of the Civil Rights Act of 1964[64] is the nation's first modern public accommodations law. It was enacted by Congress, not pursuant to the Thirteenth and Fourteenth Amendments, but to its power to regulate commerce under Article I, Section 8, Clause 3 of the Constitution. Title II provides that all persons shall be entitled to the full and equal enjoyment of goods, services, facilities, privileges, advantages, and accommodations of any place of public accommodation without discrimination or segregation on the grounds of race, color, religion, or national origin. Four classes of business establishments are covered by the act, if each serves the public, is a place of public accommodation and its operations affect commerce, or if discrimination by it is supported by state action. The covered establishments are:

1. any inn, hotel, motel, or other establishment which provides lodging to transient guests;
2. any restaurant or similar facility principally engaged in selling food for consumption on the premises, or any gasoline station;
3. any theater, sports arena, or other place of exhibition or entertainment; and,
4. any establishment which is physically located within the premises of any establishment otherwise covered, or within the premises of which is physically located any covered establishment and which serves patrons of such covered establishment.

No persons may deny or interfere with the right of access and use of any covered facility by any other person.[65]

Doesn't Title II unreasonably interfere with the rights of ownership of private property?

No. In *Heart of Atlanta Motel* v. *United States*,[66] the Supreme Court held Title II to be constitutional, rejecting the argument that it deprived private individuals of their liberty and property interests. The Court noted that thirty-two states and numerous cities had enacted similar laws and that their constitutionality had repeatedly been upheld. Not only was public accommodations legislation common, but there was no merit in the claim that prohibition of racial discrimination in public facilities interfered with personal liberty. Congress acted in light of the dramatic evidence before it of the difficulties blacks encountered in travel, and to ease the burdens that discrimination by race or color placed upon interstate commerce. Under the circumstances, the Court concluded, Title II was reasonably adapted to an end permitted by the Constitution.

May a member of a racial minority be denied access to a place of public accommodation because other patrons might object and the owner lose business?

No. The protection of Title II cannot be yielded to the subjective prejudices of patrons or the claimed economic interests of owners and managers. The exclusion of persons from public accommodations because of their race, whatever the asserted justifications, is prohibited.[67]

How is the determination made whether an establishment's operations "affect commerce" and are thus covered by Title II?

Commerce is defined by Title II basically as trade or travel among the states, the District of Columbia, and any foreign country or territory or possession of the United States.[68] Inns, motels, and similar facilities are deemed to affect commerce if they provide lodging to transient guests. Restaurants, lunch counters, and gasoline stations are covered by Title II if they serve interstate travelers or if a substantial portion of what they sell has moved in commerce. Motion picture houses and other places of entertainment affect commerce if their films, performers, or other sources of entertainment have moved in commerce. Finally, any establishment located within the premises of a facility which affects commerce, or any establishment within the premises of

PUBLIC ACCOMMODATIONS

which is located a facility which affects commerce, is itself covered by Title II.

Must an establishment have a substantial effect upon interstate commerce to be covered by Title II?

No. The success of Title II depends upon the regulation of all establishments which contribute to the problem of racial discrimination in interstate commerce. Accordingly, the fact that an establishment's effect upon interstate commerce is trivial does not remove it from coverage. Thus, a barbecue restaurant in Birmingham, eleven blocks from an interstate highway, was covered by the act since nearly half of the food it served was purchased outside the state and moved through interstate commerce.[69] The requisite interstate commerce connection has also been made to bring a billiard parlor within Title II as a place of entertainment where its snooker and pool tables and cues were manufactured out of state.[70]

What kinds of practices and facilities have been held to be covered by Title II?

Practices and facilities held by the courts to be covered by Title II have included: segregation in hotels, motels,[71] YMCA facilities,[72] trailer parks,[73] and restaurants; "freedom of choice" seating in dining rooms;[74] a local ordinance prohibiting service at bars to persons in military uniform enacted to impede integration efforts at a nearby military installation;[75] denials of facilities at a remote fishing camp,[76] an amusement park,[77] a recreational complex containing boating and swimming facilities,[78] skating rinks,[79] a tournament held on a municipal golf course,[80] a golf course,[81] beach club,[82] bowling alleys,[83] movie theatres;[84] refusal to serve a white woman at a lunch counter because she was in the company of blacks;[85] refusals at beach apartments,[86] a drive-in restaurant,[87] lunch counters,[88] snack bars,[89] a gasoline station and its rest rooms,[90] nightclubs and cabarets,[91] a country club operated by a profit-making corporation,[92] pool rooms,[93] race tracks,[94] and a swimming club.[95]

155

Are there any exemptions from coverage contained in Title II?

Yes. Excluded from Title II are private clubs not in fact open to the public, and the so-called Mrs. Murphy's boarding house—that is, any rooming house with not more than five rooms for rent and which is actually occupied by the proprietor as a residence.[96]

May an establishment that serves the general public call itself a "private club" to escape Title II coverage and practice racial discrimination?

No. A place of public accommodation may not defeat Title II coverage by the simple expedient of calling itself a private club, or even by adopting some of the formal trappings of a private club. In determining if a facility is private, the courts look at all the facts and circumstances surrounding its operation: Is it run for a profit? Who owns it? How has it been operated in the past? Does it have members? If so, how are they chosen? Do they pay dues?

In one case the Supreme Court was asked to decide if the Lake Nixon Club, a 232-acre amusement park with swimming, boating, golf, and dancing facilities, located outside Little Rock, Arkansas, was a private club. Patrons were required to pay a twenty-five-cent membership fee and were issued membership cards for entry on the premises. The Court reviewed the facts, including facts that the privately owned park had always been operated on a racially segregated basis and that whites were routinely given, and blacks denied, membership. Lake Nixon Club was found to be simply "a business operated for a profit with none of the attributes of self-government and member-ownership traditionally associated with private clubs." [97]

In a similar case, the Court held a neighborhood swimming pool was not a private facility or club, since the association which owned it granted a preference in membership to anyone living within a three-quarter-mile radius of the pool, except blacks.[98] Aside from the geographical requirement, the only condition for membership was race. The pool was no more private under Title II than the Lake Nixon Club.

Who has the burden of proving whether a club is or is not private within the meaning of the private club exemption in Title II?

Those complaining of discrimination have the initial burden of establishing a prima facie case of a violation of Title II—that is, they must show that an establishment is covered by the Act and that it discriminates on the basis of race. Thereafter, the burden shifts to the establishment to prove by significant or clear and convincing evidence that it is in fact truly private.[99]

How is Title II enforced?

Title II depends for enforcement upon both private and federal lawsuits, as well as administrative conciliation by the Community Relations Service established by Title VIII of the Civil Rights Act of 1964. Any person aggrieved by racial discrimination in access to or use of public accommodations is authorized to bring a suit for injunctive relief in the federal courts.[100] If the court deems it proper, an attorney may be appointed to represent the complainant and the payment of fees and other court costs may be waived. The Attorney General is allowed, with the permission of the court, to intervene if the case is deemed to be of general public interest. The Attorney General is also authorized to bring suit for injunctive relief against discriminatory practices where there is "reasonable cause" to believe that a pattern and practice of resistance to Title II exists.[101]

To encourage individuals injured by racial discrimination to seek judicial relief under Title II and further the purposes of the act, Congress has provided that "prevailing parties" are entitled to recover costs and reasonable attorneys' fees.[102] Damages are not authorized. The provision of costs and fees has not only facilitated access by the poor and disadvantaged to the courts, but has deterred discrimination in the operation of public accommodations.

Are the enforcement procedures contained in Title II the sole means of remedying discrimination in public accommodations?

No. Title II specifically provides that nothing in the act shall preclude any person from asserting any right under any other statute or ordinance, or from pursuing any other remedy for the vindication or enforcement of such right.[108] Thus, a person discriminated against may bring suit under Title II or, for example, under Sections 1981 and 1982.

Since Title II and Sections 1981 and 1982 provide independent remedies for discrimination in public accommodations,[104] any aggrieved person who files a lawsuit should claim violations of both Title II and Sections 1981 and 1982.

Are there any advantages to filing a lawsuit under Title II as opposed to Sections 1981 and 1982?

There are advantages under both, since the remedies provided, and often the scope of coverage, are different. Sections 1981 and 1982 authorize recovery of damages; Title II does not. Title II, however, provides for enforcement by the Attorney General and conciliation by the Community Relations Service; Sections 1981 and 1982 contain no similar provisions. As for scope of coverage, Title II requires effect upon interstate commerce, while Sections 1981 and 1982 do not.

Are there any steps which must be taken before an individual can file a lawsuit to enforce Title II?

Yes, in some instances. Title II provides that no lawsuit may be brought under the statute in any state, or political subdivision of a state, which has an agency authorized to grant or seek relief from discrimination in public accommodations, before the expiration of thirty days after written notice, by registered mail or in person, of the act or practice has been given to such agency.[105] The purpose of the provision is to give states and local governments an initial opportunity to remedy discrimination.[106] However, if they fail to do so within the thirty-day period, the discriminated-against individual is free to bring suit in the federal district court, without having to comply with any other remedy that may be provided by law.[107] The notice requirements do not apply to pattern-and-practice suits brought by the Attorney General.[108]

The District of Columbia, most states, and many cities now have laws prohibiting discrimination on the basis of race or color in places of public accommodation. However, many state courts have proved hostile to these laws and have given them restrictive application to exclude such apparently public facilities as restaurants,[109] dentists' offices,[110] golf courses,[111] apartments, hotels,[112] and saloons.[113] The reasons for exclusion have included the facts that the statutes have been strictly construed and because they are said to limit the use of private property.

Regardless, if you have been discriminated against in public accommodations in any of the jurisdictions which have laws prohibiting discrimination in public accommodations, you must file a written notice, by registered mail or in person, with the appropriate nondiscrimination agency.[114]

What is the Community Relations Service? How does it enforce Title II?

The Community Relations Service (CRS) is a federal agency established by Title VIII of the Civil Rights Act of 1964.[115] Its function is to provide assistance to communities in resolving disputes relating to discriminatory practices based on race, color, or national origin. After a lawsuit has been filed to enforce Title II, the court may refer the matter to the CRS for up to sixty days, if the court believes there is a reasonable possibility of attaining a voluntary resolution of the discrimination.[116] The court may extend the referral for an additional sixty days, not to exceed a cumulative total of one hundred twenty days.

Does the Community Relations Service play an active role in resolving complaints of discrimination in public accommodations?

No. References to the CRS are infrequent due to the relative decline in the number of lawsuits filed under

Title II, and because the CRS has no authority, other than through conciliation, to resolve disputes.[117]

Can a member of a racial minority who seeks access to a facility covered by Title II be prosecuted for trespass under state law?

No. Persons threatened with prosecution under state trespass laws stemming from their peaceful exercise of the right of equal accommodation in establishments covered by Title II have a right not even to be brought to trial on such charges.[118] Accordingly, any charges that might be brought may be removed to the federal courts and there dismissed.[119] The right of removal under Title II is an important one and is a substantial deterrent to efforts by local officials to use state criminal prosecutions to defeat implementation of Title II under the guise of protecting property rights.

Can a person be prosecuted criminally for discriminating in the operation of public accommodations?

Title II contains no criminal provisions for the punishment of proprietors and owners who merely refuse to serve persons because of race. Injunctive relief is the sole remedy available under the act. However, persons who conspire against or assault others seeking access to public accommodations can be prosecuted by the federal government under 18 U.S.C. Sections 241 and 245 for interfering with the protected rights of citizens.[120]

TITLE III OF THE CIVIL RIGHTS ACT OF 1964

What is Title III of the Civil Rights Act of 1964? What does it provide?

Title III of the Civil Rights Act of 1964 is a special public accommodations law that authorizes the Attorney General to bring suit in the name of the government to end discrimination in the use of any public facility operated, owned, or managed by a state or its political subdivisions, other than a school or college.[121]

PUBLIC ACCOMMODATIONS

Are there any limitations on the Attorney General's authority to bring suit under Title III?

Yes. Before filing suit under Title III, the Attorney General must (1) have received a complaint in writing signed by an individual to the effect that he is being discriminated against on the basis of race, color, religion, or national origin in the use of a public facility; (2) believe the complaint is meritorious; (3) certify that the signer is unable to bring a suit on his own behalf; and (4) that a lawsuit will materially further the orderly progress of desegregation in public facilities.[122]

How does the Attorney General determine whether a person is unable to bring a lawsuit on his own?

Title III provides that a person may be deemed unable to bring a lawsuit on his own behalf if the expense of litigation is too great, if the person cannot obtain effective legal representation, or if the institution of a lawsuit would jeopardize the personal safety, employment, or economic standing of such person or his family or property.[123]

Does Title III affect the right of private individuals to sue for discrimination in public accommodations?

No. Title III specifically provides that nothing in the act shall adversely affect the right of any person to sue in court against discrimination in public accommodations.[124]

How has Title III been used? What is its significance today?

Title III has been used primarily to desegregate prisons and jails.[125] Its main significance is that it allows the Attorney General to bring suit to enforce the Fourteenth Amendment in places of public accommodation, and of equal importance, spares private parties the burden and expense of litigation. Those discriminated against in use of state-owned or -operated facilities should always make a written complaint to the Attorney General, United States Department of Justice, Washington, D.C. 20530.[126]

NOTES

1. *E.g.*, 42 U.S.C. §§1981, 1982, 1983, and 1985 and 18 U.S.C. §§241, 242, and 245.
2. 24 Stat. 380, 49 U.S.C. §§3(1) and 316(d).
3. 42 U.S.C. §2000a *et seq.*
4. Burton v. Wilmington Parking Auth., 365 U.S. 715 (1961).
5. Jones v. Alfred H. Mayer Co., 392 U.S. 409 (1968), construing 42 U.S.C. §1982, derived from the Civil Rights Act of 1866, 14 Stat. 27.
6. Tillman v. Wheaton-Haven Recreation Ass'n, Inc., 410 U.S. 431 (1973); Johnson v. Railway Express Agency, 421 U.S. 454 (1975), and Runyon v. McCrary, 427 U.S. 160 (1976), construing 42 U.S.C. §1981, derived from the Civil Rights Act of 1866, 14 Stat. 27.
7. Thirteenth Amendment, §2; Fourteenth Amendment, §5.
8. 18 Stat. 335.
9. 109 U.S. 3 (1883).
10. C. Vann Woodward, *The Strange Career of Jim Crow* (New York: Oxford University Press, 1957), p. 104.
11. 163 U.S. 537 (1896).
12. *Id.*
13. 347 U.S. 483 (1954).
14. The cases include Gaines v. Canada, 305 U.S. 337 (1938); Sweatt v. Painter, 339 U.S. 629 (1950); and McLaurin v. Oklahoma State Regents, 339 U.S. 637 (1950).
15. 347 U.S. at 495.
16. Gayle v. Browder, 352 U.S. 903 (1956) (*per curiam*).
17. City of New Orleans v. Barthe, 376 U.S. 189 (1964).
18. Simkins v. Moses H. Cone Hosp., 323 F.2d 959 (4th Cir. 1963).
19. Clark v. Thompson, 313 F.2d 637 (5th Cir. 1963).
20. City of Greensboro v. Simkins, 246 F.2d 425 (4th Cir. 1957).
21. Smith v. Birmingham, 226 F.Supp. 838 (N.D.Ala. 1963).
22. Wood v. Vaughan, 321 F.2d 480 (4th Cir. 1963).
23. Schiro v. Bynum, 375 U.S. 395 (1964).
24. Lee v. Washington, 390 U.S. 333 (1968).
25. Bell v. Maryland, 378 U.S. 226 (1964).
26. Marsh v. Alabama, 326 U.S. 501 (1946).
27. Burton v. Wilmington Parking Auth., 365 U.S. 715 (1961).

PUBLIC ACCOMMODATIONS

28. Moose Lodge No. 107 v. Irvis, 407 U.S. 163 (1972).
29. Peterson v. City of Greenville, 373 U.S. 244 (1963); Lombard v. Louisiana, 373 U.S. 267 (1963).
30. Robinson v. Florida, 378 U.S. 153 (1964).
31. Griffin v. County School Bd., 377 U.S. 218 (1964).
32. Palmer v. Thompson, 403 U.S. 217 (1971).
33. 42 U.S.C. §1982.
34. 42 U.S.C. §1981.
35. Jones v. Alfred H. Mayer Co., 392 U.S. 409 (1968).
36. Johnson v. Railway Express Agency, 421 U.S. 454 (1975).
37. Sullivan v. Little Hunting Park, 396 U.S. 229 (1969).
38. Tillman v. Wheaton-Haven Recreation Ass'n, 410 U.S. 431 (1973).
39. Runyon v. McCrary, 427 U.S. 160 (1976).
40. Cf. The private-club exception in 42 U.S.C. §2000a(e).
41. E.g., 42 U.S.C. §§1981, 1982, 1983, and 1985.
42. Sullivan v. Little Hunting Park, 396 U.S. 229 (1969).
43. 42 U.S.C. §1988.
44. 18 U.S.C. §§241, 242, and 245. These statutes are discussed in more detail in Chapter IX.
45. Johnson v. Railway Express Agency, 421 U.S. 454 (1975).
46. 24 Stat. 380, 49 U.S.C. §1 *et seq.*
47. Article 1, Section 8, Clause 3.
48. 49 U.S.C. §§3(1) (rail carriers) and 316(d) (bus carriers). The Civil Aeronautics Act contains a similar provision patterned after the Interstate Commerce Act outlawing racial discrimination in the air. 49 U.S.C. §484(b). The provision has had no real significance, however, since segregation in airplanes has never been enforced by state law or air carriers themselves.
49. Cf. Bob-Lo Excursion Co. v. Michigan, 333 U.S. 28 (1948).
50. Council v. Western & A.R.R., 1 I.C.C. 339 (1887). *See also* Chesapeake & O. Ry. v. Kentucky, 179 U.S. 388 (1900), and Plessy v. Ferguson, 163 U.S. 537 (1896).
51. Mitchell v. United States, 313 U.S. 80 (1941).
52. *Id.*
53. The Court followed Mitchell, *id.*, subsequently to strike down the Southern Railway Company's practice of providing segregated dining facilities. *See* Henderson v. United States, 339 U.S. 816 (1950).
54. Morgan v. Virginia, 328 U.S. 373, 387 (1946).

THE RIGHTS OF RACIAL MINORITIES

55. NAACP v. St. Louis–San Francisco Ry. Co., 297 I.C.C. 335 (1955).
56. Keys v. Carolina Coach Co., 64 M.C.C. 769 (1955).
57. Boynton v. Virginia, 364 U.S. 454, 457 (1960); United States v. Lassiter, 203 F.Supp. 20 (W.D. La. 1962), *aff'd*, 371 U.S. 10 (1962).
58. Boynton v. Virginia, 364 U.S. 454 (1960).
59. 49 U.S.C. §§13 and 316(e). *See* NAACP v. St. Louis–San Francisco Ry., 297 I.C.C. 335, 346 (1955).
60. 49 U.S.C. §8.
61. 49 U.S.C. §16(8).
62. Wright v. Chicago, Burlington & Quincy R.R., 223 F.Supp. 660 (N.D. Ill. 1963); Lyons v. Illinois Greyhound Lines, 192 F.2d 533 (7th Cir. 1951); Lassiter v. United States, 371 U.S. 10 (1962), and United States v. Jackson, 318 F.2d 1 (5th Cir. 1963).
63. Mitchell v. United States, 313 U.S. 80 (1941).
64. 78 Stat. 243, Title II, codified as 42 U.S.C. §2000a *et seq*.
65. 42 U.S.C. §2000a-2.
66. 379 U.S. 241 (1964).
67. United States v. Gulf State Theaters, 256 F.Supp. 549 (N.D. Miss. 1966).
68. 42 U.S.C. §2000a(c).
69. Katzenbach v. McClung, 379 U.S. 294 (1964).
70. United States v. Williams, 376 F.Supp. 750 (M.D. Fla. 1974).
71. Heart of Atlanta Motel v. United States, 379 U.S. 241 (1964).
72. Smith v. YMCA, 462 F.2d 634 (5th Cir. 1972).
73. Dean v. Ashling, 409 F.2d 754 (5th Cir. 1969).
74. United States v. Gramer, 418 F.2d 692 (5th Cir. 1969).
75. United States v. Cantrell, 307 F.Supp. 259 (E.D. La. 1969).
76. United States v. Skidmore, 1 R.R.L.Sur. 267 (M.D. Fla. 1969).
77. Miller v. Amusement Enterprises, 394 F.2d 342 (5th Cir. 1968).
78. Scott v. Young, 421 F.2d 143 (4th Cir. 1970).
79. Evans v. Seamen, 452 F.2d 749 (5th Cir. 1971).
80. Wesley v. Savannah, 294 F.Supp. 698 (S.D. Ga. 1969).
81. United States v. Central Carolina Bank & Trust Co., 431 F.2d 972 (4th Cir. 1970).
82. United States v. Beach Associates, 286 F.Supp. 80 (D. Md. 1968).

83. Fazzio Real Estate Co. v. Adams, 396 F.2d 146 (5th Cir. 1968).
84. Twitty v. Vogue Theatre, 242 F.Supp. 281 (M.D. Fla. 1965).
85. Adickes v. S. H. Kress & Co., 398 U.S. 144 (1970).
86. United States v. Beach Assoc., 286 F.Supp. 801 (D. Md. 1968).
87. Newman v. Piggie Park Enterprises, 390 U.S. 400 (1968).
88. Hamm v. Rock Hill, 379 U.S. 306 (1964).
89. Daniel v. Paul, 395 U.S. 298 (1969).
90. Presley v. Monticello, 395 F.2d 675 (5th Cir. 1968).
91. Robertson v. Johnston, 249 F.Supp. 618 (E.D. La. 1966).
92. Bell v. Kenwood Golf and Country Club, 312 F.Supp. 753 (D. Md. 1970).
93. United States v. Williams, 376 F.Supp. 750 (D. Fla. 1974).
94. Bonomo v. Louisiana Downs, Inc., 337 So.2d 553 (La. App. 1976).
95. Tillman v. Wheaton-Haven Recreation Ass'n, 410 U.S. 431 (1973).
96. 42 U.S.C. §§2000a(b)(1) and (e).
97. Daniel v. Paul, 395 U.S. 298, 301 (1969).
98. Tillman v. Wheaton-Haven Recreational Ass'n, 410 U.S. 431 (1973).
99. Anderson v. Pass Christian Isles Golf Club, 488 F.2d 855 (5th Cir. 1974).
100. 42 U.S.C. §2000a-3(a).
101. 42 U.S.C. §2000a-5(a).
102. *Id.* at §2000a-3(b), applied in Newman v. Piggie Park Enterprises, 390 U.S. 400 (1968).
103. 42 U.S.C. §2000a-6(b).
104. Tillman v. Wheaton-Haven Recreation Ass'n, 367 F.Supp. 860 (D. Md. 1973), *rev'd on other grounds,* 517 F.2d 1141 (4th Cir. 1975).
105. 42 U.S.C. §2000a-3(c).
106. Harris v. Ericson, 457 F.2d 765 (10th Cir. 1972).
107. 42 U.S.C. §2000a-6(a).
108. Harris v. Ericson, *supra* note 106.
109. State v. Brown, 112 Kan. 814, 212 P. 663 (1923).
110. Coleman v. Middlestaff, 147 Cal. App. 2d 833, 305 P.2d 1020 (1957).
111. Delaney v. Central Valley Golf Club, 289 N.Y. 577, 43 N.E.2d 716 (1942).
112. Alsberg v. Lucerne Hotel Co., 46 Misc. 617, 92 N.Y.S. 851 (1905).

THE RIGHTS OF RACIAL MINORITIES

113. Gibbs v. Arras Bros., 222 N.Y. 332, 118 N.E. 857 (1918).
114. To determine whether a jurisdiction has a public accommodations law, consult the state or local legal or public information office, or one of the agencies or sources of legal assistance listed in Appendices A or B.
115. 42 U.S.C. §2000g.
116. 42 U.S.C. §2000a-3(d).
117. 42 U.S.C. §2000g-2.
118. 42 U.S.C. §2000a-2.
119. City of Greenwood v. Peacock, 384 U.S. 808 (1966) and Georgia v. Rachel, 384 U.S. 780 (1966), construing the removal provisions of 28 U.S.C. §1443. Removal is discussed in detail in Chapter VIII.
120. United States v. Johnson, 390 U.S. 563 (1968).
121. 78 Stat. 246, codified as 42 U.S.C. §2000b *et seq.*
122. *Id.*
123. 42 U.S.C. §2000b(b).
124. 42 U.S.C. §2000b-2.
125. *E.g.,* United States v. Wyandotte County, 480 F.2d 969 (10th Cir. 1973).
126. The Attorney General also has authority under 42 U.S.C. §2000h-2 to intervene in any suit to enforce the equal protection of the Fourteenth Amendment.

VII

Federally Assisted Discrimination

Government assistance is often given to institutions or organizations that practice racial discrimination. Sometimes, for example, free textbooks are provided to public or private schools that exclude or assign pupils on the basis of race; tax exemptions are granted to all-white private clubs; and federal revenue-sharing is given to discriminatory local governments. Not only is the underlying discrimination in these instances unlawful, but the provision of government assistance to the discriminatory is a separate, independent violation of the law.

The remedy for unconstitutional provision of government assistance is limited to terminating financial aid. However, threatened termination of aid frequently eliminates the underlying discrimination itself. As a federal judge recently stated: "Stopping the flow of lifeblood [federal money] to a body [recipient of that money] is certainly more fatal than enjoining that body from certain activity." [1]

This chapter will explore the advantages and methods of pursuing remedies against governmentally assisted discrimination. The most important advantage, as will become evident, is that this remedy generally is enforced by federal agencies and thus requires no more from a private individual than the filing of an administrative charge of discrimination with the appropriate federal agency.

Is government assistance to organizations and institutions engaged in discrimination very widespread?

Yes. Government assistance to institutions and organizations, many of which are engaged in discrimination, is a widespread phenomenon. There are three main types of government assistance. First, tax abatement: private clubs and not-for-profit organizations receive substantial government assistance in the form of tax exempt status and income tax deductibility of contributions. Second, direct grants: public and private schools receive funding from the Department of Health, Education and Welfare; and state and local governments receive revenue-sharing funding from the Department of the Treasury, and public housing funds from the Department of Housing and Urban Development; etc. And third, contracts: private companies and institutions of higher education receive large government contracts to build government buildings, to undertake government research, etc.

Is it *unconstitutional* for government agencies to provide assistance to organizations or institutions engaged in discrimination?

Yes. It is unconstitutional under the Fourteenth Amendment for a state government, and unconstitutional under the Fifth Amendment for the federal government, to provide assistance to entities that discriminate. There are, however, several problems in enforcing the law. First, provision of assistance is unconstitutional only if it can be proved that the government is knowingly and intentionally assisting discrimination. Second, the only effective means of terminating the unconstitutional assistance is through a lawsuit against the government.

Is it *unlawful* for federal government agencies to provide assistance to organizations or institutions engaged in discrimination?

Yes. It generally is unlawful under a variety of federal laws for agencies of the federal government to provide assistance to entities that discriminate. The theory behind this principle was explained by President John Kennedy in 1963: "Simple justice requires that public funds to which all taxpayers of all races contribute, not be spent in any fashion which encourages, entrenches, subsidizes or results in racial discrimination." [2]

There are two basic categories of federal laws that

prohibit federal agencies from providing assistance to discriminatory organizations and institutions. The first category is comprised of Title VI of the Civil Rights Act of 1964,[3] which governs the federal financial assistance provided by more than twenty agencies. In the second category are two statutes which apply respectively to the millions of dollars of revenue provided by the Office of Revenue Sharing of the Department of the Treasury and to the millions of dollars of law-enforcement funding provided by the Law Enforcement Assistance Administration. The recently amended civil rights provisions of these statutes are included in the State and Local Fiscal Assistance Amendments of 1976[4] and the Crime Control Act of 1976.[5]

Although the foregoing laws have the same objectives, and although the methods of federal enforcement are generally similar, there are important differences in the ways the various laws are implemented. Accordingly, each law is discussed separately in this chapter.

Are there advantages for minorities in seeking the protection of antidiscrimination assistance laws?

Yes. There are three important advantages. First, civil-rights enforcement is the responsibility of the assisting federal agency. This means that there usually is no need whatsoever to file a lawsuit against the discriminatory recipient. All that the discriminated-against person need do is to file an administrative charge with the assisting federal agency. Second, the federal agency usually need not show that the recipient is engaging in *intentional* discrimination. All the federal agency usually needs to find is that the recipient is engaging in practices which have a discriminatory effect. Third, if the recipient refuses to stop its discrimination, the federal agency in most instances is required to terminate its assistance. This is a powerful remedy "designed to bring [discriminatory recipients] quickly to their knees." [6]

THE FIFTH AND FOURTEENTH AMENDMENTS

What are the Fifth and Fourteenth Amendment prohibitions against government-assisted discrimination?

The Fourteenth Amendment's equal-protection clause, which applies to state and local governments, prohibits them from engaging in intentional discrimination. The Fifth Amendment's due process clause, which applies to the federal government, has been interpreted to prohibit the federal government from engaging in intentional discrimination.[7] Although the amendments generally are perceived only as prohibiting direct discrimination, they have been interpreted by the courts as prohibiting intentional participation in discrimination by others. This makes sense, of course, since government should not be able to discriminate indirectly when it is prohibited from discriminating directly.

What types of state assistance to discrimination are prohibited by the Fourteenth Amendment?

Generally, all forms of state assistance provided to recipients that the state knows are discriminatory are prohibited by the Fourteenth Amendment. For example, in 1973 the Supreme Court held that the State of Mississippi had violated the Fourteenth Amendment by providing free textbooks to students attending discriminatory private schools.[8] Similarly, lower courts have held unconstitutional state provision of tuition grants to students attending discriminatory private schools,[9] as well as state provision of tax exempt status to discriminatory private organizations.[10]

What types of federal assistance to discrimination are prohibited by the Fifth Amendment?

The same types of assistance as are prohibited when given by states under the Fourteenth Amendment: generally, all forms of federal assistance provided to recipients that a federal agency knows are discriminatory are prohibited by the Fifth Amendment. For example, the courts have held unconstitutional the federal provision of tax exempt status to discriminatory private schools[11] and private clubs.[12] Similarly, a court has held unconstitutional any recognition by the National Labor Relations Board of a discriminatory construction union.[13]

How are the Fifth and Fourteenth Amendment prohibitions against unconstitutional government assistance enforced?

Theoretically, each government agency that provides assistance is responsible for ensuring that it does not unconstitutionally aid discriminatory recipients. In practice, however, there is very little constitutional self-enforcement by assisting government agencies. Accordingly, the only effective remedy has been to sue the government agencies that are providing assistance to discriminatory recipients.

Are there any problems facing a person who wants to sue a government agency that is providing assistance to a discriminatory recipient?

Yes. Since such a lawsuit is a *big* case, an initial problem will be finding a lawyer who is willing to handle this type of lawsuit. Additionally, there are two quite significant legal problems. First, when suing under the Fifth and Fourteenth Amendments, the person suing has to prove that the agency being sued has engaged in intentional discrimination.[14] This is a heavy burden of proof. Second, even assuming you have the necessary proof, the courts increasingly are dismissing lawsuits against federal agencies on the grounds that persons discriminated against by recipients have not been harmed by the agency providing the assistance, and hence do not have legal standing to challenge it.[15]

In view of the problems with forcing government agencies to obey their Fifth and Fourteenth Amendment obligations, are there any other methods of terminating federal government assistance to discriminatory recipients?

Yes. The other methods involve filing administrative charges of discrimination with the federal agencies providing the assistance. Most federal agencies are governed by civil rights laws that specifically require the agencies to terminate assistance to discriminatory recipients. The mere filing of an administrative charge frequently leads to threatened suspension of funds and ultimately to elimination by the recipient of its discrimination.

TITLE VI OF THE CIVIL RIGHTS ACT OF 1964

What is Title VI of the Civil Rights Act of 1964?

Title VI is one of the group of statutory provisions in the omnibus Civil Rights Act of 1964. Its objective is to ensure that federal departments and agencies do not provide *federal* financial assistance to recipients engaged in discrimination. As Senator Hubert H. Humphrey explained when Congress was enacting Title VI: "The purpose of Title VI is to make sure that funds of the United States are not used to support racial discrimination." [16]

How broad are the protections of Title VI?

Fairly broad. Title VI prohibits discrimination on grounds of race, color or national origin in "any program or activity receiving federal financial assistance." [17] Despite this breadth, there are two significant exceptions. (1) Title VI applies only to federal *financial* assistance. Specifically exempted are contracts of insurance or guarantees.[18] Thus, for example, banking programs involving federally insured bank deposits are not covered by Title VI. (2) Also exempted are employment practices in any program or activity receiving federal aid unless a primary objective of the financial assistance is to provide employment.[19]

What types of federal agencies are covered by Title VI?

Title VI applies to each federal department and agency empowered to extend financial assistance through a grant, a loan, or a contract.[20] Title VI thus applies to more than twenty federal departments and agencies. For example, Title VI applies to HEW, which provides education grants; it applies to HUD, which provides grants for public housing and for community improvements; it applies to the Department of Transportation, which provides funding for highways and mass transit; etc.

Who is responsible for Title VI enforcement?

Each federal department and agency that extends financial assistance is responsible for its own Title VI enforcement. Coordination of the overall Title VI enforcement effort is provided by the Department of Justice.[21]

How do federal agencies initiate Title VI enforcement?

There are two basic methods of initiating Title VI enforcement. First, an administrative charge against a recipient filed by or on behalf of a person alleging discrimination will prompt a federal agency investigation of the alleged discrimination. Second, the agency itself, on its own initiative or in response to a large number of charges, may start a thorough compliance review of the recipient's practices. With either method, the federal agency will investigate the recipient and make a finding of discrimination (noncompliance with Title VI) or of no discrimination (compliance with Title VI).

Since most federal agencies do not initiate Title VI enforcement on their own accord, it is very important that administrative charges of discrimination be filed with the federal agencies. Unfortunately, it usually is very difficult to figure out which discriminatory institutions are receiving federal financial assistance from which federal agencies, and thus it is difficult to know which is the appropriate federal agency to receive the administrative charge. Some situations, however, are easier than others.

For example, all public schools, nearly all public and private institutions of higher education, and nearly all public and private hospitals receive substantial federal financial assistance from the U.S. Department of Health, Education, and Welfare (HEW). Accordingly, a person who has been discriminated against by a school or a hospital should send an administrative charge of discrimination to the Office for Civil Rights (U.S. Department of Health, Education, and Welfare, 330 Independence Avenue, S.W., Washington, D.C. 20201), or to any regional office of HEW.

Similarly, all public housing authorities and all local community development agencies receive federal financial assistance from the U.S. Department of Housing and Urban Development (HUD). Accordingly, a person who has been discriminated against by a housing authority or a community development agency should send an administrative charge of discrimination to the Office of Fair Housing and Equal Opportunity (U.S. Department of Housing and Urban Development, Washington, D.C. 20410), or to any regional office of HUD.

Because more than twenty federal agencies provide so many different kinds of federal financial assistance, we have listed in Appendix A the names and addresses of the federal agencies providing federal financial assistance and thus engaging in Title VI enforcement. A person who has been discriminated against should look in Appendix A for the appropriate federal agency and then mail an administrative charge of discrimination to that federal agency.

What are the requirements for filing an administrative charge of discrimination with a federal agency under Title VI?

As noted, federal agency enforcement of Title VI almost always starts with an individual filing an administrative charge of discrimination. An administrative charge under Title VI is not a formal legal document. There is no prescribed form; a letter is sufficient. The letter should fully describe the nature of the discrimination; name the institution (and its address) and the individuals that have committed the discrimination; and explain the type of federal financial assistance provided to the institution. The letter should be signed, but it need not be sworn to. And it should be mailed to the appropriate federal agency as soon as possible, and not later than 180 days after the discrimination occurred.

In order to make a finding of discrimination, must the federal agency find that the recipient was engaged in *intentional* discrimination, or is it sufficient for the agency to find that the recipient was using a practice which had a discriminatory effect with no intent to discriminate?

This, unfortunately, has not been finally resolved by the courts. In 1974, the Supreme Court held that under Title VI: "Discrimination is barred which has [a discriminatory] *effect* even though no purposeful design is present." [22] Four years later, in 1978, however, the Supreme Court held that Title VI should be interpreted the same as the Fourteenth Amendment[23]—and in order to find a violation of the Fourteenth Amendment there must be proof of *intentional* discrimination.[24] Since the Court in 1978 did not overrule its 1974 decision, it is not known whether only intentional discrimination violates Title VI.

What happens once an agency determines that a recipient has engaged in discrimination?

After an agency makes a determination of discrimination, it must take two steps. First, it must seek to obtain voluntary compliance with Title VI from the recipient.[25] This means that the recipient must be given an opportunity to stop its discrimination, rather than having its federal assistance stopped. If voluntary compliance is not achieved, the agency then must start administrative hearings to terminate the federal assistance, or the agency may refer the matter to the Department of Justice for a lawsuit against the recipient.[26] The federal courts have indicated that under Title VI, fund-termination proceedings are the preferred alternative.[27]

Once a person files a complaint with a federal agency, the agency has the responsibility to enforce Title VI. There is nothing else for the individual to do. It might be helpful, however, to write a letter to the agency once in a while to remind the federal officials that action is expected.

Do the federal agencies extending financial assistance have good reputations for enforcing Title VI?

No, but they are improving. In the late 1960s and early 1970s, many of the agencies had poor reputations for enforcing Title VI; they would investigate charges and make findings of discrimination but would not initiate the procedures to terminate funding. Most of that has changed now, and many of the agencies are beginning to earn fairly good reputations for civil rights enforcement.

If a federal agency is less than vigorous in its Title VI enforcement, is there anything that a complainant can do?

Yes. Most courts have held that an individual can sue the recipient under Title VI to eliminate the discrimination or to terminate the federal financial assistance.[28]

However, such a lawsuit can be filed only after the individual has given the federal funding agency sufficient time to act on the administrative charge.[29] Additionally, in some circumstances an individual may be able to sue the funding federal agency for Title VI nonenforcement.[30] The latter type of lawsuit can be a massive undertaking and thus is not normally recommended.

Given the uneven record of civil rights enforcement by federal agencies providing financial assistance, is it really worth the time and effort to file administrative charges against discriminatory recipients?

Yes. The administrative procedure for terminating federal assistance is highly recommended as a means for individuals to assert their civil rights to equal treatment under law. And the filing of an administrative charge is a very easy step to take, since it simply involves sending a simple letter.

THE REVENUE SHARING ACT OF 1972

What is the Revenue Sharing Act?

The Revenue Sharing Act is the common name for the Fiscal Assistance to State and Local Governments Act of 1972, which created the federal revenue sharing program. Under the revenue sharing program, the federal Office of Revenue Sharing provides billions of dollars each year to state, county, and municipal governments. Section 122 of the act prohibits state and local government recipients from engaging in discrimination on grounds of race, color, and national origin.

In 1976 the act was amended and reenacted. At that time, Section 122 was substantially amended to include the most stringent, mandatory civil rights enforcement provisions ever enacted.[31]

Do the civil rights enforcement provisions of the Revenue Sharing Act differ from those in Title VI?

Yes. Although the civil rights provisions have the same purpose (to terminate federal funding to discriminatory recipients), the civil rights enforcement provisions of the

Revenue Sharing Act are much better than those of Title VI in that they *require* investigations, *require* findings of noncompliance or compliance, and *require* suspension and termination of funding—all within set time periods.

How broad are the protections of the Revenue Sharing Act?

Very broad. Although the act applies only to state, county, and municipal government recipients of revenue sharing, the act broadly prohibits all forms of discrimination on grounds of race, color, national origin, etc., in any unit of government which receives revenue sharing.[32] Employment discrimination is not exempted.

How does the Office of Revenue Sharing initiate civil rights enforcement?

Although there are a number of triggers which initiate enforcement,[33] the one particularly relevant here is the administrative charge against a recipient filed with the Office of Revenue Sharing by or on behalf of a person alleging discrimination. Such a charge will initiate an investigation, which must be completed, and a finding made by the Office of Revenue Sharing, within ninety days after the filing of the charge.[34]

There is no prescribed form for the administrative charge of discrimination; a letter is sufficient. The letter should fully describe the nature of the discrimination, and it should state the name and address of the state or local government engaged in the discrimination. The letter need not be sworn to, but it should be signed. Significantly, the letter need not be filed within a set period of time after the discrimination occurred, but it should be filed as soon as possible. Filing the charge is accomplished by sending the letter to the appropriate office (Civil Rights Division, Office of Revenue Sharing, United States Department of the Treasury, 2401 E Street, N.W., Washington, D.C. 20226).

In order to make a finding of discrimination, must the Office of Revenue Sharing find that the recipient was engaged in *intentional* discrimination?

No. As one federal court has stated, "discriminatory conduct which violates Title VII [which does not require proof of discriminatory intent] is enough, without proof of a constitutional infirmity, to establish a violation of [the Revenue Sharing] Act's nondiscrimination provision."[35]

Must the Office of Revenue Sharing make a conclusive finding of discrimination before finding a violation of the Revenue Sharing Act?

No. The Revenue Sharing Act requires only that it be "more likely than not" that the recipient has engaged in discrimination.[36] This is a very lenient standard.

What happens once the Office of Revenue Sharing makes a finding that it is "more likely than not" that a recipient has engaged in discrimination?

At this stage there are a number of intricate mandatory steps that the Office of Revenue Sharing must take, all within very short time limits, and all leading to the suspension and termination of revenue-sharing funding.[37] For example, there is a thirty-day grace period during which the recipient may present evidence informally and at the end of which the Office of Revenue Sharing must make a formal finding of noncompliance or compliance. If the finding is noncompliance, and if a hearing is not requested by the recipient within ten days, all revenue sharing will be suspended. If a hearing is requested, it must be held within thirty days.

At any time, of course, a recipient may choose to stop its discrimination, and thereby continue to receive revenue-sharing funding.

Once a discriminated-against person has filed an administrative charge with the Office of Revenue Sharing, is there anything else for that person to do?

No. Once an administrative charge is filed with the Office of Revenue Sharing, it is the agency's responsibility to enforce the Revenue Sharing Act. A follow-up letter, however, might help to urge the agency along.

Does the Office of Revenue Sharing actually do a good job investigating complaints and making findings?

It does fairly well. Before the Revenue Sharing Act was amended in 1976, the Office of Revenue Sharing had a terrible civil rights enforcement record. That terrible record is the reason Congress in 1976 made the new civil rights enforcement procedure so stringent. After that, the agency's civil rights enforcement record has been fairly good.

If the Office of Revenue Sharing fails to act vigorously in its civil rights enforcement, is there anything that a complainant can do?

Yes. The Revenue Sharing Act creates an express cause of action pursuant to which an individual may sue the recipient directly to seek "suspension, termination, or repayment of funds." [38] However, the individual can sue only if the administrative charge has been filed for ninety days and the Office of Revenue Sharing did not make a finding of compliance within those ninety days.[39]

If a person has been discriminated against by a state, county, or municipal government, is it a good idea for that person to file an administrative charge with the Office of Revenue Sharing?

Absolutely yes! Or another person can file on behalf of that person. The 1976 amendments to the Revenue Sharing Act create the most effective remedy yet enacted to force the elimination of discrimination. Even before the 1976 amendments, an administrative charge filed with the Office of Revenue Sharing eventually led to the suspension of more than $100 million of revenue sharing to the City of Chicago.[40] Since the City of Chicago wanted to retain its federal revenue-sharing funding, it quickly ended its discrimination.

THE CRIME CONTROL ACT OF 1968

What is Section 518(c) of the Crime Control Act of 1968?

The Crime Control Act of 1968 created the Law Enforcement Assistance Administration (LEAA), a federal agency that provides millions of dollars each year to state and local law enforcement agencies, primarily police departments and prisons. With some amendments, the act was reenacted in 1973 and 1976, and the portion pertaining to LEAA will again be amended and reenacted in 1980.

Section 518(c) of the act prohibits law enforcement agencies receiving LEAA funding from engaging in discrimination on grounds of race, color, and national origin. Section 518(c), as amended in 1976, contains mandatory civil rights enforcement provisions [41] similar to those in the new Revenue Sharing Act.

Do the civil rights enforcement provisions of the Crime Control Act differ from those in Title VI?

Yes. The civil rights enforcement provisions of the Crime Control Act are different from those in Title VI, but they are similar to the provisions of the Revenue Sharing Act in that they *require* investigations, determinations of noncompliance or compliance, and suspension and termination of funding—all within set time periods.

How broad are the protections of the Crime Control Act?

Very broad. Although it applies only to the recipients of LEAA funding (*e.g.*, nearly all police departments and corrections agencies), the act broadly prohibits all forms of discrimination, specifically including employment discrimination, on grounds of race, color, and national origin, in any department or agency which receives LEAA funding.[42] There is no exemption, as there is in Title VI, for employment discrimination.

How does the LEAA initiate civil rights enforcement?

Although there are a number of triggers which will initiate enforcement,[43] one is particularly relevant here. An administrative charge of discrimination against a recipient filed by or on behalf of a person alleging discrimination will initiate an investigation. The investigation must be completed and a determination made by the LEAA, normally within 180 days after the filing of the administrative charge.[44]

As with the Revenue Sharing Act, there is no prescribed form for the administrative charge of discrimination; a letter is sufficient. It should fully describe the nature of the discrimination, and should state the name and address of the law-enforcement agency which has engaged in the discrimination. The letter need not be sworn to, but it should be signed. It must be filed within one year of the date on which the discrimination occurred, unless the LEAA determines that there is good cause for investigating a charge alleging older discrimination.[45] Filing is accomplished by mailing the letter to the compliance office: Office of Civil Rights Compliance, Law Enforcement Assistance Administration, U.S. Department of Justice, 633 Indiana Avenue, N.W., Washington, D.C. 20531. Once the LEAA receives the charge, it must investigate the matter and make a determination.

Before finding a violation of the Crime Control Act, does the LEAA have to make a finding of *intentional* discrimination?

No. The legislative history of the Crime Control Act makes clear that "the standards of Title VII of the Civil Rights Act of 1964 apply"[46]—that is, proof of discriminatory intent is not required. The LEAA's regulations incorporate this standard of discriminatory effect.[47]

What happens once the LEAA makes a determination that a recipient has engaged in discrimination?

At this stage there are a number of mandatory steps the LEAA must take, all within specified time periods, and all leading to the suspension or termination of LEAA funding. For example, after a formal determination has been made, the LEAA must suspend all funding unless the recipient comes into compliance or unless the recipient convinces an administrative law judge that it is "likely" to prove nondiscrimination at a full administrative law hearing.[48]

Once a discriminated-against person has filed a timely administrative charge with the LEAA, there is nothing else for that person to do. But a follow-up letter to the LEAA might help to speed its investigation.

Does the LEAA do a good job investigating charges and making determinations of discrimination?

Yes and no. In recent years, the LEAA has improved upon its past failure to engage in civil rights enforcement. But it still acts too slowly, and it does not fully comply with the requirements set forth in the Crime Control Act.

If the LEAA fails to act vigorously, or if an individual wishes to take action against the recipient prior to the completion of the LEAA investigation, etc., is there anything that the person can do?

Yes. The Crime Control Act creates an express cause of action pursuant to which an individual may sue the recipient directly.[49] Such a lawsuit can be filed, however, only after the administrative charge has been filed with the LEAA for a period of sixty days.[50]

If a person has been discriminated against by a recipient of LEAA funding, is it a good idea to file an administrative charge with the LEAA?

Absolutely yes! Like the civil rights provisions of the Revenue Sharing Act, the civil rights provisions of the Crime Control Act create a very effective remedy to force the elimination of discrimination. In fact, since most recipients of LEAA funding also receive revenue sharing funding, any individual discriminated against by a state or local law enforcement agency also should file an administrative charge with the Office of Revenue Sharing.

NOTES

1. United States v. Chicago, 549 F.2d 415, 448 (7th Cir. 1977) (Pell, J., dissenting), *cert. denied*, 434 U.S. 875 (1978).
2. 109 CONG. REC. 11161 (June 19, 1963).
3. 42 U.S.C. §§2000d *et seq.*
4. 31 U.S.C. §§1242 *et seq.*
5. 42 U.S.C. §3766(c).
6. United States v. Chicago, 549 F.2d 415, 447 (7th Cir. 1977) (Pell, J., dissenting), *cert. denied*, 434 U.S. 875 (1978).

7. Although the Bill of Rights (which applies to the federal government) nowhere contains a guarantee of equal protection of the laws, the courts consistently have applied equal-protection principles through the due-process clause of the Fifth Amendment. *E.g.*, Bolling v. Sharpe, 347 U.S. 497 (1954).
8. Norwood v. Harrison, 413 U.S. 455 (1973).
9. Coffey v. State Educ. Fin. Comm'n, 296 F.Supp. 1389 (S.D. Miss. 1969), and cases cited at 1390 n.1.
10. Pitts v. Department of Revenue for Wisconsin, 333 F.Supp. 662 (E.D. Wis. 1971).
11. Green v. Kennedy, 309 F.Supp. 1127 (D.D.C. 1970) (three-judge court), and Green v. Connally, 330 F.Supp. 1150 (D.D.C. 1971) (three-judge court), *aff'd sub nom.* Coit v. Green, 404 U.S. 997 (1971).
12. McGlotten v. Connally, 338 F.Supp. 448 (D.D.C. 1972) (three-judge court).
13. NLRB v. Mansion House Center Management Corp., 473 F.2d 471 (8th Cir. 1973).
14. *E.g.*, Arlington Heights v. Metropolitan Dev. Corp., 429 U.S. 252 (1977); Washington v. Davis, 426 U.S. 229 (1976).
15. Simon v. Eastern Kentucky Welfare Rights Org., 426 U.S. 26 (1976).
16. 110 CONG. REC. 6544.
17. 42 U.S.C. §2000d.
18. 42 U.S.C. §2000d-4.
19. 42 U.S.C. §2000d-3.
20. 42 U.S.C. §2000d-1.
21. Executive Order 11764. The Attorney General's coordinating regulations are at 28 C.F.R. §§42.401 *et seq.*
22. Lau v. Nichols, 414 U.S. 563, 568 (1974) (emphasis in original). *See also, e.g.*, HEW's implementing regulation, 45 C.F.R. §80.3(b)(2).
23. Regents of the Univ. of California v. Bakke, 438 U.S. 265 (1978).
24. Washington v. Davis, 426 U.S. 229 (1976).
25. 42 U.S.C. §2000d-1.
26. *Id.*
27. Adams v. Richardson, 480 F.2d 1159, 1163 n.4 (D.C. Cir. 1973) (*en banc*).
28. *E.g.*, Uzzell v. Friday, 547 F.2d 801 (4th Cir. 1977), *vacated on other grounds*, 438 U.S. 912 (1978); Chambers v. Omaha Pub. School Dist., 536 F.2d 222 (8th Cir. 1976); Serna v. Portales Mun. Schools, 497 F.2d

1147 (10th Cir. 1974). *Cf.* Cannon v. University of Chicago, 99 S.Ct. 1946, 60 L.Ed.2d 560 (1979).
29. *E.g.,* NAACP v. Wilmington Med. Center, 426 F.Supp. 919 (D. Del. 1977); Johnson v. County of Chester, 413 F.Supp. 1299 (E.D. Pa. 1976); Mendoza v. Lavine, 412 F.Supp. 1105 (S.D.N.Y. 1976).
30. *See, e.g.,* the massive lawsuit under Title VI against HEW, Adams v. Richardson, 351 F.Supp. 636 (D.D.C. 1972), *supplemental order,* 356 F.Supp. 92 (D.D.C. 1973), *aff'd per curiam, en banc,* 480 F.2d 1159 (D.C. Cir. 1973), *supplemental order on remand, sub nom.* Adams v. Weinberger, 391 F.Supp. 269 (D.D.C. 1975). *Cf.* Gautreaux v. Romney, 448 F.2d 731 (7th Cir. 1971).
31. 31 U.S.C. §§1242 *et seq.*
32. 31 U.S.C. §1242(a)(1).
33. Omitted from the text is any discussion of one of the primary triggers initiating civil-rights enforcement. This trigger concerns the receipt by the Office of Revenue Sharing of a "holding" of discrimination rendered by a federal court, state court, or federal administrative agency. Once such a holding against a recipient is received, the Office of Revenue Sharing automatically must begin its procedures for suspending and terminating all revenue sharing to the recipient. *See, generally,* 31 U.S.C. §1242.
34. 31 U.S.C. §1242(c)(4) and 31 U.S.C. §1245.
35. United States v. Chicago, 549 F.2d 415, 442 (7th Cir. 1977), *cert. denied,* 434 U.S. 875 (1978). *See also* the pertinent regulation promulgated by the Office of Revenue Sharing, 31 C.F.R. §51.53(e).
36. 31 U.S.C. §1242(c)(4).
37. These procedures and time limits are set forth in full at 31 U.S.C. §1242.
38. 31 U.S.C. §1244(a) & (b).
39. 31 U.S.C. §1244(d).
40. United States v. Chicago, 549 F.2d 415 (7th Cir. 1977), *cert. denied,* 434 U.S. 875 (1978).
41. 42 U.S.C. §3766(c).
42. 42 U.S.C. §3766(c)(1).
43. Omitted from the text is any discussion of one of the primary triggers initiating civil rights enforcement. Whenever LEAA receives notice of a "finding" of discrimination made by a federal or state court or by a federal or state agency after a hearing, LEAA automatically must begin its procedures for suspending and terminating all

LEAA funding to the recipient. *See, generally,* 42 U.S.C. §3766(c)(2). Additionally, whenever the Attorney General files a pattern-and-practice discrimination lawsuit against a recipient, LEAA automatically must suspend funding to the recipient forty-five days after the lawsuit was filed, unless the recipient obtains a preliminary injunction enjoining the suspension. 42 U.S.C. §3766(c)(3) and 42 U.S.C. §3766(c)(2)(E).
44. 28 C.F.R. §42.205.
45. 28 C.F.R. §42.205(b).
46. CONFERENCE REPORT, H.R. REP. No. 94-1723, 94th Cong., 2d Sess., at 32 (Sept. 29, 1976).
47. 28 C.F.R. §42.203.
48. 42 U.S.C. §3766(c)(2) and 28 C.F.R. §42.210–16.
49. 42 U.S.C. §3766(c)(4).
50. *Id.*

VIII

Jury Selection and Trials

Racial discrimination in the administration of justice has been chronic. Not only have physical facilities such as courtrooms and prisons and jails been segregated, but minority members were traditionally deemed not competent to serve on juries, were denied employment in law enforcement, and because of limited opportunities for education, had no chances to become members of the bar, judges, or prosecutors. The inevitable consequence of all-white justice was that racial minorities were not simply denied the protection of the law, they were frequently its victims.

This chapter will focus primarily on discrimination in jury selection and trials, for it is through the institution of trial by jury that citizens have an opportunity to exercise the ultimate control over the administration of justice and insure its fairness.

What are the basic federal laws which protect minorities against discrimination in the administration of justice?

Minorities are protected against discrimination in the administration of justice by the Sixth Amendment, which guarantees a fair and impartial trial; by the Fourteenth Amendment, which prohibits intentional discrimination by public officials; by a Reconstruction-era statute making it a crime to exclude any person from jury service because of race or color;[1] by the Federal Jury Selection and Service Act of 1968, which prohibits racial discrimination in federal jury selection;[2] and by a provision of the Civil Rights Act of 1968 making it a crime willfully to interfere with any person who has served as a juror.[3]

CONSTITUTIONAL PROTECTION AGAINST DISCRIMINATION IN THE ADMINISTRATION OF JUSTICE

How are juries chosen?

Jury selection varies from jurisdiction to jurisdiction, but generally involves several common, distinct steps. Selection officials, or jury commissioners, meet periodically and compile master lists of persons in the jurisdiction eligible to serve on juries. Eligibility is variously defined, but includes those who meet age, residency, and other requirements and are free of any specified disability, such as felony conviction, insanity, or physical infirmity. Selection laws also allow exemptions which may be claimed by individuals who have hardships or hold critical employment. In compiling the master lists, the commissioners typically consult voter rolls, telephone directories, etc., or even add the names of their personal acquaintances. The names on the master lists are then placed in separate boxes or wheels for grand and trial jury, from which they are drawn and placed on lists, or venires, as jurors are needed for particular terms of court. Finally, the parties to a lawsuit are permitted to "strike" a juror from the venire by asking the court to excuse persons for prejudice or other cause, or excusing a predetermined number peremptorily for no stated cause at all.

Does the Constitution protect against racial discrimination in jury selection?

Yes. Perhaps no right of minorities has been more constitutionally protected, at least in theory, than the right to be free of racial discrimination in jury selection. As early as 1880, the Supreme Court reversed the conviction of a black man by a West Virginia court because state law had disqualified blacks from sitting on his jury.[4] The disqualification was found to be stigmatizing to the defendant and "a stimulant to that race prejudice which is an impediment to securing . . . equal justice" in violation of the Fourteenth Amendment.[5]

Discrimination in jury selection also offends the Sixth and Fourteenth Amendment right to representative juries drawn from a cross-section of the community and the right of all citizens to be considered on a basis of equality for jury duty.[6] Not only are those eligible for jury service found in every stratum of society, but the jury is a democratic institution deriving its legitimacy from the fact that it is representative of the community. To allow the exclusion of racial minorities would tend to establish the jury as an instrument of the racially privileged and to that extent would undermine it as an institution of democratic government.

Is discrimination which falls short of total exclusion also prohibited by the Fourteenth Amendment?

Yes. The early jury cases, such as the one from West Virginia, involved total exclusion, but later decisions make clear that any purposeful discrimination against minorities in jury selection violates the Fourteenth Amendment. Examples of discriminatory practices found to be unconstitutional include the token inclusion or restriction of the number of minority persons on lists of persons eligible for jury duty;[7] the selection of jurors from segregated tax digests;[8] placing the names of black and white jurors on different colored tickets so that race could be identified prior to juror selection;[9] assigning blacks to special jury panels;[10] and, placing blacks at the end of jury lists so that they would be called last, if at all.[11]

Does underrepresentation of minorities in jury selection violate the Fourteenth Amendment, if there is no direct proof of individual acts of discrimination by selection officials?

Yes. Even in the absence of proof of individual acts of discrimination, a prima facie case of violation of the Fourteenth Amendment may be shown by proof that the selection procedures employed resulted in substantial underrepresentation of a racial minority.[12] The assumption is that if the disparity is sufficiently large, it likely did not occur because of accident or chance, but race or other class-related factors played a part in selection. The prima facie case, or presumption of intentional racial discrimination, is enhanced if selection procedures allow for the exercise of subjective judgment by selection officials or are otherwise susceptible to abuse.[13]

How large must a disparity be to violate the Fourteenth Amendment?

In one leading case, Swain v. Alabama,[14] the Supreme Court indicated that a disparity as great as 10 percent between blacks in the population and blacks summoned for jury duty would not prove a prima facie case of unconstitutional underrepresentation. Conversely, the case has generally been read to mean that disparities in excess of 10 percent would be unconstitutional.[15] *Swain* has been criticized both for tolerating a relatively large disparity and for the formula it used for calculating underrepresentation. This is called the absolute deficiency standard, by which the percent of blacks summoned was merely subtracted from the percentage of blacks in the population presumptively eligible for jury duty. This standard may be an acceptable measure where the percent of the group in the general population is relatively large. However, it does not give a true measure of underrepresentation when the excluded group is small. For example, if the excluded group were 20 percent of the population and 10 percent of those summoned for jury duty, the absolute deficiency would be only 10 percent, whereas in fact the group would be underrepresented by one-half.

To meet the limitations of the absolute deficiency standard, some courts have used a comparative deficiency test for measuring underrepresentation, by which the absolute disparity is divided by the proportion of the population comprising the specified category.[16] Using the figures in the example above, the comparative deficiency test would yield a 50 percent underrepresentation of minorities. The courts that have used the comparative deficiency standard have not adopted a maximum tolerable deviation similar to the one in *Swain*.

The Supreme Court has also referred to, without adopting, a third method of calculating underrepresentation in jury selection, the statistical significance test.[17] The test measures representativeness by calculating the probability of a disparity occurring by chance in a random drawing from the population. If the probability is low, the conclusion is warranted that the disparity did not occur by chance but was caused by intentional discrimination. The statistical significance test involves relatively complicated calculations of probabilities and standard deviations, and must generally be done by an expert statistician.

In summary, the courts have not adopted a single mathematical formula or standard for measuring underrepresentation in all jury selection cases. Instead, the courts have looked at the particular facts of each case, taking into account the size of the minority group relative to the general population and other relevant factors, in order to develop a distortion-free picture of the group's participation in jury selection and to determine whether a prima facie case of exclusions has been made.

Can a prima facie showing of discrimination in jury selection be rebutted?

Yes. Once a prima facie case of discrimination is established, selection officials then have the burden of proving that selection procedures were racially neutral. Mere protestations of good faith that no discrimination, intentional or otherwise, was practiced are not sufficient to rebut a prima facie case.[18] Otherwise, the right to equal service upon juries would be illusory, for public officials can hardly be expected to admit to violations of the law. Neither the administrative convenience of jury commissioners nor their subjective notions about who might be willing to serve have been found adequate to overcome a prima facie case on the theory that officials have a duty not to pursue a course which operates in fact to exclude minorities.[19] Rebuttal might be made, however, by showing that the underrepresented group was not proportionately available or eligible for jury duty because of age or similar disqualification.

Is the fact that some jury selection officials are members of a racial minority enough to overcome a prima facie case of discrimination?

No. Because human behavior and motivation are complex, the courts will not presume as a matter of law that members of racial minorities will not discriminate against other members of their own group. In Castaneda v. Partida,[20] for example, a jury discrimination case from Texas, the Supreme Court ruled that a prima facie case of exclusion of Mexican-Americans was not rebutted, even though three of the five jury commissioners were Mexican-American, the judge who appointed the commissioners and later presided over the defendant's trial was Mexican-American, both grand and trial juries included Mexican-Americans, and a majority of local elected officials were Mexican-American. The Court refused to assume without evidence that where a minority was in fact the "governing majority" that no discrimination could exist, and concluded that the only way discriminatory intent could be rebutted was "with evidence in the record about the way in which the commissioners operated and their reasons for doing so."[21]

Which racial minorities are protected from discrimination in jury selection?

In order to claim the protection of the Fourteenth Amendment in jury selection, the group in question must establish that it is a recognizable, distinct class, singled out for different treatment under the laws, as written or applied. Applying this test, the Supreme Court has found blacks and Mexican-Americans to be clearly identifiable racial classes.[22] Lower federal and state courts have found other racial groups entitled to equal protection status including Puerto Ricans,[23] "non-Caucasians,"[24] Indians,[25] and those with "Spanish-sounding names."[26]

Are jury laws constitutional if they require the selection of persons for jury duty who are "upright and intelligent," or are of "good character and sound judgment"?

Yes. The charge has been made that subjective standards for jury selection allow officials to give effect to their beliefs that racial minorities are generally inferior to whites, and less likely to measure up to the statutory requirements,[27] but the Supreme Court has held such laws to be constitutional.[28] The Court reasoned that the statutes do not refer to race and are capable of being administered on a nondiscriminatory basis. While the use of such laws in fact to exclude minorities is plainly prohibited, the statutes themselves are not unconstitutional merely because they vest a certain amount of discretion in selection officials.

May jury commissioners impose their own standards, in addition to or different from those set out by applicable statutes, in selecting jurors?

No. Selection officials may not use standards different from those prescribed by law in selecting jurors, even though their motives may be to choose "the best" jurors or excuse people for whom service would be inconvenient.[29] They are required, rather, to comply strictly with applicable laws, both as to selection procedures and substantive standards.

May jury commissioners use source lists for jurors, such as voter registration or tax lists, which underrepresent minorities?

Yes and no. No source list may be used for juror selection which itself is discriminatory or which fails reasonably to reflect a cross-section of the population.[30] Thus, the use of segregated tax digests in drawing grand and trial jurors has been held to be unconstitutional.[31] By the same token, use of voter registration lists from which minorities have been excluded should also be unconstitutional. However, without exception the courts have approved the use of voter lists, either as the sole or primary source for jurors, even though they underrepresent minorities and even in jurisdictions in which there has been a long history of discrimination in registering and voting.[32] The justification for use of voter lists has been the practical one, that in spite of their deficiencies, they are probably the most broadly based lists available. That justification does not, however, explain why multiple or supplementary lists should not be required where voter lists are in fact underrepresentative.

Is discrimination in jury selection still a significant problem?

Yes. In many jurisdictions, minorities remain chronically underrepresented in the jury system. Because selection procedures are complex, they allow for the exploitation, deliberate or otherwise, of the historic disadvantages of the minority community, such as lower rates of voter registration and the entire heritage of separate but equal. Discrimination can occur at any step in the selection process, whether in choosing source lists, determining eligibility or granting exemptions, compiling master lists, or even as we have seen, in selecting names from the box or wheel and assigning persons to particular venires. Although the law of nondiscrimination in jury selection has always been plain, the continuing and steady stream of jury litigation is tribute to the enduring problem of racial discrimination in this crucial phase of the administration of justice.

How are constitutional challenges raised to discrimination in jury selection?

Challenges to discriminatory jury selection practices may be raised in affirmative civil suits under the Fifth or Fourteenth Amendments by those who have been excluded from jury service because of their minority status,[33] by potential parties in civil cases who desire representative cross-sectional juries,[34] as well as by criminal defendants, black and white, at their trials or in postconviction proceedings. Although no court has expressly so held, members of majority groups included on jury lists should also have standing to complain of exclusion of racial minorities because of the unequal burden of jury service such practices cast upon them.

What is the remedy for discrimination in jury selection?

Parties in civil suits who prevail in affirmative lawsuits are entitled to declaratory and injunctive relief prohibiting continued discrimination and requiring selection officials to recompile constitutional jury lists that adequately represent a cross-section of the community.[35] Attorneys' fees are authorized for prevailing parties against state defendants.[36] Criminal defendants who prove racial discrimination in selection of their juries are entitled to have the indictments against them dismissed and their convictions, if any, reversed.[37] They may, however, be reindicted and retried, but only by procedures which conform to constitutional requirements.[38]

In recompiling jury lists to remedy past discrimination, how close must the percentages be between minority members eligible to serve on juries and those actually on the master jury lists?

The Supreme Court has not adopted a specific mathematical formula, but has said that, in correcting past underrepresentation, the courts have not merely the power but the duty to render a decree which will so far as possible eliminate the discriminatory effects of the past.[39] Lower federal courts in implementing this directive have rejected the argument based upon *Swain* v. *Alabama* that a 10 percent disparity is tolerable in a remedial list, drawing a distinction between proving discrimination in the first instance and measuring the adequacy of a remedy for discrimination once it has been found to exist.[40] Accordingly, selection officials are held to a very high standard of comparability between population percentages and those on jury lists in correcting past underrepresentation.[41] Unless there is some compelling reason why such a high degree of comparability cannot be achieved, there seems no reason to tolerate any deviation at all.

Is a criminal defendant required to show actual prejudice to be entitled to a new trial where racial minorities have been excluded or underrepresented in grand or trial jury selection?

No. The Supreme Court has held that due process is denied by circumstances that create the likelihood or the appearance of bias in the trial of a case.[42] Moreover, illegal jury-selection procedures cast such doubt on the integrity of the whole judicial process that convictions secured in violation of constitutional selection norms may not stand, irrespective of a showing of actual prejudice in a particular case.[43]

Is there any particular time during a criminal proceeding when the issue of jury discrimination must be raised?

Yes. Great care should be taken in criminal cases to raise the issue of discrimination promptly. In federal prosecutions, Rule 12(b)(2) of the Federal Rules of Criminal Procedure requires that all challenges to the grand jury be raised by motion prior to trial. Otherwise, if the motion is made after trial, the defendant is deemed to have waived objection except for "cause shown." Cause is a technical term which means that the defendant had a legally valid excuse for not objecting, such as the incompetence or physical incapacity of his attorney. In addition to showing cause, however, the defendant must also show the case was actually prejudiced by the discrimination in grand jury selection.[44] Since jurors are not likely to admit that they voted in a prejudicial way, it is generally impossible to prove actual prejudice. As a practical matter the issue of discrimination in grand jury selection cannot be raised after trial. Many states have procedural rules comparable to the federal rule, and they have been held constitutional.[45]

Challenges to trial juries are not specifically covered by Rule 12 and may be raised after trial or in post-conviction proceedings, unless a defendant has deliberately bypassed applicable procedures or knowingly and deliberately elected not to raise the jury issue for some reason of trial strategy.[46] Although the government has the burden of showing that a criminal defendant waived the fundamental constitutional right to a representative jury, the courts have become increasingly hostile to attempts by defendants to raise the issue of jury discrimination for the first time after trial.[47]

Are such courtroom practices as segregated seating and refusing to use courtesy titles when addressing blacks permissible?

No. Segregation in seating and other discriminatory courtroom practices such as referring to black witnesses and defendants solely by their first names violate equal protection under the Fourteenth Amendment.[48]

May race ever be considered in determining guilt or sentence?

No. Historically, state laws made race a factor in assessing guilt or in determining sentence. During the days of Jim Crow, it was generally a crime to integrate common carriers, prisons and jails, etc.[49] But in no situation was race more crucial in determining guilt or sentence than in violations of laws regulating sexual conduct and marriage.

Alabama, for example, had one statute which punished fornication between members of the same race by imprisonment for six months, but had another statute punishing fornication between members of different races by imprisonment for two to seven years. The statutory scheme was initially upheld in 1883 by the Supreme Court on the grounds that all persons, black or white, who committed violations were punished the same.[50] Eighty-one years later, however, the Court concluded that such a narrow view of equal protection had been "swept away" and invalidated a Florida statute which made it a crime for an interracial couple to live in and occupy the same room at night.[51] The Court found no compelling justification for the racial classification and held it to be invidious discrimination forbidden by the Fourteenth Amendment. Subsequently, the Court struck down Virginia's miscegenation statutes (which made interracial marriage a crime) on the grounds that mere equal application of a racial classification was not enough to remove it from the reach of the Fourteenth Amendment, and that the definition of criminal conduct could not be made to turn on the color of a person's skin.[52] Many state criminal statutes embodying racial classifications remain on the statute books, but there is no doubt that they would be declared unconstitutional if challenged today.

The problem of racial discrimination in discretionary sentencing, as opposed to racial classifications written into the law, is more difficult to remedy. Race has often made the difference in sentences handed down in cases involving black defendants and white victims. The most documented instance of the discriminatory imposition of sentencing is use of the death penalty against blacks for the crime of rape. Although more than half of all convicted rapists are white, of 455 men executed for rape since 1930, 405 (nearly 90 percent) have been black.[53] During the same period, blacks have comprised 76 percent of those executed for robbery, 83 percent for assault by a life prisoner, and 100 percent of those executed for burglary. Of all persons executed since 1930, more than 50 percent have been black. Not only have greater numbers of blacks been executed for crimes, but the rate of execution for blacks exceeds the proportion of capital crimes committed by blacks. No court, however, has ever held that such a statistical showing would render unconstitutional the death penalty in a given case.[54] Of course, direct proof that sentence was imposed intentionally because of race would constitute reversible error.

STATUTORY PROTECTION AGAINST DISCRIMINATION IN JURY SELECTION

Do any federal criminal statutes specifically protect minorities from discrimination in jury selection?

Yes. An early federal criminal statute, enacted in 1875, makes it a crime for any person charged with any duty in selecting or summoning jurors, to exclude persons from jury service in any state or federal court because of race or color.[55] The penalty for violation of the act is a fine of not more than $5000.

A second criminal statute enacted as part of the Civil Rights Act of 1968 makes it a crime for any person willfully to interfere with another who has served as a juror.[56]

Have the criminal laws against jury discrimination been effectively enforced?

No. In spite of the volume of jury litigation in the courts and the admitted discrimination that has occurred against minorities, there has only been one reported prosecution under the 1875 Act, that of a Virginia state judge in 1878 who refused to consider blacks for jury duty in his court.[57] In that case, the Supreme Court sustained the indictment and found the act to be a proper exercise of congressional power under the Fourteenth Amendment to protect the right to an impartial jury trial by jurors "indifferently selected" without discrimination because of their color.[58]

Are there any federal civil statutes designed specifically to protect minorities from discrimination in jury selection?

Yes. The Federal Jury Selection and Service Act of 1968 (Federal Jury Act) declares it to be national policy that all litigants have the right to grand and trial juries in the federal courts selected at random from a fair cross-section of the community, and that all citizens have the opportunity for consideration for jury service.[59] In furtherance of that policy, the act prohibits exclusion of any person from service upon grand and trial juries in federal courts on account of race, color, religion, sex, national origin, or economic status.[60] Each federal trial court is required to devise a written plan for random selection of jurors designed to achieve the statute's objectives of representativeness.[61] No plan may be put into operation until it has been reviewed and approved by a panel of the members of the judicial council of the circuit and the chief judge of the district whose plan is being reviewed, or his or her designee.[62]

What general provisions must be included in jury plans required to be adopted by the Federal Jury Act?

The selection plans devised under the Federal Jury Act must provide for establishment of a jury commission, or authorize the clerk of court to manage the jury selection process. They must specify whether jurors are to be selected from voter registration lists or lists of actual voters, and whether any other additional source of names is to be used to insure that a representative cross-section of the community is chosen. Detailed procedures must be specified to ensure random selection of a fair cross-section, including provision for the excuse of individuals for whom service would entail "undue hardship or extreme inconvenience," and exemption of those "in the public interest," such as members of fire or police departments or the Armed Forces.[63] Through use of qualification forms mailed to those who have been randomly selected, a "qualified jury wheel" must be prepared containing the names of all those determined to be eligible and not excused or exempted from jury duty.[64] Persons are required to be publicly drawn at random from the qualified jury wheel, assigned to grand and trial jury panels, and summoned for service.

Can persons be required to give their race in responding to federal juror questionnaires?

No. The Federal Jury Act provides, however, that the forms sent to prospective jurors elicit such information as address, age, occupation, etc., as well as race.[65] The purpose of gathering racial data is solely to aid in the enforcement of nondiscrimination in jury selection and has no bearing on an individual's qualification for jury service. Accordingly, each juror questionnaire must contain words clearly informing the person that the furnishing of any information with respect to race or national origin is not a prerequisite to qualification for jury service and need not be furnished if the person finds it objectionable to do so.[66]

Is there a constitutional, as opposed to a statutory, requirement that juries be randomly selected in addition to representing a cross-section of the community?

No. Random selection is required for federal juries by the Federal Jury Act, but there is no separate, constitutional requirement that either federal or state juries be randomly selected.[67]

How is the Federal Jury Act enforced?

The Federal Jury Act is enforced by parties to federal trials and by the Attorney General.[68] Either may file motions in civil or criminal cases to dismiss or stay the proceedings on the grounds of "substantial failure" to comply with the provisions of the act.[69] The motion must be accompanied by a sworn statement of facts describing the failure to comply and must be filed before the voir dire (examination of jurors) begins, or within seven days after the noncompliance was discovered or could have been discovered by the exercise of diligence, whichever is earlier. Great care must be taken to follow the procedures prescribed, for they are the only means by which a party may challenge a jury on the grounds that it was not selected in conformity with the act. The absolute insistence by the courts on strict and complete compliance with procedural requirements has inevitably resulted in hardships to individual litigants who did not know until after their trials that selection officials had not complied with the act.[70]

Are all failures of selection officials to comply with the Federal Jury Act and local selection plans deemed substantial and thus unlawful?

No. Mere technical violations of the act or those that involved good faith efforts to comply and which do not affect the random nature or objectivity of the selection process and which do not frustrate the goals of the act are not regarded as "substantial." [71] Thus, a grand jury selection in which the drawing took place in a room in the clerk's office which, though open to the public, contained only clerk personnel was not deemed a substantial failure to comply with the act's requirement that jurors be "publicly" drawn from the jury wheel.[72]

What kinds of failures in compliance with the Federal Jury Act have been regarded as substantial?

In one case,[73] a district court in Georgia had a rule that if there was an unexpected shortage of trial jurors drawn from the qualified jury wheel, the deficiency could be made up by asking jurors who had served at the previous term of court to volunteer for additional service. The court of appeals declared the policy to be in violation of the Federal Jury Act, on the grounds that a volunteer was quite the opposite of a person selected at random.

In another case,[74] the failure of selection officials in Guam to require prospective jurors to answer questions in the juror questionnaire was deemed a substantial failure to comply with the act, requiring dismissal of an indictment. The procedures used were found to create a serious risk that jurors selected were not proficient enough in English to understand the proceedings and did not represent a fair cross-section of the community.

In addition to showing substantial noncompliance with the Federal Jury Act, must a challenger also show prejudice or show that the violation tended to exclude some racial group?

No. Once it had been established that selection officials failed substantially to conform to the requirements of the Federal Jury Act, it is not necessary that the challenger show any actual or specific prejudice to his or her case.[75] Congress, in passing the act, was more concerned that regular procedures be established to ensure that juries were representative than that individual challengers show actual prejudice arising from statutory violations.[76] Thus, a departure from the statutory scheme that affects randomness is a distinct violation independent of its impact in a particular case.[77]

Does the fact that a jury selection plan has been approved by the federal judicial council of the circuit court foreclose challenge to the plan or the representativeness of jury lists?

No. Approval of a jury selection plan by a circuit-court judicial council does not validate the plan. Not only does the Federal Jury Act itself provide procedures by which a party may attack the validity of a plan, making such an attack proper,[78] but serious constitutional issues would be presented by substituting judicial council approval for judicial determination in a live case presented by adversary parties.[79]

What are the remedies for noncompliance with the Federal Jury Act?

The only remedy for noncompliance provided by the Federal Jury Act is a court order staying the proceedings pending selection of a new grand or trial jury or dismissing the indictment, whichever is appropriate.[80]

Are the challenge procedures in the Federal Jury Act also the sole means of attacking constitutional infirmities in jury selection?

No. The Federal Jury Act specifically provides that nothing in the act shall preclude any person or the United States from pursuing any remedy, civil or criminal, which may be available for the vindication or enforcement of any law prohibiting discrimination on account of race, color, religion, sex, national origin, or economic status in the selection of persons for service on grand or trial juries.[81] Failure to comply with the statute does not, therefore, preclude resort to other remedies to enforce the Constitution's ban on race discrimination.[82]

ADDITIONAL PROTECTIONS AGAINST RACIALLY BIASED TRIALS

Does a defendant have the right to question prospective jurors prior to trial, to determine if they might be racially biased?

Yes, where there is a significant likelihood that racial prejudice might affect the trial. The right, called the right of voir dire, derives from a defendant's entitlement under the Sixth Amendment and under the due process clause of the Fourteenth Amendment to a fair and impartial jury.[83] The right is not, however, absolute. In one case the defendant claimed that South Carolina police officers had framed him on a narcotics charge in retaliation for his civil rights activities. Under the circumstances, the Supreme Court held it was an error not to allow questions to be asked to prospective jurors specifically directed to racial prejudice.[84] But in a later case from Massachusetts in which the only racial factor was assault by a black on a white security guard, the Court held that a general inquiry into the impartiality of potential jurors was sufficient and no specific questions related to race were required to be asked.[85] Two Supreme Court justices in the Massachusetts case dissented, charging that the Court had written "an epitaph" for voir dire questioning of jurors about their possible racial prejudice.[86] The Massachusetts case has in fact severely limited the voir dire rights of minority defendants.

What remedy does a defendant have if a prospective juror admits, or is suspected of having, racial bias?

If a potential juror admits to racial bias which would preclude the rendering of a fair and impartial verdict, then the juror is disqualified from service and must be excused for cause by the court.[87]

Jurors who deny racial bias, or whom the court refuses to excuse for cause, may still be excused by the defendant through exercise of what are called peremptory challenges. Peremptory challenges may be for any or no reason at all, but are designed to rid the jury of real or suspected bias and to ensure that jurors will decide cases solely on the basis of evidence before them.

There is no constitutional right to peremptory challenges, but their use is provided in all jurisdictions and is deeply rooted in our jury system.

Do both sides get peremptory challenges? How many?

Yes, both sides get them. In federal trials in capital cases, each side is entitled to twenty peremptory challenges. In felony cases, the defendant gets ten and the prosecution six peremptory challenges, while in misdemeanor trials each side is entitled to three peremptory challenges.[88] The practice in state trials may be different, and local rules or statutes should be consulted.

May a prosecutor use peremptory challenges to exclude blacks from service on a particular jury panel?

Yes, provided such use does not reflect a pattern and practice of exclusion of blacks in case after case, whatever the circumstances, whatever the crime, and whoever the defendants or victims may be.[89] Parties have traditionally been permitted to exercise peremptory challenges without showing cause or reason, and without being subject to the court's control. Because of its historical status, the courts have been loath to interfere with use of peremptory challenge to exclude blacks, even though it is acknowledged to be a crime to exclude a person from jury service because of race,[90] except in those cases where it constitutes a clear perversion of the cross-sectional ideal. Predictably, the burden of proving misuse of peremptory challenges has been so severe that only one reported case has involved a successful challenge, and it was overturned on appeal.[91] In a second case in which the prosecutor used peremptory challenges to exclude blacks, the conviction was reversed, but not based on the Fourteenth Amendment, but on the basis of Rule

33 of the Federal Rules of Criminal Procedure, which allows the court to grant a new trial "in the interest of justice." [92]

Are there other remedies, in addition to voir dire, for combatting an atmosphere of racial prejudice at trial?

Yes. The courts have recognized that a questioning of potential jurors, no matter how searching and in spite of denials by jurors of prejudice, cannot disclose and neutralize all racial bias jurors might have.[93] Accordingly, defendants may move for a change of venue (place of trial) to a site less affected by prejudice,[94] or request postponement of trial until prejudicial feelings may have subsided. The Supreme Court has also indicated that if a conviction is so permeated by racial feelings "that counsel, jury and judge were swept to the fatal end by an irresistible wave of public passion," it violates constitutional standards of due process and cannot be sustained.[95] Very few cases, however, can be expected to meet such a strict standard for reversal, or to overcome the problem of waiver inherent in going to trial without having sought to neutralize prejudice through a venue change.

What are the standards for determining whether to grant a change of venue?

In a line of cases beginning in 1959, some of them unrelated to race, the Supreme Court has held that a motion to change venue, based upon the Sixth Amendment's guarantee of an impartial jury and due process, should be granted where there is a "probability" or "reasonable likelihood" of prejudice if the trial is held at the scheduled site.[96]

When must a request for change of venue be made?

In federal trials, Rule 21 of the Federal Rules of Criminal Procedure requires that a motion for change of venue be made before the plea is entered or within such "reasonable time thereafter as permitted by the court." In other trials, local rules will govern and should be scrupulously followed to avoid waiver or by-pass.

How can a defendant prove likelihood of prejudice to gain a venue change?

Likelihood of prejudice may be shown by evidence of bias in the community,[97] pretrial publicity such as assertions of guilt in the media,[98] and publication of alleged confessions,[99] prior criminal record,[100] allegations of bad character, and evidence in the case.[101] Pretrial publicity emanating from the government or the prosecution is regarded as particularly prejudicial because of the enhanced credibility likely to be attached to it and because of the prosecution's overriding responsibility of providing a fair trial.[102] Evidence of the absence of prejudice in the surrounding jurisdictions should also be developed to assist the court in locating a bias-free alternate site for trial.

Can anything be done to combat prosecutorial bias in a particular case?

Sometimes. If a law is being enforced to discriminate against persons because of their race, the defendant is entitled to have the prosecution dismissed on the grounds of selective enforcement. This doctrine was developed and applied in a famous case decided in 1886, *Yick Wo v. Hopkins*,[103] involving an ordinance of the City of San Francisco which required all laundries to be located in buildings of brick or stone. Two Chinese, Yick Wo and Wo Lee, requested permission to operate their laundries in wooden buildings, were refused, and were subsequently convicted of violating the ordinance. The facts were, however, that two-hundred others, all Chinese, had similarly been denied permission to operate laundries in wooden buildings, but that eighty others, none of whom were Chinese, had been exempted from compliance with the restriction. Under the circumstances, the Supreme Court held the convictions violated the Fourteenth Amendment and could not stand:

> Though the law itself be fair on its face, and impartial in appliance, yet, if it is applied and administered by public authority with an evil eye and an unequal hand, so as practically to make unjust and illegal discriminations between persons in similar

circumstances, material to their rights, the denial of equal justice is still within the prohibition of the Constitution.[104]

The defense of selective enforcement has been exceedingly difficult to establish, however, because of the requirement of proof of intent to discriminate and because the Supreme Court has more recently held that the conscious exercise of "some selectivity" in enforcement of the law by the prosecution does not establish a constitutional violation.[105]

Will the federal courts ever enjoin state court prosecutions or expunge the record of convictions on the grounds of discriminatory, selective enforcement?

Yes, but only in the most limited of circumstances. Generally, federal courts will not interfere with state criminal proceedings because of federal statutory prohibitions,[106] and because of the three doctrines of "comity," or respect for state court functions, "equity," or avoiding a duplication of legal proceedings where the defendant has an adequate state court remedy, and "federalism," a policy of noninterference with legitimate state activities in recognition of the fact that the country is a union of separate state governments.[107]

During the days of the civil rights movement, federal courts occasionally enjoined state proceedings in extreme cases where the law was clearly being enforced in a discriminatory manner. In one such case, a state prosecution had been brought against a SNCC worker who had assisted blacks in registering to vote in Walthall County, Mississippi.[108] The defendant, John Hardy, whose conduct had been entirely peaceful, was assaulted by the voter registrar and charged by the sheriff with "disturbing the peace and bringing an uprising among the people."[109] The court of appeals, relying upon the Civil Rights Act of 1957[110] prohibiting interference with voting, held that the state proceedings should be enjoined to give the defendant Hardy a chance to prove his allegations that the prosecution was depriving him and other blacks in the county of protected rights. In a similar case, blacks leaving a voter registration meeting in Dallas County, Alabama, were arrested en masse, and charged and prosecuted for "improper license-plate lighting." [111] The court of appeals found that the prosecutions had been brought, not "to eradicate the sinful practice of driving with burned-out license-plate lights," but solely to harass voting workers and interfere with voter registration, purposes prohibited by the Civil Rights Act of 1957.[112] To remedy the violations, the court ordered county officials to return all fines, expunge from the record all arrests and convictions, and reimburse the defendants for the costs, including reasonable attorneys' fees, incurred in defense of the state criminal prosecutions.

Such cases must be regarded as exceptional, however, for the Supreme Court has more recently indicated that when federal courts are asked to enjoin state proceedings, normally they must refuse. The only exception to the rule is where the state prosecution poses a danger of "irreparable loss" that is "both great and immediate." [113] Such a loss must involve more than prosecution under a law that may be unconstitutional but must include bad faith and harassment or other "extraordinary circumstances." [114] As a practical matter, it is prohibitively hard to prove irreparable loss.[115]

Is there any way to remove state prosecutions to the federal courts if it is necessary to protect constitutional rights?

Yes, but the scope of removal has been so narrowed by the Supreme Court as to be almost nonexistent. The present removal statute is a descendant of a portion of the Civil Rights Act of 1866,[116] and provides that any civil or criminal action in a state court may be removed by the defendant to the federal district court where the action is pending when the defendant is denied or cannot enforce in the state court a right under any law providing for the equal civil rights of citizens of the United States. In a series of cases beginning in 1880 and ending in 1906,[117] the Supreme Court established a quite narrow area in which pretrial removal of state prosecutions could be sustained. The cases held essentially that a law providing for equal civil rights referred to in the statute meant a law couched in terms of racial equality, as distinguished from

THE RIGHTS OF RACIAL MINORITIES

a law of general application such as the due process clause of the Fourteenth Amendment, and secondly, that the denial of rights protected by such a law must be manifest in a formal expression of state law. Applying this test, removal was proper in a case in which a black defendant was prosecuted in a state court which excluded blacks from jury service.[118]

After 1906 the Supreme Court did not consider the removal statute again until sixty years later, a principal reason being that an order denying removal, or sending the case back to the state court, could not be appealed after the year 1887.[119] As part of the Civil Rights Act of 1964, however, Congress specifically provided for appeals from orders denying removal to give the federal reviewing courts an opportunity to supervise administration of the removal statute.[120] In a pair of cases decided in 1966, the Supreme Court adopted the earlier construction of the removal statute, consigning it once again nearly to the status of dead letter.

The first of the two cases[121] involved black defendants who sought removal of state prosecutions for trespass growing out of sit-in demonstrations at a Georgia restaurant. The Supreme Court held that the prosecutions could be removed, applying the two pronged test developed in the earlier cases. The defendants showed that the law providing for equal civil rights upon which they relied was the Civil Rights Act of 1964 guaranteeing the equal enjoyment of public accommodations, and that the right was denied or could not be enforced in the courts of the state because the Civil Rights Act of 1964 granted an absolute right not to be prosecuted for seeking access to public accommodations. The defendants had a right, in other words, not even to be brought to trial on trespass charges in the state court. The case was sent back to the federal district court to establish whether or not the defendants had been ordered to leave the restaurant because of their race or some other reason. If the defendants were correct in their allegation that a racial motivation was present, then their right to removal would be clear.

In the second case,[122] however, the Court denied removal, showing the exceedingly narrow range of cases which could be exempted from state prosecution. The defendants were members of a civil rights group engaged in a Mississippi voter registration drive. They satisfied the law providing for equal civil rights requirement by alleging a denial of equal voting rights under the Civil Rights Acts of 1866 and 1964. The Court concluded, however, that the second requirement, that the right involved would be denied or could not be enforced, was not met since neither of the civil rights acts conferred immunity from state prosecution as did the public-accommodations provisions of the Civil Rights Act of 1964, nor did they confer an absolute right for the defendants to engage in the conduct involved, that is, obstructing a public street in connection with voter registration efforts. The Court also held that it was not enough to support removal to prove that the defendants' federal equal civil rights had been illegally and corruptly denied in advance of trial, that the charges were false, or that the defendants would be unable to obtain a fair trial. Removal was proper only in those cases where it could be clearly predicted by reason of the operation of a pervasive and explicit state or federal law, that the protected rights would inevitably be denied by the very act of bringing the defendant to trial in the state court. Such a burden can rarely be carried. The Supreme Court supported the result it reached by observing that federal judges were not permitted "to put their brethren of the state judiciary on trial," and that a contrary holding would revolutionize the relationship of state and federal courts by depriving states of authority to prosecute in certain cases and at the same time dramatically expanding the jurisdiction of the federal courts.[123]

The removal statute was last considered by the court in 1975, but it adhered to its earlier decisions and refused to make any changes in the long-settled interpretation of the provisions of the century-old removal statute.[124]

NOTES

1. 18 Stat. 336, presently codified as 18 U.S.C. §243.
2. 28 U.S.C. §§1861 *et seq.*
3. 18 U.S.C. §245.
4. Strauder v. West Virginia, 100 U.S. 303 (1880).

5. *Id.* at 308.
6. Thiel v. Southern Pacific Co., 328 U.S. 217 (1946); Carter v. Jury Commission, 396 U.S. 320 (1970).
7. Cassell v. Texas, 339 U.S. 282 (1950).
8. Whitus v. Georgia, 385 U.S. 545 (1967).
9. Avery v. Georgia, 345 U.S. 559 (1953).
10. Billingsley v. Clayton, 359 F.2d 13 (5th Cir. 1966).
11. Smith v. Texas, 311 U.S. 128 (1940).
12. Castaneda v. Partida, 430 U.S. 482 (1977).
13. *Id.;* Turner v. Fouche, 396 U.S. 346, 360 (1970); Alexander v. Louisiana, 405 U.S. 625, 630 (1972).
14. 380 U.S. 202 (1965).
15. Foster v. Sparks, 506 F.2d 805, 811-37 (5th Cir. 1975) (appendix to the opinion by Judge Walter P. Gewin).
16. Alexander v. Louisiana, 405 U.S. 625, 629-30 (1972) (using both the absolute and comparative deficiency methods); Stephens v. Cox, 449 F.2d 657 (4th Cir. 1971); Thompson v. Sheppard, 502 F.2d 1389, 1390 n. 1 (5th Cir. 1974) (Brown, J., dissenting); and Berry v. Cooper, 577 F.2d 322, 326 n. 11 (5th Cir. 1978).
17. Castaneda v. Partida, 430 U.S. 482 n. 17 (1977); Whitus v. Georgia, 385 U.S. 545, 552 n. 2 (1967); Alexander v. Louisiana, 405 U.S. 625, 630 n. 9 (1972).
18. Alexander v. Louisiana, 405 U.S. 625, 632 (1972).
19. Hill v. Texas, 316 U.S. 400 (1942); United States v. Zirpolo, 450 F.2d 424 (3rd Cir. 1971).
20. Castaneda v. Partida, 430 U.S. 482 (1977).
21. *Id.* at 500.
22. Strauder v. West Virginia, 100 U.S. 303 (1800); Hernandez v. Texas, 347 U.S. 475 (1954).
23. United States *ex rel.* Leguillou v. Davis, 115 F.Supp. 392 (D.V.I. 1953).
24. United States v. Fujimoto, 105 F.Supp. 727 (D.. Haw. 1952), *cert. denied,* 344 U.S. 852 (1953).
25. State v. Plenty Horse, 184 N.W.2d 654 (1971).
26. Montoya v. Colorado, 141 Colo. 9, 345 P.2d 1062 (1959).
27. Carter v. Jury Commission, 396 U.S. 320 (1970).
28. *Id;* Turner v. Fouche, 396 U.S. 346 (1970).
29. Ballard v. United States, 329 U.S. 187 (1946); Labat v. Bennett, 365 F.2d 698 (5th Cir. 1966). *cert. denied,* 386 U.S. 991 (1967); Rabinowitz v. United States, 366 F.2d 34 (5th Cir. 1966).
30. Brown v. Allen, 344 U.S. 443 (1953).

JURY SELECTION AND TRIALS

31. Whitus v. Georgia, 385 U.S. 545 (1967); Sims v. Georgia, 389 U.S. 404 (1967).
32. Simmons v. United States, 406 F.2d 456 (5th Cir. 1969); Blackwell v. Thomas, 476 F.2d 443 (4th Cir. 1973); Berry v. Cooper, 577 F.2d 322, 328 n. 16 (5th Cir. 1978).
33. Carter v. Jury Commission, 396 U.S. 320 (1970).
34. Peters v. Kiff, 407 U.S. 493 (1972); Taylor v. Louisiana, 419 U.S. 522 (1975).
35. Turner v. Fouche, 396 U.S. 346 (1970); Carter v. Jury Commission, 396 U.S. 320 (1970).
36. 42 U.S.C. §1988.
37. Whitus v. Georgia, 385 U.S. 545 (1967).
38. Hill v. Texas, 316 U.S. 400 (1942).
39. Carter v. Jury Commission, 396 U.S. 320, 340 (1970).
40. Berry v. Cooper, 577 F.2d 322 (5th Cir. 1978).
41. Broadway v. Culpepper, 439 F.2d 125 (5th Cir. 1971); Berry v. Cooper, 577 F.2d 322 (5th Cir. 1978).
42. Tumey v. Ohio, 273 U.S. 510 (1927).
43. Peters v. Kiff, 407 U.S. 493 (1972).
44. Davis v. United States, 411 U.S. 233 (1973).
45. Francis v. Henderson, 425 U.S. 536 (1976).
46. Fay v. Noia, 372 U.S. 391 (1963); Johnson v. Zerbst, 304 U.S. 458 (1938).
47. *Compare* United States *ex rel.* Goldsby v. Harpole, 263 F.2d 71 (5th Cir. 1959), *with* Winters v. Cook, 489 F.2d 174 (5th Cir. 1973).
48. Johnson v. Virginia, 373 U.S. 61 (1963); Hamilton v. Alabama, 376 U.S. 650 (1964). Segregation beyond the courtroom, *i.e.*, in prisons and jails, is also unconstitutional. Lee v. Washington, 390 U.S. 333 (1968). *See* THE RIGHTS OF PRISONERS in this series.
49. Plessy v. Ferguson, 163 U.S. 537 (1896).
50. Pace v. Alabama, 106 U.S. 583 (1883).
51. McLaughlin v. Florida, 379 U.S. 184 (1964).
52. Loving v. Virginia, 388 U.S. 1 (1967).
53. U.S. BUREAU OF PRISONS, NATIONAL PRISONER STATISTICS: CAPITAL PUNISHMENT 1930–1970 (Washington, D.C.: U.S. Department of Justice, 1971).
54. Moorer v. South Carolina, 368 F.2d 458 (4th Cir. 1966); Maxwell v. Bishop, 398 F.2d 138 (8th Cir. 1968).
55. 18 Stat. 336, presently codified at 18 U.S.C. §243.
56. 18 U.S.C. §245.
57. *Ex parte* Virginia, 100 U.S. 339 (1880).

58. *Id.* at 345.
59. 28 U.S.C. §1861.
60. 28 U.S.C. §1862.
61. 28 U.S.C. §1863.
62. 28 U.S.C. §1863(a).
63. 28 U.S.C. §1863(6).
64. 28 U.S.C. §1866(a).
65. 28 U.S.C. §1869(h).
66. For a discussion of disclosure of race on state voter registration forms, see Chapter II.
67. United States v. Kennedy, 548 F.2d 608 (5th Cir. 1977).
68. 28 U.S.C. §1867.
69. 28 U.S.C. §1867(d).
70. United States v. Hawkins, 566 F.2d 1006 (5th Cir. 1978).
71. United States v. Davis, 546 F.2d 583 (5th Cir. 1977); United States v. Evans, 529 F.2d 523 (5th Cir. 1976); United States v. Geelan, 509 F.2d 737 (8th Cir. 1974).
72. United States v. Dalton, 465 F.2d 32 (5th Cir. 1972).
73. United States v. Kennedy, 548 F.2d 608 (5th Cir. 1977).
74. United States v. Okiyama, 521 F.2d 601 (9th Cir. 1975).
75. United States v. Okiyama, 521 F.2d 601 (9th Cir. 1975); United States v. Coleman, 429 F.Supp. 792 (E.D. Mich. 1977).
76. United States v. Armsbury, 408 F.Supp. 1130, 1143 (D. Ore. 1976).
77. United States v. Kennedy, 548 F.2d 608 (5th Cir. 1977).
78. 28 U.S.C. §1867.
79. United States v. Hyde, 448 F.2d 815 (5th Cir. 1971).
80. 28 U.S.C. §1867(d).
81. 28 U.S.C. §1867(e).
82. United States v. Kennedy, 548 F.2d 608 (5th Cir. 1977).
83. Duncan v. Louisiana, 391 U.S. 145 (1968); Irvin v. Dowd, 366 U.S. 717 (1961).
84. Ham v. South Carolina, 409 U.S. 524 (1973).
85. Ristaino v. Ross, 424 U.S. 589 (1976).
86. 424 U.S. at 599.
87. Aldridge v. United States, 283 U.S. 308 (1931).
88. Rule 24(b), Fed. R. Crim. P.
89. Swain v. Alabama, 380 U.S. 202 (1965).
90. United States v. Pearson, 448 F.2d 1207, 1216 (5th Cir. 1971).
91. United States v. Robinson, Crim. No. N–76–63, October

JURY SELECTION AND TRIALS

15, 1976, D. Conn., *vacated,* United States v. Newman, 549 F.2d 240 (2d Cir. 1977).
92. United States v. McDaniels, 370 F.Supp. 298 (E.D. La. 1973).
93. Irvin v. Dowd, 366 U.S. 717 (1961); Rideau v. Louisiana, U.S. 723 (1963).
94. Groppi v. Wisconsin, 400 U.S. 505 (1971).
95. Moore v. Dempsey, 251 U.S. 86, 91 (1923); Shepherd v. Florida, 341 U.S. 50 (1951).
96. Marshall v. United States, 360 U.S. 310 (1959); Estes v. Texas, 381 U.S. 532 (1965); Sheppard v. Maxwell, 384 U.S. 333 (1966).
97. Johnson v. Beto, 469 F.2d 1396 (5th Cir. 1972).
98. Sheppard v. Maxwell, 384 U.S. 333 (1966).
99. Rideau v. Louisiana, 373 U.S. 723 (1963).
100. Marshall v. United States, 360 U.S. 310 (1959).
101. Sheppard v. Maxwell, 384 U.S. 333 (1966).
102. Henslee v. United States, 246 F.2d 190 (5th Cir. 1957).
103. 118 U.S. 356 (1886).
104. *Id.* at 373–74.
105. Oyler v. Boles, 368 U.S. 448, 456 (1962). *See also* United States v. Falk, 479 F.2d 616 (7th Cir. 1973); United States v. Steele, 461 F.2d 1148 (9th Cir. 1972).
106. *E.g.,* 28 U.S.C. §2283, forbidding injunctions against proceedings in a state court, and 28 U.S.C. §2254, forbidding the issuance of habeas corpus unless the petitioner has exhausted state remedies. Civil rights suits under 42 U.S.C. §1983, however, are an exception to the anti-injunction provisions of 28 U.S.C. §2283. Mitchum v. Foster, 407 U.S. 225 (1972).
107. Younger v. Harris, 401 U.S. 37 (1971).
108. United States v. Wood, 295 F.2d 772 (5th Cir. 1961).
109. 295 F.2d at 776.
110. 42 U.S.C. §1971(b).
111. United States v. McLeod, 385 F.2d 734, 742 (5th Cir. 1967).
112. *Id.* at 744.
113. Younger v. Harris, 401 U.S. 37, 46 (1971).
114. *Id.* at 54.
115. Allee v. Medrano, 416 U.S. 802 (1974); Huffman v. Pursue, Ltd., 420 U.S. 592 (1975).
116. 14 Stat. 27, now codified as 28 U.S.C. §1443(1).
117. Strauder v. West Virginia, 100 U.S. 303 (1880); Kentucky v. Powers, 201 U.S. 1 (1906).

118. Strauder v. West Virginia, 100 U.S. 303 (1880).
119. Georgia v. Rachel, 384 U.S. 780, 786 (1966).
120. 28 U.S.C. §1447(d).
121. Georgia v. Rachel, 384 U.S. 780 (1966).
122. Greenwood v. Peacock, 384 U.S. 808 (1966).
123. 384 U.S. at 828.
124. Johnson v. Mississippi, 421 U.S. 213 (1975).

IX

Federal Criminal Statutes Protecting the Rights of Minorities

One of the most melancholy chapters in the history of race relations in the United States has involved the failure of the criminal law to protect the lives and property of minorities. That failure was a predictable consequence of racial exclusion in the justice system discussed earlier, as well as the entire way of life which placed a different valuation on people according to the color of their skin. The law, no matter what its theory, in practice worked first and always to protect the rights of whites, and only thereafter, if at all, to protect the rights of minorities.

Racial violence and terrorism, the ultimate forms of discrimination, have been rampant and often unobstructed by the normal operation of state laws prohibiting criminal misconduct. During the 1880s and 1890s, for example, there were about 100 reported lynchings of blacks every year in the United States. In 1892 there were 155. Lynchings continued briskly over the next twenty years. There were 75 in 1909, 80 in 1910, 63 in 1911, and rarely less than 50 per year from then until 1923.[1]

A lynching in 1922 in Moultrie, Georgia, was all too typical of the times. A black man named Will Anderson was suspected of having attempted a criminal attack on a white woman. Before he could be tried, Anderson was seized by a mob, handcuffed, taken to the scene of the crime, shot, and then dragged behind an automobile. A grand jury was hurriedly convened the next day to investigate the lynching, but the panel adjourned after a few hours because it was unable, it said, to get any evidence upon which to base indictments. The Moultrie *Observer,* the town's only newspaper, soft-pedaled the affair and speculated that the lynch mob was small: "It was pointed out that he was not swung to a tree and that he was shot less than twenty-five times. . . . It was hardly believed that this would have been the way the body would have been found if the crowd that participated had been of the proportion mobs usually assume on such occasions." [2] A local judge condemned the violence, but no person was ever charged or tried for Anderson's death.

There are criminal laws, however, enacted by the Congress specifically to meet the problem of racial violence and related discrimination against minorities. These laws, and their enforcement, will be discussed in the following pages.

RECONSTRUCTION-ERA CRIMINAL STATUTES

Have any federal criminal statutes been enacted to give minorities general protection against racial violence and other forms of discrimination?

Yes. Although under our federal system the states are regarded as having primary responsibility for prosecuting criminal offenses, including those which are racially motivated, Congress did enact two laws during the Reconstruction period to give minorities general protection against violence and discrimination. 18 U.S.C. §242, enacted in 1866, makes it a misdemeanor punishable by fine of not more than $1000 or imprisonment for not more than one year or both, for any person acting "under color of law" willfully to deprive another of any right protected by the Constitution or laws of the United States.[3] Four years later, in 1870, Congress enacted a companion statute, 18 U.S.C. §241, to curb the terrorist activities of organizations such as the Ku Klux Klan and the Knights of the White Camelia, which were becoming increasingly active during the post–Civil War years.[4] Section 241 prohibits conspiracies by two or more persons to injure or intimidate any

FEDERAL CRIMINAL STATUTES

citizen in the exercise of any right protected by the Constitution or laws of the United States. The section also applies if two or more persons go in disguise on the highway or onto the premises of another with the intent to prevent or hinder the free exercise of protected rights. Those convicted may be punished by a fine of not more than $5000 or imprisoned for not more than ten years, or both.

What does "under color of law" mean in Section 242?

"Under color of law" refers to a misuse of power possessed by virtue of state or federal law and made possible because the wrongdoer is clothed with the authority of law.[5] Acts are deemed done under color of law even though they may be themselves violations of the law. Thus, a law enforcement officer who beats a prisoner or turns him over to a lynch mob or fails to protect him from such a mob acts under color of law.[6]

Are private individuals ever subject to prosecution under Section 242?

Yes, if they act under color of law, or if they engage in criminal conduct with others who act under color of law. In one case, for instance, several private individuals conspired during the summer of 1964 with the sheriff and deputy sheriff of Neshoba County, Mississippi, to murder three young men, Michael Schwerner, James Chaney, and Andrew Goodman, who had been taken into custody because of their civil rights activities.[7] As part of the conspiracy, the young men were released at night from the jail in Philadelphia, Mississippi, then later intercepted by eighteen people (including the sheriff, the deputy, and the private individuals), taken from their car, and murdered; their bodies were buried in an earthen dam five miles southwest of the city. All eighteen of the conspirators were indicted and found to be acting under color of law for purposes of prosecution under Section 242. The deputy, Cecil Ray Price, and six others were eventually convicted in federal court and sentenced to six years in prison for depriving the youths of their civil rights. There were never any state convictions, however, for murder or any other state crime.[8]

217

THE RIGHTS OF RACIAL MINORITIES

Is state action also required for prosecution of conspiracies under Section 241?

No. In two cases in 1966, a majority of the Supreme Court indicated, without expressly deciding the question, that Congress clearly had the power to punish all conspiracies that interfere with constitutional rights under Section 241—with or without state action.[9] As one of the justices pointed out, Senator Pool of North Carolina, who introduced Section 241 into Congress, intended the section to apply to the acts of individuals whether they acted as "officers or whether they are acting upon their own responsibility."[10] Then, in a case decided two years later in 1968, the Court simply assumed without lengthy discussion that Section 241 applied to private conspiracies and reversed a trial court that had dismissed indictments against several people who had assaulted blacks seeking to exercise their right to receive service at a restaurant.[11]

What kind of offenses are generally punishable under Sections 241 and 242?

The Supreme Court has made it clear that Sections 241 and 242 do not make all wrongful acts of racial discrimination federal crimes. Only those acts which are "willful" and deprive a person of some right made specific either by the express terms of the Constitution or laws of the United States or by decisions interpreting them are indictable. The requirement of willfulness was elaborated upon in a 1945 case in which a Georgia sheriff bludgeoned a Negro prisoner to death.[12] The sheriff was indicted for violating Section 242 by depriving the prisoner of due process, of a trial by jury, and of the right to be punished in accordance with the law. The indicted sheriff argued that Section 242 contained no ascertainable standard for guilt since the definition of constitutional rights, especially the right to due process, was fluid and subject to interpretation by the judiciary. The Supreme Court ruled that the problem of vagueness was cured by requiring the prosecution to prove willfulness—that is, that the sheriff acted with "the purpose to deprive the prisoner of a constitutional right, e.g., the right to be tried by a court rather than by ordeal."[13]

In addition to prosecutions brought against persons who engaged in police brutality and denied due process, prosecutions have been brought under Sections 241 and 242 for interference with the right to vote,[14] with the right to perfect a homestead,[15] with the right of federal officers to perform their duties,[16] with equal protection under the Fourteenth Amendment, with the full enjoyment of public accommodations, and with the right to interstate travel.[17]

Has the requirement of willfulness for violations of Sections 241 and 242 proved to be an insurmountable barrier to successful prosecution for denial of constitutional rights?

No. Proof of willfulness has not been as difficult to present as it originally appeared. In a subsequent case involving assault of a black prisoner by state law enforcement officers, the Supreme Court held that willfulness could be inferred from the circumstances of the attack and the relationship between the victim and the officers.[18] The fact remains, however, that requiring proof that a defendant acted willfully to deprive one of a specific constitutional right, as opposed to showing that the defendant acted in general with a bad purpose, the standard for most criminal prosecutions, has hampered enforcement of Sections 241 and 242.[19]

Have Sections 241 and 242 been effectively enforced?

Generally, no. Immediately after the Civil War the federal government made a concerted effort to enforce Sections 241 and 242 as well as other civil rights laws enacted for the protection of minorities. A number of prosecutions were brought against persons interfering with the rights of blacks to vote in congressional elections and to be secure in their persons and property.[20] However, only about 20 percent of all prosecutions resulted in actual convictions, while some major decisions severely limited the application of the statutes.[21]

From the turn of the century until 1939, the enforcement of Sections 241 and 242 declined dramatically. Only four cases involving Section 241 reached the Supreme

Court during this period, and none involving Section 242.[22]

In 1939, however, a civil rights section was established in the Department of Justice charged with the duty "to pursue a program of vigilant action in the prosecution of infringement" of civil liberties.[23] More prosecutions were brought under Sections 241 and 242 than during prior years, and the Supreme Court upheld indictments against election officials who made a fraudulent ballot count[24] and who stuffed ballot boxes in federal elections.[25] But the federal policy of enforcement was for the most part cautious and restrained. Indeed, in one of the first of the modern cases arising under Section 242 to reach the Supreme Court, the Justice Department's policy of enforcement was noted to be one of "strict self-limitation" to avoid unnecessary interference by the federal government with the administration of local criminal laws by the states.[26]

CRIMINAL STATUTES PROHIBITING SLAVERY, INVOLUNTARY SERVITUDE, AND PEONAGE

Has Congress made slavery, involuntary servitude, and peonage criminal activities?

Yes. In addition to Sections 241 and 242, which are general prohibitions on unconstitutional conduct, Congress enacted a variety of criminal statutes during Reconstruction prohibiting such specific discriminatory practices as slavery,[27] involuntary servitude (compulsory service of one person to another)[28] and peonage (involuntary servitude with the additional factor of indebtedness of one person to another).[29]

Punishments for violations of these statutes range from fines of $2000 to $10,000, and imprisonment for up to five years.[30]

Are slavery, involuntary servitude, and peonage widespread practices today?

Slavery and involuntary servitude, except in a few isolated cases,[31] no longer exist in this country. Peonage in the form of holding and forcing a person to work to pay off a debt is more common, though admittedly not as widespread as it was during the years following the Civil War, when debt-labor was often little more than a substitute for slavery.[32]

The federal peonage statute, though enacted in 1867, lay dormant throughout the nineteenth century, while many states enacted, and strictly enforced, laws making it a crime for a person to quit work if he owed money to his employer. As a consequence of federal inaction and state enforcement of debt law, the Immigration Commission in 1910 reported that cases of probable peonage had been found in all but two states in the Union.[33] Maine was said to have had the most complete system of peonage in the entire country in its lumber camps.

In 1905, the first case under the antipeonage statute reached the Supreme Court and the statute was held constitutional.[34] A series of subsequent cases struck down state laws in Alabama, Georgia, and Florida that made it a crime for a person to fail to perform work for which he had been paid.[35] In the last of these cases, decided in 1944, the Court reversed the state court conviction of a Negro laborer who had received a $5 advance but failed to perform promised work. The states are free to punish fraud, the Court held, but "no state can make the quitting of work a component of a crime, or make criminal sanctions available for holding unwilling persons to labor."[36] The employer's remedy for failure to perform work for which he has paid was said to be the civil one—suing for breach of contract.

With the demise of state debt-labor statutes, however, and the establishment of the Civil Rights Section of the Department of Justice in 1939, peonage has steadily declined. One of the last reported peonage prosecutions was of a Connecticut chicken farmer in 1962 who imported a Mexican family to work on his farm.[37] Although there was evidence that he threatened his workers with deportation if they failed to fulfill the terms of their work contract, the prosecution was dismissed on the grounds that there was insufficient evidence of the use of law or force in compelling performance, and the Mexicans had not been effectively deprived of their option voluntarily to leave the farm.

Are there any forms of compulsory service that are constitutional?

Yes. Neither the draft,[38] compulsory civilian labor as an alternative to military service,[39] nor hard labor pursuant to a lawful prison sentence[40] violate the Thirteenth Amendment's ban on slavery and involuntary servitude.

MODERN CRIMINAL STATUTES

Has there been any modern legislation imposing criminal penalties for interference with minority rights?

Yes. Congress enacted 18 U.S.C. §245 as part of the Civil Rights Act of 1968[41] providing for criminal penalties for willful interference by force or threat with certain enumerated rights and activities. The statute prohibits anyone, whether or not acting under color of law, from injuring or interfering with one who has voted, campaigned for office, or qualified as an election official; participated in any federal program; applied for or secured federal employment; served as a grand or trial juror; or participated in any program receiving federal financial assistance. The statute also proscribes racial discrimination in public schools and colleges; in state programs; in employment by states, private individuals, or labor unions; in jury duty; in interstate commerce; and in public accommodations. Persons who interfere with interstate commerce during riot or civil disorder are also subject to prosecution, as are those who intimidate others participating in speech and assembly opposing racial discrimination. The penalties for violation of the statute are a fine of not more than $1000 or imprisonment for not more than one year, or both. If bodily injury occurs the fine may be up to $10,000 or imprisonment for not more than ten years, or both, while if death results, imprisonment may be for any term of years or for life.

Has Section 245 been effectively enforced?

No. The sweep of Section 245 appears to be great, but a number of provisions considerably restrict its application. In an obvious attempt to minimize friction resulting from federal prosecution of civil rights offenders, the statute provides that no prosecution may be undertaken except upon the certification in writing of the Attorney General or the Deputy Attorney General that prosecution "is in the public interest and necessary to secure substantial justice." [42] The function of certification may not be delegated. The statute also makes clear that state prosecution of offenses is not preempted and that no law-enforcement officer shall be considered to be in violation of the statute for lawfully carrying out official duties or enforcing the laws of the United States or any state. Finally, the statute places the heavy burden upon the government of proving willfulness and the use of force or threat of force. Given these strictures, and the deference required to be paid to state law enforcement, it is not surprising that there have been few reported prosecutions for violations of Section 245.[43]

What should a person do who believes that another has committed an act made a crime by federal laws prohibiting racial discrimination?

Notify the Department of Justice, Washington, D.C. 20530, and request that it prosecute the alleged offender. The state prosecutor should also be notified, since the offense may be a violation of state law as well.

If an act is a violation of both federal and state criminal laws, may it be prosecuted by both governments?

Yes. The Supreme Court has held that when an act is made a crime by both federal and state governments, it is a separate offense to the peace and dignity of each and may be punished as such.[44] However, the Department of Justice has adopted a policy of not prosecuting individuals previously tried in a state court for offenses involving the same acts, unless there exists "most compelling reasons" and then only after the specific approval of the appropriate Assistant Attorney General has been obtained.[45]

NOTES

1. Emerson, Haber, and Dorsen, *Political and Civil Rights in the United States*, 1356–65 (Little, Brown & Co., Boston, 1967), and sources cited therein.
2. *Moultrie Observer*, July 28, 1922.
3. 14 Stat. 27, enacted as part of the Civil Rights Act of 1866.
4. 16 Stat. 141, enacted as part of the Enforcement Act of 1870.
5. United States v. Price, 383 U.S. 787 (1966); United States v. Classic, 313 U.S. 299 (1941); Screws v. United States, 325 U.S. 91 (1945).
6. Screws v. United States, 325 U.S. 91 (1945); Lynch v. United States, 189 F.2d 476 (5th Cir. 1951).
7. United States v. Price, 383 U.S. 787 (1966).
8. *See also* Williams v. United States, 341 U.S. 97 (1951), holding that a private detective, who held a special police card and who used brutal methods to extract confessions from suspects, acted under color of law and was subject to prosecution under §242.
9. United States v. Guest, 383 U.S. 745, 762, 781–84 (1966), United States v. Price, 383 U.S. 787 (1966).
10. United States v. Price, 383 U.S. 787, 805 (1966).
11. United States v. Johnson, 390 U.S. 563 (1968).
12. Screws v. United States, 325 U.S. 91 (1945).
13. 325 U.S. at 107.
14. United States v. Classic, 313 U.S. 299 (1941).
15. United States v. Waddell, 112 U.S. 76 (1884).
16. United States v. Mason, 213 U.S. 115 (1909).
17. United States v. Guest, 383 U.S. 745 (1966).
18. Williams v. United States, 341 U.S. 97 (1951).
19. Pullen v. United States, 164 F.2d 756 (5th Cir. 1947).
20. *Ex parte* Yarbrough, 110 U.S. 651 (1884); *ex parte* Siebold, 100 U.S. 371 (1880); United States v. Waddell, 112 U.S. 76 (1884); Logan v. United States, 144 U.S. 263 (1892).
21. United States v. Cruikshank, 92 U.S. 542 (1876).

FEDERAL CRIMINAL STATUTES

22. United States v. Mosley, 238 U.S. 383 (1915); United States v. Gradwell, 243 U.S. 476 (1917); United States v. Bathgate, 246 U.S. 220 (1918); United States v. Wheeler, 254 U.S. 281 (1920).

23. Emerson, Haber and Dorsen, *Political and Civil Rights in the United States,* 104 (Little, Brown & Co., Boston, 1967).

24. United States v. Classic, 313 U.S. 299 (1941).

25. United States v. Saylor, 322 U.S. 385 (1944).

26. Screws v. United States, 325 U.S. 91, 159–61 (1945).

27. 18 U.S.C. §1582 (using vessels for slave trade); 18 U.S.C. §1585 (selling, transporting, or detaining slaves); 18 U.S.C. §1586 (serving on a slave ship); 18 U.S.C. §1587 (possessing slaves on such a ship); 18 U.S.C. §1588 (transporting slaves from the United States); and 18 U.S.C. §1583 (enticing a person into slavery).

28. 18 U.S.C. §1584 (holding, selling, or bringing into the country a person in involuntary servitude).

29. 18 U.S.C. §1582 (holding, arresting, or returning anyone to a condition of peonage).

30. In addition to criminal laws, Congress has enacted a civil statute abolishing peonage and declaring void any law, regulation, or usage which maintains a system of peonage. 42 U.S.C. §1994. The statute has been held to create a cause of action for damages against one who has held another in such involuntary servitude. Bryant v. Donnell, 239 F.Supp. 681 (W.D. Tenn. 1965).

31. *See, e.g.,* United States v. Ingalls, 73 F.Supp. 76 (S.D. Cal. 1947).

32. For a discussion of the subject, see Pete Daniel, THE SHADOW OF SLAVERY: PEONAGE IN THE SOUTH, 1901–1969 (Urbana: University of Illinois Press, 1972).

33. Pollock v. Williams, 322 U.S. 4 (1944).

34. Clyatt v. United States, 197 U.S. 207 (1905).

35. Bailey v. Alabama, 219 U.S. 219 (1911); United States v. Reynolds, 235 U.S. 133 (1914); Taylor v. Georgia, 315 U.S. 25 (1942); Pollock v. Williams, 322 U.S. 4 (1944).

36. Pollock v. Williams, 322 U.S. 4, 18 (1944).

37. United States v. Shackney, 333 F.2d 475 (2d Cir. 1964).

38. Selective Draft Law Cases, 245 U.S. 366 (1918).

39. Badger v. United States, 322 F.2d 902 (9th Cir. 1963).

40. Linsey v. Leavy, 149 F.2d 899 (9th Cir. 1945).
41. 82 Stat. 73.
42. 18 U.S.C. §245(a)(1).
43. Johnson v. Mississippi, 421 U.S. 213 (1975).
44. Bartkus v. Illinois, 359 U.S. 121 (1959); Abbate v. United States, 359 U.S. 187 (1959).
45. Watts v. United States, 422 U.S. 1032, 1033 (1975).

Appendix A

Federal Agencies Responsible for Enforcing the Rights of Racial Minorities

Under the hundred-year-old Reconstruction constitutional amendments and civil rights acts, little power of enforcement was delegated to federal agencies. Instead, the rights of racial minorities were enforced and obtained almost exclusively through lawsuits filed by racial minorities themselves.

The civil rights legislation of the past two decades altered the previous reliance on private enforcement by authorizing and sometimes requiring federal agencies to enforce the rights of racial minorities. The impact of this authorization is twofold. First, the authorization usually means that federal agencies will receive administrative charges of discrimination, will negotiate informally with alleged discriminators, and ultimately may sue the discriminators, thereby making private lawsuits by racial minorities unnecessary. Second, the authorization means that administrative charges of discrimination (*e.g.*, a letter to the federal agency describing the discrimination) should and sometimes *must* be filed with the federal agencies before racial minorities are permitted to file private lawsuits.

The authorization of civil rights enforcement by federal agencies does not mean that the federal agencies adequately perform their enforcement obligations. Nonetheless, when those obligations are performed, it always is helpful to have the power of the federal government on one's side.

APPENDIX A

In each of the chapters of this book, the names and addresses of the specific federal agencies responsible for enforcement of a particular area of law have been provided. In this appendix, some of that information is repeated.

All of the federal agencies mentioned in this book maintain their central offices in Washington, D.C. Most of them also have regional offices in the ten federal regions centered in the following cities:

Boston, Region I
New York, Region II
Philadelphia, Region III
Atlanta, Region IV
Chicago, Region V
Dallas, Region VI
Kansas City, Mo., Region VII
Denver, Region VIII
San Francisco, Region IX
Seattle, Region X

In addition to their regional offices, some federal agencies maintain district offices in nearly every city in the United States.

A person who needs information about the rights of racial minorities, about the filing of administrative charges of discrimination, or about the nature and extent of federal agency enforcement should contact the appropriate federal agency. This can be accomplished by contacting the agency either at its main office in Washington, D.C., *or at any of the regional or district offices throughout the United States*. The addresses and phone numbers of the latter offices are not listed in this book but are readily available through local telephone directories.

The one federal agency which has been delegated the broadest responsibility for civil rights enforcement is the Department of Justice:

U.S. Department of Justice
10th & Constitution
Washington, D.C. 20530
(202) 737-8200

It maintains at least one office and sometimes more than one in each of our 50 states. These offices, usually referred to as offices of the United States Attorney, are located in or near the federal court buildings in the major city or cities of each state. A person who needs information about the rights of racial minorities, about how to file an administrative charge of discrimination with the Department of Justice, or about the nature and extent of civil rights enforcement by the Department of Justice should contact the Department of Justice in Washington, D.C., or a nearby office of the United States Attorney.

As we have indicated in this book, the Department of Justice is not the only federal agency responsible for federal civil rights enforcement. The various agencies, with their Washington addresses and phone numbers, are listed below.

Voting, Chapter II

The federal agency with responsibility for insuring nondiscrimination in voting is the U.S. Department of Justice. The Department has the duty to preclear changes in voting procedures submitted under Section 5 of the Voting Rights Act of 1965; to register voters and assign poll watchers where necessary to guarantee equal voting rights; to insure that language minorities are provided with bilingual voting information and instructions; to file lawsuits against jurisdictions which continue to discriminate against minorities in the elective process; and to defend lawsuits brought by jurisdictions seeking exemption from Voting Rights Act coverage. The address of the Department of Justice is given above.

Employment, Chapter III

The primary federal agency responsible for enforcing the rights of racial minorities to nondiscrimination in employment is the Equal Employment Opportunity Commission (EEOC). It is responsible under Title VII of the Civil Rights Act of 1964, as amended, for receiving and investigating administrative charges of discrimination, for issuing right to sue letters to persons who intend to sue private employers and unions, for suing private employers and unions, and for resolving appeals involving discrimination in federal employment.

APPENDIX A

Equal Employment Opportunity Commission
2401 E St., N.W.
Washington, D.C. 20506
(202) 634-7040

Another federal agency with civil rights enforcement powers in employment is the U.S. Department of Justice. The Department of Justice is responsible, under Title VII, for issuing right to sue letters to persons who intend to sue state and local government employers, and for filing "pattern or practice" lawsuits against discriminatory employers. The address of the department of justice is given above.

A federal agency with civil rights enforcement responsibilities in state and local government employment is the Office of Revenue Sharing (ORS). The ORS is responsible for insuring that the state and local government recipients of millions of dollars of revenue-sharing funding do not engage in discrimination. The ORS is required to receive, investigate, and attempt to resolve administrative charges of discrimination, and to suspend funding to state or local governments which are engaged in discrimination.

Civil Rights Division
Office of Revenue Sharing
U.S. Department of the Treasury
2401 E St., N.W.
Washington, D.C. 20226
(202) 634-5157

A federal agency with similar responsibilities relating to state and local law enforcement agencies is the Law Enforcement Assistance Administration (LEAA). The LEAA, under the Crime Control Act, provides millions of dollars of federal funding to state and local law enforcement agencies, is required to receive, investigate, and attempt to resolve administrative charges of discrimination filed against its recipients, and is required to suspend funding to recipients which are engaged in discrimination.

APPENDIX A

Office of Civil Rights Compliance
Law Enforcement Assistance Administration
U.S. Department of Justice
633 Indiana Ave., N.W.
Washington, D.C. 20531
(202) 633-3286

Education, Chapter IV

The federal agency responsible for receiving administrative charges of discrimination and for filing lawsuits against discriminatory school systems is the Department of Justice (address above).

Another federal agency responsible for insuring nondiscrimination in education is the U.S. Department of Health, Education, and Welfare (HEW). HEW both provides extensive federal funding to educational institutions and is responsible, under Title VI of the Civil Rights Act of 1964, for ensuring that recipients of that funding do not engage in discrimination. Specifically, HEW is responsible for receiving, investigating, and attempting to resolve administrative charges of discrimination, and for suspending funding to educational institutions that do engage in discrimination.

Office for Civil Rights
U.S. Department of Health,
  Education, and Welfare
330 Independence Ave., S.W.
Washington, D.C. 20201
(202) 245-6671

Housing, Chapter V

The federal agency responsible, under Title VIII of the Civil Rights Act of 1968, for receiving and investigating administrative charges of discrimination and for suing persons, companies and state and local governments that do engage in discriminatory housing practices is the U.S. Department of Housing and Urban Development (HUD). HUD also is responsible, under Title VI of the Civil Rights Act of 1964, for receiving and investigating administrative charges of discrimination filed against recipients

APPENDIX A

of federal housing funding, and for suspending the funding to those recipients which do engage in discrimination.

> Office of Fair Housing and Equal Opportunity
> U.S. Department of Housing and Urban Development
> 451 Seventh St., S.W.
> Washington, D.C. 20410
> (202) 755-6422

Public Accommodations, Chapter VI

Three federal agencies have basic responsibility for insuring equal access to and use of public accommodations.

The Department of Justice has the duty under Titles II and III of the Civil Rights Act of 1964 to investigate complaints and bring (or intervene in) lawsuits against discrimination in public accommodations. The address is given at the beginning of this appendix.

The Community Relations Service (CRS) is a special agency established under Title VIII of the Civil Rights Act of 1964 and has the general responsibility of receiving complaints and assisting communities in resolving disputes relating to racial discrimination. After a lawsuit has been filed to enforce Title II, the federal court has authority to refer the matter to the CRS to seek a voluntary resolution of the discrimination.

> Community Relations Service
> U.S. Department of Justice
> 10th & Constitution
> Washington, D.C. 20530
> (202) 724-7361

The Interstate Commerce Commission (ICC), established under the Interstate Commerce Act of 1887, has the duty to hear and resolve administrative complaints of discrimination in interstate commerce. The ICC is also authorized to file lawsuits in the federal courts against common carriers who discriminate in the provision of services and accommodations.

APPENDIX A

Interstate Commerce Commission
Washington, D.C. 20423
(800) 424-9312

Federally Assisted Discrimination, Chapter VII

There are more than twenty agencies that distribute federal funds to state, local, and private entities, and which therefore are required to insure nondiscrimination in the use of those funds by Title VI of the Civil Rights Act of 1964. Each agency is responsible for receiving and investigating administrative charges of discrimination filed against recipients and for suspending federal funding to recipients engaging in discrimination.

U.S. Department of Agriculture
Office of Equal Opportunity
Compliance and Enforcement Division
Washington, D.C. 20250
(202) 447-4031

Nuclear Regulatory Commission
1717 H St., N.W.
Washington, D.C. 20006
(202) 492-7000

Small Business Administration
1441 L St., N.W.
Washington, D.C. 20416
(202) 653-6887

Civil Aeronautics Board
1825 Connecticut Ave., N.W.
Washington, D.C. 20428
(202) 673-5990

National Aeronautics and Space Administration
600 Independence Ave., S.W.
Washington, D.C. 20546
(202) 755-2320

Tennessee Valley Authority
1426 H St., N.W.
Washington, D.C. 20444
(202) 566-1401

APPENDIX A

Agency for International Development
U.S. Department of State
320 21st St., N.W.
Washington, D.C. 20523
(202) 632-8628

Department of State
2201 C St., N.W.
Washington, D.C. 20520
(202) 632-9884

U.S. Department of Housing and Urban
   Development
451 Seventh St., N.W.
Washington, D.C. 20410
(202) 755-6422

Department of Justice
10th & Constitution
Washington, D.C. 20530
(202) 737-8200

Department of Labor
200 Constitution Ave., N.W.
Washington, D.C. 20210
(202) 523-6666

Veterans' Administration
810 Vermont Ave., N.W.
Washington, D.C. 20420
(202) 393-4120

General Services Administration
F & 18th & 19th Sts., N.W.
Washington, D.C. 20405
(202) 566-1231

Department of the Interior
C & 18th & 19th Sts., N.W.
Washington, D.C. 20240
(202) 343-1100

National Science Foundation
1800 G St., N.W.
Washington, D.C. 20550
(202) 632-5728

APPENDIX A

Community Services Administration
1200 19th St., N.W.
Washington, D.C. 20506
(202) 653-5675

Department of Health, Education, and Welfare
300 Independence Ave., S.W.
Washington, D.C. 20201
(202) 245-6671

Department of Energy
1000 Independence Ave., S.W.
Washington, D.C. 20545
(202) 252-5000

In addition to the foregoing agencies, the Office of Revenue Sharing is responsible under Title VI and under its governing statute for insuring that state and local governments that receive federal revenue-sharing funds are not engaged in discrimination. Its address is given in the employment section of this appendix.

Similarly, the Law Enforcement Assistance Administration is responsible under Title VI and under its governing Crime Control Act for insuring that state and local law enforcement agencies which receive LEAA funding are not engaged in discrimination. Its address also is in the Employment section.

Jury Selection and Trials, Chapter VIII

As a practical matter, the enforcement of nondiscrimination in jury selection and trials is implemented by defendants in criminal cases and private individuals in affirmative civil lawsuits. There is no federal agency with general supervisory authority over the courts as, for example, the Department of Justice has over changes in voting practices by state and local governments.

Criminal Statutes Protecting the Rights of Minorities, Chapter IX

The President has the duty under Article II, Section 3 of the Constitution to "take Care that the Laws be faithfully executed." This prerogative of the executive branch of government of enforcing the criminal laws has been implemented by Congress by giving the exclusive power to prosecute federal offenses, including violations of federal statutes protecting racial minorities, to the Department of Justice and the offices of the United States attorney in the various federal districts. The address of the Department of Justice is given at the beginning of this appendix.

Appendix B

Legal Resources for Racial Minorities Who Need Legal Assistance

Most of the civil rights laws guaranteeing the rights of minorities are, as we have seen, enforced by the federal government. Thus, in most instances, information about your rights and about enforcement of your rights can and should be obtained from the federal agencies listed in Appendix A.

There will be occasions, however, where you may need information more quickly, where you may need help against the federal government, or where you may need representation in a lawsuit which you intend to file to obtain your rights. In these and other instances you may need a lawyer.

Finding a lawyer is easier than you might think. Finding the right lawyer for you is sometimes more difficult.

In looking for a lawyer you should be aware of four sources of legal assistance: (1) lawyers in private practice; (2) federally and/or locally supported legal services organizations; (3) national civil liberties and civil rights organizations with local offices; and (4) regional, local, or specialized civil liberties and civil rights organizations. When looking for a lawyer, you should contact the lawyer or organization you think is most appropriate for you. You need not, of course, limit yourself to only one source.

1. Lawyers in Private Practice

There simply are not enough lawyers on the staffs of civil liberties and civil rights organizations to assist, much less to represent in lawsuits all of the people who have had their rights to nondiscrimination violated. Accordingly, much of the advice and representation provided to such people is supplied by lawyers who practice law in private law firms. Many of these lawyers, incidentally, have worked with and remain affiliated with one or more of the civil liberties and civil rights organizations listed below.

There are two ways to find a lawyer in private practice to assist you. The first method is basically by word of mouth. Ask your friends and colleagues about their lawyers. Find out about lawyers in your area who have assisted persons in positions similar to yours. And look in the telephone book for the names of local groups of lawyers (such as the local bar association's lawyers' referral service). Once you find an attorney, you should briefly interview him or her to assure yourself that he/she has some knowledge about civil rights law.

A second way to find a lawyer in private practice is through the civil liberties and civil rights organizations listed below. Although the organizations themselves might not be able to assist you, they usually will be able to refer you to private lawyers who will. If you are having difficulty finding an attorney, you should contact such an organization for a referral.

Before you obtain your own private lawyer, you should be aware that lawyers, like doctors, have fees which you will have to pay. Remember, though, that if you have a good case and have to go to court, you usually are able to recover your attorneys' fees from your opponent when you win.

2. Legal Services Organizations

If you are poor or unemployed, you may be eligible for free legal assistance from a local legal-services organization supported by federal and local funding. These organizations, usually referred to as Legal Aid Societies or Legal Services Organizations, employ from a handful to dozens of lawyers who provide legal assistance to poor people in all areas of law, including discrimination law. These organizations exist in nearly every city and county in the country.

APPENDIX B

In order to find your nearest legal services organization, you should look through the phone book or call your local goverment for advice. If you have difficulty finding the appropriate local organizations, there are several national organizations you might want to contact.

National Legal Aid and Defender Association
2100 M St., N.W., Suite 601
Washington, D.C. 20037
(202) 452-0620

Most legal services lawyers or their organizations are members of the NLADA. The NLADA might be able to refer you to the appropriate legal services office in your area.

Legal Service Corporation
733 Fifteenth St., N.W.
Washington, D.C. 20005
(202) 376-5100

The Legal Services Corporation is an independent agency which provides federal funding to most legal services organizations. It should be able to refer you to an appropriate legal services office in your area.

3. National Civil Liberties and Civil Rights Organizations

There are several national civil liberties and civil rights organizations which have state and local offices (usually called chapters or affiliates) throughout the United States. Generally, the national offices will not be able to assist you directly, but will refer you to one of their local offices, which will assist you.

The local offices of the following major organizations are listed in your telephone directory. If you can't find them, you should write to the national offices for referrals.

APPENDIX B

American Civil Liberties Union
22 East 40th St.
New York, N.Y. 10016
(212) 725-1222

The ACLU specializes in free speech law but also is very much involved in discrimination law. There are state affiliates and local chapters of the ACLU in nearly every state.

Mexican Legal Defense and Education Fund
28 Geary St.
San Francisco, Calif. 94108
(415) 981-5800

MALDEF specializes in discrimination law and represents Mexican-Americans almost exclusively. Its offices are located primarily in the Midwest, the Southwest, and the West.

National Association for the Advancement of
  Colored People
1790 Broadway
New York, N.Y. 10019
(212) 245-2100

The NAACP, the oldest and largest of the civil rights organizations, specializes in racial discrimination law on behalf of black persons. It has state and local chapters throughout the United States.

National Urban League
425 Thirteenth St., N.W.
Washington, D.C. 20024
(202) 393-4332

Like the NAACP, the National Urban League specializes in racial discrimination law on behalf of black people, and has offices throughout the United States.

Puerto Rican Legal Defense Fund
95 Madison Ave.
New York, N.Y. 10016
(212) 532-8470

The PRLDF specializes in discrimination law and particularly in bilingual education law. It maintains several offices, primarily in the Northeast.

4. Regional, Local, and Specialized Civil Liberties and Civil Rights Organizatons

There are vast numbers of regional, local, and specialized civil liberties and civil rights organizations across the United States. Many of them are very small and operate primarily or solely through volunteer help. Others employ staff attorneys.

Because of the variety and large numbers of such organizations, it is impossible to list them all here. A few of the better known organizations, however, are listed here. In order to learn about other organizations in your area, you should begin by asking your friends and colleagues and by contacting the organizations that you do know about.

ACLU Southern Regional Office
52 Fairlie St., N.W.
Atlanta, Ga. 30303
(404) 523-2721

The ACLU Southern Regional Office specializes in voter discrimination law and jury discrimination law in the South.

Center for Constitutional Rights
853 Broadway
New York, N.Y. 10003
(212) 673-3303

The Center for Constitutional Rights focuses on numerous constitutional issues, including discrimination issues.

APPENDIX B

Center for Law and Social Policy
1751 N St., N.W.
Washington, D.C. 20036
(202) 872-0670

The Center for Law and Social Policy is involved in numerous civil liberties and civil rights issues, including discrimination issues.

Lawyers Committee for Civil Rights Under Law
733 Fifteenth St., N.W.
Washington, D.C. 20005
(202) 628-6700

The Lawyers Committee concentrates on all aspects of racial discrimination law, primarily on behalf of black persons. It maintains a number of regional and local offices, and it widely uses the volunteer services of lawyers in private law firms.

NAACP Legal Defense Fund
10 Columbus Circle
New York, N.Y. 10019
(212) 568-8397

The Legal Defense Fund, an organization entirely separate from the NAACP (except for the shared name), has the largest national legal staff of any civil rights organization. It concentrates on all aspects of racial discrimination law and represents black persons almost exclusively. Although the Legal Defense Fund has no local offices, it maintains a close relationship with hundreds of lawyers, many of whom are black, most of whom are in small private law firms specializing in civil rights law, and most of whom are located in the South.

National Committee against Discrimination
  in Housing
1425 H St., N.W.
Washington, D.C.
(202) 783-8150

APPENDIX B

NCDH, as its name implies, specializes in housing discrimination law.

National Conference of Black Lawyers
126 West 119th St.
New York, N.Y. 10026
(212) 866-3501

NCBL, an organization of black lawyers, focuses on all aspects of discrimination law through its national network of black lawyers.

National Lawyers Guild
853 Broadway
New York, N.Y. 10003
(212) 260-1360

The Guild, a membership organization of civil rights lawyers, focuses upon unpopular legal causes, including the rights of minorities. It maintains offices in most major cities.

Native American Rights Fund
1506 Broadway
Boulder, Colo. 80302
(303) 447-8760

The Native American Rights Fund specializes in Native American issues and represents indigent Native Americans exclusively. It has several offices in the West and in the Southwest.

Southern Poverty Law Center
1001 South Hull St.
Montgomery, Ala. 36101
(205) 264-0268

The Southern Poverty Law Center specializes in the legal problems of the poor, and primarily represents poor black people. It focuses its efforts throughout the South.

APPENDIX B

Suburban Action Institute
257 Park Ave. So.
New York, N.Y. 10010
(212) 777-9119

The Suburban Action Institute specializes not only in housing discrimination law but particularly in suburban exclusionary zoning law. Geographically, it operates primarily in the North and Northeast.

Index

Index

Advertising
  discrimination in, 118
Affirmative Action
  employment, 72-73, 83-88
  education, 109-112
Alaskan Natives
  voting, 54
American Indians
  jury selection, 191
  voting, 54
Asian-Americans
  voting, 54
  employment, 71
At-Large voting, 55-58
  see also voting rights
Attorneys Fees (generally), 20-21, 27, 149, 193
  education, 103
  employment, 23-24, 72
  housing, 26, 124-125, 128
  public accommodations, 157
  voting, 25
Attorney General, *see* Department of Justice

Back pay (remedy for employment discrimination), 24, 26, 72
Bilingual Education (generally), 104, 106-107
  Act, 106
Black Codes, 14
Busing, *see* Desegregation

Capital Punishment, 196-197
Census
  Voting Rights Act, 45, 47
  voting surveys, 42-43
Chicanos, 71
Chinese, 106-107
Civil Rights Act of 1866 (generally), 14, 17, 19-20
  contracts, 20, 108
  education, 20, 108
  employment, 20, 64, 70, 74, 78, 82
  housing, 20, 25, 117, 121-123, 128-129
  public accommodations, 20, 148-149, 158
  removal, 207, 209

247

Civil Rights Act of 1871, 18-21, 63-70, 78, 103
Civil Rights Act of 1875, 19, 22, 143-144, 148
Civil Rights Act of 1957, 38, 206-207
Civil Rights Act of 1964
    Title I (voting), 34, 38-39
    Title II (public accommodations), 22, 143, 152-161, 208-209
    Title III (state facilities), 160
    Title IV (education), 103
    Title VI (federally assisted discrimination), 107-108, 111, 169, 172-176, 180
    Title VII (employment), 23-24, 26-27, 63-88, 177-178, 181
    Title VIII (community relations service), 157-159
Civil Rights Act of 1968 (Fair Housing Act), 25-26, 116-133, 222
Civil Rights Movement, 16, 21, 142, 206
Civil War, 13, 34, 36, 216, 219, 221
Color of Law Doctrine, 217, 222, *see also* State Action
Commission on Civil Rights, 38
Community Relations Service, 22, 157-160

Compelling State Interest Standard, 18
Compromise of 1877, 14
Conspiracies, 21, 160
Constitution of the United States
    Article 1, Sec. 4, 41
    Interstate Commerce Clause, 150, 153
    slavery, 13
    see also Fifth Amendment (due process and equal protection)
    Sixth Amendment (fair trial)
    Thirteenth Amendment (no slavery)
    Fourteenth Amendment (equal protection)
    Fifteenth Amendment (equal voting)
    Twenty-fourth Amendment (voting)
Crime Control Act of 1968, 27, 79, 169, 179-182
Criminal Laws
    protection of minority rights, 149, 160, 186, 197, 215-235
    18 U.S.C. §241, 160, 216, 218-220
    18 U.S.C. §242, 216-220
    18 U.S.C. §245, 160, 222-223

Damages (remedy for discrimination)

INDEX

education, 20
employment, 20, 21, 74
housing, 20, 26, 124-125, 128
public accommodations, 20, 157
see also Punitive Damages

Declaration of Independence, 13

Department of Health, Education and Welfare (HEW), 103, 107, 130, 168, 172-173

Department of Housing and Urban Development (HUD), 25, 122, 124-125, 130-131, 168, 172-174

Department of Justice, enforcement of non-discrimination in
education, 103
employment, 23-24, 78-79, 82
federally assisted programs, 173, 175
housing, 25-26, 122-123
prosecution of civil rights violations, 219-221, 223
public accommodations, 22, 152, 157-161
voting, 19, 24-25, 38, 43-45, 48-50, 52-55

Department of Transportation, 172

Department of the Treasury, 168-169

Desegregation, 96, 98, 100, *see also* Education

DuBois, W.E.B., 15

Education (generally), 15, 95-112, 145, 149, 167-168, 170-173
affirmative action, 109-112
bilingual education, 104, 106-107
desegregation, 96, 98, 100
interdistrict desegregation, 101-102
private schools, 107-108, 149, 167-168, 170-171, 173
school financing, 104-106
termination of federal assistance, 167-168, 170-173

Employment (generally), 17-18, 20, 23-24, 63-88
Civil Rights Act of 1866, 20, 70, 78
Civil Rights Act of 1871, 21, 70, 78
Civil Rights Act of 1964, Title VII, 23-24, 63-82, 87
affirmative action, 72-73, 83-84
charge of discrimination, 76
coverage, 65
procedures, 75-82
prohibited practices, 65-71
remedies, 72-75

249

Equal Education Opportunities Act of 1974, 103

Equal Employment Opportunity Commission (EEOC), 23-24, 64, 66, 72, 75-82

Fair Housing Act, *see also* Civil Rights Act of 1968

Federal Housing Administration, 116

Federal Jury Selection and Service Act of 1968, 186, 197-202

Federal Rules of Criminal Procedure
    Rule 12, 194-195
    Rule 21, 204
    Rule 33, 203-204

Federal Voter Registrars and Examiners, 24, 34, 38, 52-53

Federally Assisted Discrimination (generally), 27, 103-104, 107-108, 167-182
    Civil Rights Act of 1964, Title VI, 27, 105-104, 107-108, 169, 172-176, 180
    Crime Control Act of 1968, 27, 79, 169, 179-180
    Fiscal Assistance to State and Local Governments Act of 1972, 27, 79, 169, 176-181

Fifth Amendment (due process and equal protection), 82, 87, 168, 170-172, 193

Fifteenth Amendment (equal voting), 14, 16, 18-19, 34-44

Fiscal Assistance to State and Local Governments Act of 1972 (Revenue Sharing Act), 27, 79, 169, 176-181

Fourteenth Amendment (equal protection) (generally), 14-18, 20-21, 149
    affirmative action, 87, 111
    criminal laws, 149, 219
    education, 15, 97-98, 101, 103-108, 111
    employment, 18, 63, 70, 78, 87
    federally assisted discrimination, 168, 170-172, 175
    housing, 25, 117, 130-133
    jury selection and trials, 186-188, 191, 193, 195-197, 202-203, 205-206, 208
    public accommodations, 142-147, 149, 151, 153, 161
    voting, 34, 41

Gerrymandering, 42, 57-58
see also Voting Rights
Grandfather Clause, 36-38

Hospitals, discrimination by, 173
Housing (generally), 15, 20, 25-26, 102, 116-134

INDEX

Civil Rights Act of 1866, 116-117, 121-122, 128-129
Civil Rights Act of 1968, Title VIII (Fair Housing Act), 25-26, 116-133
    discriminatory practices, 116-120
    enforcement, 122-129
    proof of discrimination, 120-121
    zoning, 129-134
Humphrey, Hubert H., 172

Immigration Commission, 221
Interstate Commerce
    Act, 142, 150-152
    Commission, 150-152
    discrimination in, 15, 150-155
    travel, 219
Involuntary Servitude, 16, 220-222

Jim Crow, 14-15, 144-148, 151, 195
Jury Selection and Trials (generally), 186-209
    criminal statutes, 186, 197, 222
    Federal Jury Selection and Service Act, 186, 197, 202
    juror challenges, 193-195, 199-204
    proof of discrimination, 188-191
    prosecutorial bias, 205-207
    race as factor in guilt and sentence, 195-197
    racial data, disclosure of, 199
    remedies, 193-194
    removal, 207-209
    selection process, 187, 191-192, 198
    venue change, 204-205
    voir dire, 202, 204

Kennedy, John F., 168
Kerner Commission, report, 16
King, Martin Luther, Jr., 124
Knights of the White Camelia, 216
Ku Klux Klan, 216

Language Minorities
    education, 96, 104, 106-107
    voting, 24, 44, 53-55
Law Enforcement Assistance Administration (LEAA), 27, 79, 82, 169, 179-182
Literacy Tests, 15, 24, 34, 36, 38-41, 44-45
Lynching, 15, 215, 217

Mexican-Americans, 54, 71, 191
Miscegenation, 196
Missouri Compromise of 1820, 13
Mitchell, Arthur W., 151

Niagara Movement, 15
National Association for the

Advancement of Colored People, 15
National Labor Relations Board, 171

Office of Revenue Sharing (ORS), 27, 79, 169, 176-179, 182

Parks, Rosa, 142
Peonage, 220-222
Political Parties, 37, 39-40
Poll Tax, 15, 37, 40
Presidential Executive Order, 63, 110, 116, 131
Prisons and Jails, 161
Private
    clubs, 22, 146-149, 156-157, 167-168
    schools, 20, 107-108, 149, 167-168, 170-171, 173
Prosecutorial Bias, 205-207
Public Accommodations, 17-19, 22, 142, 261
    Civil Rights Act of 1964,
        Title II, 22, 143, 153-160
        Title III, 160-161
    criminal statutes, 142, 218-219
    Interstate Commerce Act, 142, 150-152
    removal of state trespass prosecutions, 160, 207-209
Public Housing, 130-131, 172-174
Puerto Ricans, 54, 71, 191
Punitive Damages (remedy for discrimination)
    employment, 74
    housing, 26, 124-125, 128
    public accommodations, 157
Racial Violence, 15, 215-217
Reconstruction, 14-21, 34-37, 63-64, 69-70, 74, 144, 186, 220
Removal of State Criminal Trials, 160, 207-209
Revenue Sharing, 27, 167, 176-179, 182, see also Fiscal Assistance to State and Local Governments Act of 1972
Revenue Sharing Act, see also Fiscal Assistance to State and Local Governments Act of 1972

Section 5, see also Voting Rights Act of 1965
Selective Enforcement of Criminal Laws, 205-207
Sixth Amendment, 186-188, 202, 204
Slavery, 13, 16, 220-222
Spanish Heritage, 54, 71, 106-107, 191
State Action, 217, 222

Thirteenth Amendment (generally), 13-14, 16-20, 222
    employment, 63, 70, 78
    public accommodations, 143-144, 148-149, 153

INDEX

Tillman, "pitchfork" Ben, 36
Twenty-Fourth Amendment, 40

Venue Change, 204-205
Veterans Administration, 116
Voir Dire (examination in jury selection), 202, 204
Voting Rights (generally), 14-15, 24-25, 34-58
    criminal laws, 34, 37-38, 43, 219-222
    dilution of minority voting strength, 55-58
    gerrymandering, 42, 57-58
    grandfather clause, 36-38
    language minorities, 24, 44, 53-55
    literacy tests, 15, 24, 34, 36, 38-41, 44-45
    poll tax, 15, 37, 40
    racial data collection, 42-43
    voter registrars and observers, 24, 34, 38, 52-53
    white primaries, 37, 39-40
    see also Voting Rights Acts of 1967, 1960, 1964 and 1965
Voting Rights Act of 1957, 34, 39
Voting Rights Act of 1960, 34, 39
Voting Rights Act of 1964, 34, 39
Voting Rights Act of 1965 (generally), 19, 24-25, 34, 39, 42-55
    census surveys, 42-43
    criminal penalties, 52
    language minorities, 24, 44, 50, 53-55
    Section 5 preclearance, 24-25, 42-55
    suspension of literacy tests, 24, 44-45, 53
    voter registrars and examiners, 24, 52-53

White Primaries, 37, 39-40

Zoning, 18, 25, 102, 129-134

Are you a member?

The ACLU needs the strength of your membership to continue defending civil liberties. If you have not renewed, we urge you to do so today. If you are not a member, please join.

Fill out the membership form below and send, with the mailing label on the right, to: **American Civil Liberties Union, 22 East 40 Street, New York, N.Y. 10016. Att: Membership Dept.**

If you have already renewed, give this issue to a friend and ask them to join.

	Individual	Joint
Basic Membership	☐ $20	☐ $30
Contributing Membership	☐ $35	☐ $50
Supporting Membership	☐ $75	☐ $75
Sustaining Membership	☐ $125	☐ $125
Life Membership	☐ $1,000	☐ $1,000

☐ $5 Limited Income Member   ☐ Other $_____

Enclosed is my check for $_____.
(Make your check payable to the American Civil Liberties Union.)

PLEASE PRINT
☐ Renewal of membership
☐ New membership

NAME_____

ADDRESS_____

CITY_____ STATE_____ ZIP_____

ACLU-H

ACLU HANDBOOKS

THE RIGHTS OF GOVERNMENT EMPLOYEES		
Robert O'Neil	38505	1.75
THE RIGHTS OF CANDIDATES AND VOTERS		
B. Neuborne and A. Eisenberg	28159	1.50
THE RIGHTS OF LAWYERS AND CLIENTS		
Stephen Gillers	42382	1.95
THE RIGHTS OF MENTAL PATIENTS		
Bruce Ennis and Richard Emery	36574	1.75
THE RIGHTS OF THE POOR		
Sylvia Law	28001	1.25
THE RIGHTS OF PRISONERS		
Rudovsky, Bronstein, and Koren	35436	1.50
THE RIGHTS OF OLDER PERSONS		
Robert Brown	44362	2.50
THE RIGHTS OF STUDENTS (Revised Ed.)		
Alan H. Levine and Eve Cary	47019	1.75
THE RIGHTS OF SUSPECTS		
Oliver Rosengart	28043	1.25
THE RIGHTS OF TEACHERS		
David Rubin	25049	1.50
THE RIGHTS OF WOMEN		
Susan Deller Ross	27953	1.75
THE RIGHTS OF REPORTERS		
Joel M. Gora	38836	1.75
THE RIGHTS OF EX-OFFENDERS		
David Rudenstine	44701	1.95
THE RIGHTS OF HOSPITAL PATIENTS		
George J. Annas	39198	1.75
THE RIGHTS OF GAY PEOPLE		
E. Boggan, M. Haft, C. Lister, J. Rupp	24976	1.75
THE RIGHTS OF MENTALLY RETARDED PERSONS		
Paul Friedman	31351	1.50
THE RIGHTS OF ALIENS		
David Carliner	31534	1.50
THE RIGHTS OF YOUNG PEOPLE		
Alan Sussman	42077	1.75
THE RIGHTS OF MILITARY PERSONNEL		
(Revised Ed. of THE RIGHTS OF SERVICEMEN)		
Robert R. Rivkin and Barton F. Stichman	33365	1.50
THE RIGHTS OF VETERANS		
David Addlestone and Susan Hewman	36285	1.75

Wherever better paperbacks are sold, or direct from the publisher. Include 50¢ per copy for postage and handling; allow 4-6 weeks for delivery.

Avon Books, Mail Order Dept.,
224 West 57th Street, New York, N.Y. 10019

ACLU 7-79

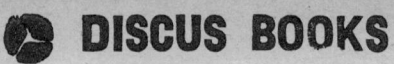

DISCUS BOOKS
DISTINGUISHED NON-FICTION

Title	Code	Price
MOZART Marcia Davenport	45534	3.50
NATURE OF POLITICS M. Curtis	12401	1.95
THE NEW GROUP THERAPIES Hendrick M. Ruitenbeek	27995	1.95
NOTES OF A PROCESSED BROTHER Donald Reeves	14175	1.95
OF TIME AND SPACE AND OTHER THINGS Isaac Asimov	24166	1.50
DELMORE SCHWARTZ James Atlas	41038	2.95
THE RISE AND FALL OF LIN PIAO Japp Van Ginneken	32656	2.50
POLITICS AND THE NOVEL Irving Howe	11932	1.65
THE POWER TACTICS OF JESUS CHRIST AND OTHER ESSAYS Jay Haley	11924	1.65
PRISONERS OF PSYCHIATRY Bruce Ennis	19299	1.65
THE LIFE OF EZRA POUND Noel Stock	20909	2.65
THE QUIET CRISIS Stewart Udall	24406	1.75
RADICAL SOAP OPERA David Zane Mairowitz	28308	2.45
THE ROMAN WAY Edith Hamilton	33993	1.95
SHOULD TREES HAVE STANDING? Christopher Stone	25569	1.50
STUDIES ON HYSTERIA Freud and Breuer	16923	1.95
THE TALES OF RABBI NACHMAN Martin Buber	11106	1.45
TERROR OUT OF ZION J. Bowyer Bell	39396	2.95
THINKING ABOUT THE UNTHINKABLE Herman Kahn	12013	1.65
THINKING IS CHILD'S PLAY Evelyn Sharp	29611	1.75
THOMAS WOODROW WILSON Freud and Bullitt	08680	1.25
THREE NEGRO CLASSICS Introduction by John Hope Franklin	16931	1.65
THREE ESSAYS ON THE THEORY OF SEXUALITY Sigmund Freud	29116	1.95
TOO STRONG FOR FANTASY Marcia Davenport	45195	3.50
TOWARDS A VISUAL CULTURE Caleb Gattegno	11940	1.65
THE WAR BUSINESS George Thayer	09308	1.25
WHAT WE OWE CHILDREN Caleb Gattegno	12005	1.65
WHEN THIS YOU SEE, REMEMBER ME: GERTRUDE STEIN IN PERSON W. G. Rogers	15610	1.65
WILHELM REICH: A PERSONAL BIOGRAPHY I. O. Reich	12138	1.65
WOMEN'S ROLE IN CONTEMPORARY SOCIETY	12641	2.45
WRITERS ON THE LEFT Daniel Aaron	12187	1.65

Wherever better paperbacks are sold, or direct from the publisher. Include 50¢ per copy for postage and handling; allow 4-6 weeks for delivery.

Avon Books, Mail Order Dept.
224 W. 57th St., New York, N.Y. 10019

(3) DDB 11-79